MORE HOW YOUR HORSE WANTS YOU TO RIDE

Also by Gincy Self Bucklin:

How Your Horse Wants You to Ride: Starting Out—Starting Over

What Your Horse Wants You to Know: What Horses' "Bad" Behavior Means and How to Correct It

MORE HOW YOUR HORSE WANTS YOU TO RIDE

Advanced Basics: The Fun Begins

GINCY SELF BUCKLIN

Howell Book House™

For general information on our other products and services or to obtain technical support please contact our Customer Care Department within the U.S. at (800) 762-2974, outside the U.S. at (317) 572-3993 or fax (317) 572-4002.

Wiley also publishes its books in a variety of electronic formats. Some content that appears in print may not be available in electronic books. For more information about Wiley products, please visit our web site at www.wiley.com.

Library of Congress Cataloging-in-Publication Data:
Bucklin, Gincy Self.
More how your horse wants you to ride : advanced basics—the fun begins / Gincy Self Bucklin.
     p. cm.
  Includes index.
  ISBN-13: 978-0-7645-9914-9 (cloth)
  ISBN-10: 0-7645-9914-3 (cloth)
  1. Horsemanship. I. Title.
  SF309.B885 2006   798.2—dc22

                                          2005025256

Printed in the United States of America

10 9 8 7 6 5 4 3 2 1

Cover design by Wendy Mount
Book production by Wiley Publishing, Inc. Composition Services

To all the patient horses and students who bore with me over the many years during which I struggled to learn my trade. Thank you all from the bottom of my heart.

"There is only one kind of mistake, that is, the fundamental mistake. Regardless of how advanced the exercise, if the performance is defective, one can directly trace that fault to a lack in the fundamental training of either the horse or the rider."

—Erik Herbermann

Contents

Preface

Horse and rider together on a beautiful fall day, galloping through fields and over fences, totally relaxed and happy, both of them having a wonderful time!

That is every horse's and every rider's dream. The details might vary a bit—for one pair, the scene might be the dressage ring at Devon, for another, a 100-mile competitive trail ride—but what is important is that, whatever they are doing, both rider and horse are having the time of their lives.

The question is, how can you make that dream come true? Time and money are certainly factors, but there is more to it than that. We have all seen the overmounted rider on her expensive—and angry—horse, being taken for a ride in the show ring or the hunt field, and it's not the ride she had in mind.

In my earlier book *How Your Horse Wants You to Ride: Starting Out— Starting Over*, we explored the skills you need to ride comfortably at the walk and trot, and perhaps a little canter, on a horse who already knows what to do and just needs to have his rider keep out of the way and allow him to do it. Many riders, especially those with many commitments and little time, are very content to remain at that level. They can ride with their friends, and perhaps participate in hunter paces or small shows. Lots of fun for everyone and not too much work.

But there are others for whom riding becomes the major passion. They can never ride enough or know enough. If you are one of those riders, this book is intended for you! While there are many great horsemen doing advanced work effortlessly, for all too many riders seeking to reach advanced levels the process seems to be a painful struggle. In most if not all of these cases, the trouble results from the lack of a strong foundation and a lack of understanding of the reasons why we do what we do. Horses are generally very cooperative animals by nature, but like all of us, if their work is uncomfortable—even painful—and confusing, they become seemingly uncooperative, either because they don't understand or because they are unable to respond to the rider's wishes. And nobody is having any fun.

With a few notable exceptions, books offered for the more advanced rider are concerned almost entirely with work at the advanced level, while books that focus on the basics are usually directed at the novice. However, as every truly skilled horseman knows, it is the lack of understanding of basic skills that leads to failure at the advanced level. No matter how well trained the horse, if the rider is making fundamental mistakes in her riding the horse will not be able to perform consistently well. Further, the lack of a solid foundation is the major reason why riders lose confidence, both in themselves and in their horses.

The fortunate few may either luck into a horse who forgives their mistakes or be able to afford the horses and the trainers to fix their problems. But for the rest of the world, especially those who are forced to work alone or with a minimum of exposure to lessons or clinics, this book will fill a great gap. Each horsehandling or riding skill is described carefully, the need for it explained clearly, and the techniques for successfully learning it demonstrated in depth with both text and illustrations. In many cases, especially for the more basic skills, the work in this book is covered in much greater depth in the earlier volume. Where appropriate, there will be chapter references to that book so you can find what you need if you want to know more.

We will also see how each skill lays a foundation for others, so you can clearly understand how work on your basic skills will improve your overall riding and eventually improve your horse as well. My goal in writing this book and its predecessor was to provide the reader with all the tools she needs to build a strong foundation. From this foundation she can go on in the discipline of her choice, with every likelihood of success.

As in the previous volume, in the interests of clarity the horse is always referred to as "he" and the rider as "she"—an idea for which I am indebted to Mary Wanless. I apologize to any male riders or female horses who may be offended.

Gincy Self Bucklin
Narragansett, R.I., July 2005

Acknowledgments

Since this book is a continuation of the previous volume, acknowledgments are due to many of the same people for its existence. Among them are Brigit Van Loggem, who insisted on it; Pat Snell, my agent, who made it happen; Karen Hayes, my daughter, who kept up my courage; and Beth Adelman, my editor, who keeps me from making any horrendous errors while keeping my nose firmly to the grindstone. There are many others who act as an ongoing support group, including the members of my Tuesday writer's group, and my Riding With Confidence e-group, all of whom give me ideas and constructive criticism as necessary.

A special thank you to John and Robert Clements of Zephyr Designs, in Brattleboro, Vermont, for their invaluable advice and assistance to me in drawing the diagrams. Any faults are mine, not theirs.

For their generous contributions of time and their patience, I am most grateful to the following:

Photographers: Terri Miller for the cover; Deb Bunker, Randy Connor, Jerry Ferreira, Karen Hayes, Chelsea Kaspar, Josh Sprague, Susan Stone, Ron Whittemore

Models: Human, other than the author: Peg Megan, Douglas Murray, Ian McBean

Equine (and their owners): Lily and Lisa Connor, Sammy and Edie Johnson, Prince William (Wills) and Maggie Clarke, Miss Kitty Coker and Kathy Bowser, Cree's Bold Time (T.B.O.) and Susan Stone, Dream Weaver (Pie) and Lucille Bump, Brandy and the McBean family

Helping Hands: Sam Bunker, Nancy Kelleigh, Dottie Lester, Ron Stearns, Holly Wilber

Locations: Belle Terre Farm, Clouds Hill Farm, Cherry Croft Farm, Castlefield Farm, Stone Ledge Farm, Southmowing Farm

And thank you to publisher J. A. Allen & Co., Ltd., and Mr. Herbermann himself, for allowing me to include the quote on page vi from Erik Herbermann's 1999 book *Dressage Formula, Third Edition*.

Introduction

What's in the Book, Where It Came from, Why You Need to Know It

Many years ago, I was at a local hunt club the day before their big show of the year. All the best riders were there. I happened to be out on the hunt course when one of them whom I had known for many years, David Kelley, was schooling a horse. He was very quiet, working in circles, then cantering a fence, stopping smoothly, then choosing another fence or another line. At no time did the horse ever appear flustered or insecure, and the whole procedure seemed effortless for both horse and rider.

A day or two later I was watching an Amateur Owner hunter class at the show and there was the same horse again, this time with his owner aboard. The difference in the horse's performance was astounding: He was unsure, his fences were uneven, he even stopped a couple of times. It was hard to believe it was the same horse I had seen before with David.

The difference, of course, was the rider. What made David a consummate professional was his ability to help the horse—to make the right result easy for the horse to find. And, of course, what makes a result the right one is the very fact that it *is* easy for the horse. The more difficult something is, the less likely the horse will be to want to do it, the tenser he will be, and the more likely he will be to injure himself—perhaps immediately, but certainly over time.

So the main object of this book is to teach you how to make your goals easy for the horse, both by the way you choose your goals and by how you help the horse to achieve them. That's How Your Horse Wants You to Ride.

First, I'd like to touch on my background. Until fairly recently in history, much of the knowledge of English riding rested with the military, where the needs of the cavalry resulted in an enormous store of knowledge that was passed on from generation to generation. I was fortunate enough to be exposed, directly and indirectly, to much of that knowledge before it was lost with the passing of the cavalry. After my mother and first teacher, Margaret Cabell Self, I learned from Colonel Polkovnikoff, who had been in the White Russian

1

Cavalry in World War I. One of my most influential teachers, William Hillebrand, studied in a German State Equestrian School immediately following that same war. Michael Miller and his wife, Ruth, of Sleepy Hollow Stable in Tarrytown, New York, were a generation older than me and had studied the work of many classical trainers. They all taught me an enormous amount about horses and how they function. More recently and most importantly, Sally Swift and Centered Riding helped me understand how the rider must function in order to help the horse.

What are the factors we have to consider when we are thinking about making something easy for the horse? After all, in most disciplines we are not asking the horse for anything he can't do perfectly well on his own—walk, trot, canter, gallop, turn, stop, jump, move over different kinds of terrain. Think of how effortlessly a young, sound horse plays in the field. He doesn't have to think, he just *does*. Barring accident or illness, it is only when we introduce a rider into the equation that the horse begins to have problems. So we need to think about how we affect the horse and what we need to know to affect him in a positive, not a negative, way.

There are three true riding fundamentals on which all correct horse performance is based. The first is developing a good relationship with the horse. This goes well beyond bringing a carrot every time you ride. It means considering your horse's needs in every way: his comfort, his fears, his health, his need for emotional support, and in fact, all the same things we must consider in any close relationship. Such apparently unimportant details as how you put on and take off the bridle can tell your horse that you are a considerate person who can be trusted to take care of him, or a rude, uncaring boor. When a horse who has been treated carelessly is eventually faced with a decision about jumping a scary fence, he is far more likely to decide *not* to jump than a horse who has learned that his rider cares about him and can be trusted not to hurt him.

Relationships are cemented on the ground. Besides the obvious—patting, scratching, grooming, treats—there is training that conditions the horse to accept a predator (you!) as a friend while still giving you the respect that is necessary for safety and trust. The horse must learn to accept the unusual, and surprises, without overreacting. In effect, he must learn that no matter how odd a new situation appears to him, if you (the trainer) say it's okay, then it's okay and he should go on with what he's doing. Once you're on the horse, it's too late. If he lacks confidence in you or in himself, it can be difficult to prevent serious problems from arising.

The more elementary ground/relationship skills, such as approaching, grooming, and tacking—which were covered in depth in *How Your Horse Wants You to Ride: Starting Out—Starting Over*—are covered briefly in the first few chapters of this book, to touch on some of the more common errors I have observed in advanced riders over the years. Leading is covered in some depth, because "you ride what you lead." It is during leading that the horse finds out whether he or his handler is the one who is really in charge, and therefore the one who must accept the responsibility for making decisions in difficult situations. A horse who knows his handler is capable feels that he can relax and trust her.

Free-longeing—working a loose horse in a large, enclosed space—is an essential skill that is rarely taught. Free-longeing helps the horse learn about his own body and how to release his tensions safely, and develops his natural skills in turns and transitions. The handler learns a great deal about the horse from watching him move freely, and also learns some of the many ways one can communicate with a horse without using any restraining equipment.

There are also a number of ground training/relationship building programs already in place. You can find the web sites for the main ones in appendix C, and they are also summarized in another book of mine: *What Your Horse Wants You to Know: What Horses' "Bad" Behavior Means and How to Correct It.*

The second fundamental skill is the ability to work around the horse on the ground and sit on him at all gaits in a way that does not disturb either horse or rider. Unfortunately, riding may be the worst-taught sport, at the introductory level, in the whole field of athletics. Many, if not most, beginners are expected to groom, tack up, walk, trot, post, steer, and stop—all in the first lesson. Talk about information overload! As a result of this poor start, probably better than 75 percent of riders have fears, recognized or not, that create tensions in their bodies that interfere with the horse's ability to function.

This is where *How Your Horse Wants You to Ride: Advanced Basics—The Fun Begins* comes into its own. Most advanced riders know what they are doing wrong, but very few of them know exactly what they have to do to correct the problems. My lengthy experience in teaching not only advanced riders, but many, many beginners and intermediates, has given me the knowledge to solve almost any fundamental problem. You will learn what causes the problem, what steps to take to fix it, and most important, why it is essential to do so. That is, what other problems it leads to that cannot be fixed unless the cause is first dealt with.

For example, Jeanne has the habit of riding with tense thighs and buttocks (as a result of moving ahead in her riding before her body had found its balance), which causes her to have trouble with her heels coming up. This is because her overall tense legs result in tense ankles that lack shock-absorbing qualities, which means she has too much body movement at the faster gaits. This unbalances her horse, Dancer, making him unable to go forward smoothly. When she rides dressage, Dancer's more advanced movements are noticeably incorrect and are scored accordingly. If she jumps, he jumps unevenly.

Frequently, her heels coming up cause her center to come forward ahead of Dancer's center, so he tends to refuse fences unless he happens to meet them exactly right. His confidence has been undermined and eventually will be lost. All because of an apparently unimportant position fault.

Since most trainers of advanced riders are focused on the advanced levels, there are many basic skills that they assume their students have mastered. My interest in teaching basic skills in greater depth began when I was teaching two group lessons of teenagers back to back, one with novice riders and the other an advanced class. One day I suddenly realized that the advanced riders were making exactly the same mistakes as the novice riders. They had, of course, learned ways of coping with the resulting effects on their horses, but I knew that in order to reach a high level of competence they would have to go back and relearn the skills they had never fully developed. The solid foundation they needed to ride really well just wasn't there.

A large portion of this book is devoted to these riding skills, starting with the Seven Steps—a method of quickly releasing tensions and restoring the body to a centered, grounded place. With the Seven Steps as a starting point, we'll go on to work on the different seats. Where most English trainers only teach two seats—full seat and half seat—I break them out into seven seats: three seated and four standing, which are the variations that are actually used by all riders in different situations. For example, the position of your body when you are in the seated phase of posting is quite different from your position at the sitting trot. Understanding and learning the different seats enables you to be secure and comfortable under virtually any conditions except the most extreme, and even then you can usually find a way to emerge safely.

Only from this secure place can you successfully develop the third fundamental skill: communicating with the horse and understanding what he is telling you.

Communication must be a two-way street. In discussing the aids—the methods by which we communicate with the horse—not only do we cover, in great detail, all the different aids, but also how they affect the horse and what to look for in the way of response. The horse's response is the way the rider learns whether her aids are correct, whether the horse understands them, and whether he is able and willing to perform the desired action. The rider who simply assumes, when she gets an undesired response, that the horse is at fault, is not truly communicating.

"Control" is a word that is frequently used by riders and trainers when they talk about responses. "You have to *control* that horse!" "You'll feel more secure once you have better control." The reality is that control *cannot* originate with the rider. Control must be *given* by the horse, either willingly through understanding and trust, or reluctantly through pressure and fear. The latter, of course, is likely to be withdrawn at any time, when a source of greater fear appears. This is why the relationship aspect is so important for successful riding.

Because of my many years of teaching experience (about sixty, as of this writing), I have a knowledge of the aids and their function that is shared by very few. It's not that many advanced riders don't use their aids correctly, but most of them do so instinctively with no real awareness of how they do things.

I recall a lesson I took many years ago with one of the top instructors in the country at the time. My horse, a very large, heavy-necked animal, kept bolting with me down the side of the ring toward the gate, no matter what I did to try to stop him. My instructor kept yelling at me to pull him up, but I was unable to do so. Finally he got on the horse himself, and I watched carefully as the horse tried unsuccessfully to break away from him. I saw that he was doing something with his hands that I had never noticed. I have since realized that this simple little trick, which all successful riders use, is at the root of rein communication. But he had no idea that he was doing it, so he never taught it. I have never seen it in any other book, or at least not described in a simple, recognizable way. You'll find it in Chapter 8.

Finally, with all your tools in place, you will get detailed descriptions of more advanced work—cantering, galloping, lead changes, cross-country riding (with in-depth explanations of riding up and down hills), and a little bit about collection and lateral work.

Jumping is given special attention. Some years ago, after working with General Humberto Mariles of the Mexican Olympic Team and with many good American trainers, I came up with a method of teaching jumping position that is simple to learn and just about foolproof. It enables both rider and horse to stay centered, grounded, comfortable, and secure throughout the whole sequence of the jump. The result is an enormous increase in confidence in both rider and horse.

The overall theme of this book is the importance of a respectful and caring relationship between rider and horse. Such a relationship must be based on your desire to please the horse; that is, the horse must enjoy his work, and, of course, you should be having fun too. This mutual love and enjoyment of horse and rider as they work together is what the sport of riding is all about.

Part I

Building Trust Through Ground Work

1

The Stone Horse

Working in the Barn

When I am introducing a beginner to a horse for the first time, the last thing I want is for her to be frightened by him. The size of the horse is bad enough; "I had no idea they were so *big*!" is a comment I often hear. If, in addition, the horse is fidgety, it is very difficult to get the student to relax. So in describing the sort of horse I like to use, I refer to him as "like a large boulder": a horse who just stands there as though nothing in the world would upset him enough to make him a threat. Hence, the "stone horse."

∞

Even for the more advanced rider, a horse who is fidgety on the ground is annoying to work with, and a surprising number of otherwise well-trained horses do not stand quietly in the barn. Since riding begins with grooming and tacking, and our ride is affected by how we get along with the horse on the ground, let's begin by examining how our actions affect the horse on the ground.

The information in this chapter has been covered in much greater depth in my previous book *How Your Horse Wants You to Ride: Starting Out—Starting Over*, which is intended for the novice rider. But I have found over the years that many experienced riders have not been exposed to handling concepts that are important for the horse's comfort, both mental and physical. Therefore, I will cover these concepts briefly in this chapter, so that you too may have a "stone horse."

THE EMOTIONAL CONNECTION

At one time or another, all of us have experienced the way horses seem to pick up on our emotions, especially when we're nervous. People will say things like "They can smell your fear," and assume there's nothing we can do about it. Perhaps horses do smell your fear, especially if you're terrified, but transmitting

To learn more about this topic, read Chapters 2, 3, and 4 of the companion volume to this book, *How Your Horse Wants You to Ride: Starting Out—Starting Over.*

emotions is actually a physical occurrence, and *one that can be controlled.* It is dependent on two phenomena, one observed and one scientifically researched.

The observed phenomenon I call muscular telepathy, and I initially learned about it at a Centered Riding clinic some time ago. The best way to understand it is to think of a school of fish, all scooting along at high speed. Suddenly they all turn almost simultaneously and shoot off in another direction. How did they do that? Obviously the lead fish didn't say to the next fish, "At the big rock I'm going to turn right and go up. Pass it on." No. Something occurs at some deep level in the fishes' brains that enables their bodies to pick up muscle signals from the other fish. You may have observed it in horses when you are on a trail ride: You are trotting along briskly when the horse in front of you breaks into a canter without increasing speed, and your horse almost simultaneously changes into the canter as well.

This phenomenon works between species just as well as it does within the species. That is, you and the horse communicate at the muscular level. For example, it has been shown that if a trainer has some serious muscular limitation, such as fused vertebrae in her lower back, the horses she trains will all have rigid backs in the same area.

The second, scientific, phenomenon was discovered comparatively recently. It was always thought that emotions originated in the brain and then were transmitted to the body as various physical tensions or expressions. Now scientists know that the transmission is the other way around. That is, the body observes something through the senses and reacts accordingly. The brain processes this reaction and interprets it as fear, anger, joy, or whatever.

Putting these two things together, we realize that if you are fearful, the horse's body, through muscular telepathy, will pick up the tensions in your body associated with fear. His brain will then also interpret those tensions, now in himself, as fear—and suddenly you're both in trouble.

"So," you might say, "now I know that the horse and I can scare each other without meaning to. But what good does that knowledge do me?" Simple. Just as there are muscular patterns for fear and insecurity, there are also muscular patterns for confidence. All you have to do is put your body in "confident mode," and not only will your fear dissipate, but so will your horse's. If this sounds like magic, it really isn't, and it has proved itself over and over with my students and their horses, some of whom had serious hurdles to surmount.

Tidbits & Supplements

When I lost my husband, of course I informed my friends in my e-group, ridingwithconfidence. Among the expressions of sympathy was one in which the writer said, "Are you using the Seven Steps to help you work through your grief?" At first I was rather startled at the idea, but then I tried them and they did indeed help. I concluded that grief is, after all, another form of fear, so telling my body that it wasn't afraid helped me handle my grief.

THE SEVEN STEPS

To teach students how to put their bodies in confident mode, I use something I call the Seven Steps, which are a series of exercises derived from Centered Riding and such disciplines as yoga and t'ai chi. I find they work best for most people when they are performed in the order you see here, but there is no law about it and you may find that you need to work on one step more than the others. It is important, however, that you do not try to force perfection in yourself, but simply make the best effort you can at the time and then go on to the next task.

When you are first learning the Seven Steps, wear comfortable clothes. Begin each exercise by standing with your feet comfortably apart and your arms relaxed at your sides. If you're at home and have a full-length mirror you can use, it will help you visualize what you are trying to achieve in some of the exercises.

In this chapter I describe how you do the steps on the ground and discuss how they relate to ground work. Later in the book you will see how they apply to riding. Once you have learned them, and the resulting feeling in your body, you can go through them in a minimalist way any time. Besides helping your riding, they are very useful in stressful situations in the real world.

Step 1. Growing

Growing lengthens and stretches your body so that all the muscles become softer and more flexible, especially in your hips and lumbar spine area.

1. Bring your left hand up in front of your face with the thumb facing toward you.

2. Raise your arm up and watch it as it goes up until the whole arm is straight up. Drop your head again until your face is vertical and reach up a little further so that you feel the pull at your waist.

Peg growing her right side. That side now appears longer than the left and her right foot is well grounded.

3. Bring your arm down but leave your body up there.

4. Repeat with your right arm, but instead of bringing your arm all the way down, first tap the top of your head, right where a line drawn from ear to ear and one drawn straight back from your nose would cross. Imagine that your body is suspended from that point, like a Halloween skeleton that you hang on the door.

5. Drop your arm by your side. Your body is being gently pulled upward and your arms and legs are hanging down from it.

Step 2. Shakeout

Shakeout further releases tension in your muscles, especially in your limbs.

1. Allow your arms to hang naturally at your sides. Begin with your fingers, shaking them as if you were shivering or as if you had water on your hands and were trying to shake it off.

2. After a few seconds, begin shaking your hands as well, then your wrists, forearms, elbows, upper arms, and finally, shoulders, in that order.

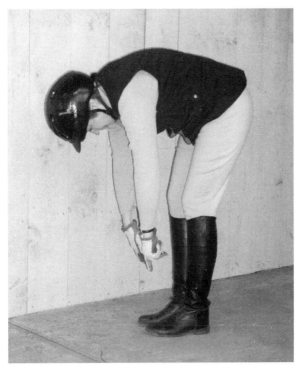

The final shakeout relaxes your whole body.

3. Then, one leg at a time, shake your feet, ankles, calves, knees, and thighs. Be sure you shake, not twist or turn your ankles.

4. Finally, allow your body to bend at the hips and fall forward until you are bent over as far as is comfortable, and shake all over like a dog. Come up slowly and finish by growing again.

Step 3. Breathing

Holding our breath is something we all do when we're scared. But your breathing is noticeably copied by the horse, so good breathing is good first aid for releasing tensions in both of you in scary situations. Good breathing comes from the diaphragm, not the chest, so you need to learn how it feels.

1. Place your hand on your belly, palm in with your little finger on your navel, and try to push your hand out each time you inhale. You should feel your diaphragm pushing out and your lower rib cage expanding all the way around. Do not allow your shoulders to lift.

2. Relaxation breathing means exhaling for about twice as long as you inhale. You can inhale through your nose and exhale through your mouth. Breathe out very slowly as though you were gently blowing out a candle. Exhale as long as you comfortably can. Feel your rib cage contracting and your diaphragm lifting to expel the air.

Step 4. Soft Eyes

Hard eyes are predatory and tend to make the horse nervous when you are working around him, especially if he is loose (which is why many people have trouble catching their horses). Soft eyes are less threatening and improve your awareness of where you are in relation to your horse as you work together on the ground.

1. Pick an object about five feet away and stare at it for a minute, trying to block out everything else. This sharply focused look is called hard eyes.

2. Without moving your head or eyes, keeping the object in the center of your field of vision, allow your focus to soften and spread out so that you can see all around you at once. This unfocused way of seeing is called soft eyes.

3. Hold both arms extended in front of you.

4. Wiggling your fingers vigorously, bring both arms out to the sides like airplane wings until they almost disappear from your line of sight. With soft eyes you can be conscious of the wiggling fingers of both hands at once, without looking to either side.

Step 5. Teeter-Totter (Longitudinal Centering)

Standing and moving with your longitudinal center too far forward, both of which are common, cause tension in your feet, which the horse interprets as preparation for flight, making him less inclined to stand or move in a relaxed manner. The teeter-totter improves your awareness of how you are centered longitudinally (that is, back to front).

1. Stand on level ground with your feet close together. Notice where the pressure is distributed on your feet.

2. Keeping the rest of your body straight and bending only at the ankles, allow your body to sway forward until you are forced to take a step to keep from falling. Repeat, swaying to the back.

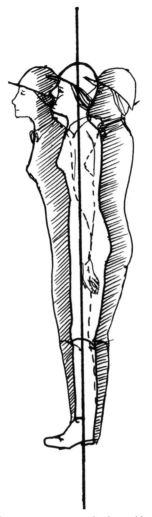

In the teeter-totter, only the ankle joint
opens and closes.

3. Try it again, but this time stop just *before* you have to take a step.

4. Next, sway forward while being aware of the pressure on the soles of your feet. Stop as soon as it begins to change.

5. Sway back the same way, but now notice that there is also some tension in your lower back as you sway.

6. Sway slowly forward from your position in step 5, and stop *as soon as the tension leaves your back*. You have found your longitudinal center.

Step 6. Lateral Centering

Lateral (side to side) centering is primarily a concern while you are riding, since the horse can be made unbalanced to the side quite easily. Becoming conscious of lateral centering on the ground will make it easier to learn when you ride. But it's useful on the ground, too. Especially when you are doing such tasks as leading or asking the horse to pick up a foot, keeping your own lateral balance square will help the horse do the same. Of course, if you want him to shift his balance, shifting yours will help.

   1. Stand facing a full-length mirror. Raise both arms over your head and grow as much as you can without getting stiff. Imagine that in your center, which is located just below and behind your navel, there is a big, heavy ball.

   2. Without twisting your body, carry both arms to the right. At the same time, imagine that the heavy ball is rolling to the left. Your body should form a smooth bow shape. You should feel more pressure on your left foot. You have moved your lateral center to the left.

   3. Bring both arms back up over your head and allow the ball to roll back to the center.

   4. Now bring your arms to the left and allow the ball to roll to the right. To do this successfully, you must really lengthen as you raise your arms. If you don't, the top of your pelvis will move to the right but the lower section will stay where it is and the ball won't really roll to the right. Look in the mirror and make sure the point on the right side of your pelvis that is lined up with your navel is also the point farthest to the right.

   5. Allow yourself to center again. Then repeat in both directions. Try to stay long and soft so that you sway easily from one side to the other.

   Try to make a habit, whether you're sitting or standing, of checking your lateral balance now and then. Think of keeping your spine at twelve o'clock, then feeling the pressure on your feet or seat bones to see if it is even.

Step 7. Following Seat

This step is also more important in riding, but learning it on the ground will help you ride and also (believe it or not) have an influence on your horse's way of moving. That is, if he is following you and you move freely and athletically, he will tend to copy you.

| Moving my center to the left. The vertical left leg shows clearly that my weight is over my left foot. | Moving my center to the right. It's not so easy, and not just because I'm not as young as I used to be! |

You need a fairly large open space for this exercise. Use a full-length mirror if possible. Begin by doing all the previous exercises, then start walking in place as follows.

1. Keep your feet solidly on the floor and your torso upright and still from the waist up, and place your hands on your hips.

2. Now bend your left knee by pushing it forward; straighten it by pulling it back, but don't lock it. Do this several times and feel how your hip drops as your knee bends. This is very clear visually in the mirror. Keep your spine vertical and don't allow your hip to sway to the side.

3. Try the same thing with your right knee. See if one side feels different from the other—which is true for many people. If there is a noticeable differ-ence, try putting both hands over your head and stretching and growing as much as you comfortably can; then, with your arms still extended, walk in place again and see if you feel looser and smoother.

4. Thinking about how your hips drop, and not allowing them to sway from side to side, start walking around. First let your arms swing, even exagger-ating the movement to free up your shoulders and give yourself room.

5. Now tighten your shoulders and neck, stop swinging your arms, and feel how this restricts your leg movement.

6. Return to the vigorous swinging, and when you are moving freely, bring your arms down to your sides.

7. Imagine that you have a bicycle pedal sticking out of each hip joint. Hold your imaginary pedals in your hands and start pedaling backwards while walking forward. Try the pedaling while walking in place. Also try it running in place (you do have to lift your feet to run).

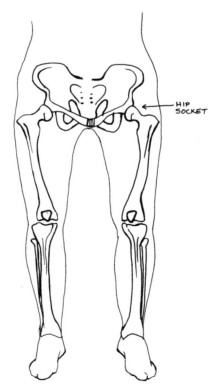

The location of the hip joint within the pelvis.

Working on the following seat on the ground will raise your awareness of the movement in your pelvis that is necessary to enable you to follow the horse's movement when you're sitting in the saddle. You should also be aware that the following movement is exactly the same whether you are absorbing the motion of your own legs or the horse's. This is why riding, in the sense of following the horse's movement, can and should be extremely easy, because it is already hard-wired in our bodies.

GROUNDING

In any athletic endeavor, or indeed any physical activity, to perform your best you must be free of tension yet still muscularly alert. You also need to have a solid connection with something in order to control your movements. If you're trying to run and you hit a patch of ice, you become an instant comedy act— at least until you hit the ground!

The name for this connection is *grounding*. I find the best way to create a clear image of grounding is to think of playing dodge ball. Your feet are firmly connected to the ground, while the rest of you is flexible and able to move in any direction that is consistent with the laws of gravity. Waiting to receive a serve in tennis is another example. In fact, in any sport you can name, what you see in the good players that you *don't* see in the novices is the ability to ground. The lack of grounding is particularly evident in riders, mostly because of their wiggly stirrups and the body's almost unconquerable desire to hang on with the legs! Let's look at what we have to do to become grounded.

Tidbits & Supplements

At a recent seminar on Feldenkrais for singers, we were given an exercise for our feet. Sitting on the front of a chair, first we lifted the toes of the left foot several times, then the heel, then one after the other, being careful to find the most comfortable position to place our feet. Next we lifted the inside and the outside of each foot. We were to be very conscious of each movement, repeating it several times and being careful not to cause tension or strain. Then we lifted each section in turn, moving around the foot first in the "easy" direction, then in the "hard" direction. Finally, we repeated the whole exercise with the right foot. A little later on we were standing and walking around, and I realized I had rarely felt so thoroughly grounded!

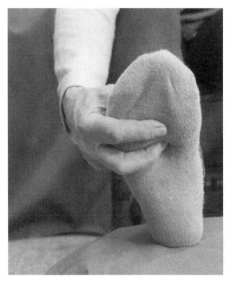

Finding the bubbling spring.

The Bubbling Spring

Sit down and take one shoe off, then feel around on the sole of your foot, just at the back of the ball, behind the second toe. You'll find a little hollow there that's a tiny bit sensitive. The martial arts people call this the *bubbling spring*, and it's the point at which, they say, the energy of the earth enters your body and gives you power. Certainly it is the point that must be connected to the ground for you to maintain standing balance. Try your teeter-totter and notice that when your bubbling springs leave the ground, *that* is the moment at which you lose your balance and are forced to take a step to regain it, whether forward, back, or sideways.

Now go through the Seven Steps again and when you finish, think about your bubbling spring points, then imagine that your feet are becoming very wide and flat, like a duck's feet, allowing your bubbling springs to really connect to the ground. Next, imagine roots growing into the ground from these points, spreading out to make a wide, secure base. Or make up your own images to create the idea of being totally connected with the ground.

Finding Freedom from Tension in Balance

Next, start mentally "looking" at your body, beginning with your feet, and trying to locate areas of tension. As you find tense areas, release them by breathing out, imagining that they are made of something soft and melting or that the space they occupy is actually empty. Think of allowing your shins to rest on your ankles, your thigh bones on your shins, and so on up your body, but don't lose your growing in the process. If you can find true balance and release from tension, so that you are solidly grounded, you will discover that you feel very confident and secure, and very athletic at the same time.

Sometimes tension can be released with something as simple as the thigh and shoulder squeezes found on pages 118–119. If you find it difficult or impossible to release all your tensions, it may be because your body is structurally misaligned. Often this can be corrected through disciplines such as the Feldenkrais technique described in the box on

> ### *Tidbits & Supplements*
>
> If your leg bones don't form a straight line there will be some compensatory tension when you try to ground. Sometimes this can be corrected with orthotics (shoe inserts that level your foot). It is worthwhile for the serious horseman to be fitted with them. For such things, I happen to be a fan of applied kinesiology, a diagnostic technique used by some chiropractors, in which your own body determines whether the device is correct for you.

page 19. There are many such programs available, and what you decide to learn at least partly depends on what is available in your area.

You will need to practice the Seven Steps and grounding over and over until you are very comfortable with them and can use them with little or no thought or effort. At first you may need to do them in their entirety, using the exercises above, but with practice you will find you can simply picture the Seven Steps in your mind and your body will release its tensions with a minimum of external effort.

The Seven Steps assist you in grounding, so by going through the steps first, then envisioning the grounding, you will find that, too, becomes fixed in your muscle memory and more easily available. I find a very useful way to practice them daily is when I'm walking downstairs, especially if I'm carrying something. Many people use them in stressful situations such as turnpike driving. However you use them, the more you do, the easier they become and the more secure you become, both physically and emotionally.

EQUIPMENT FOR GROUND WORK

The basic equipment you use on the ground with your horse is a halter and a lead rope, but there are a number of variations. The standard English halter is made of either leather or nylon strapping, about an inch wide. It has a number of rings that allow different ways of fastening the horse. Both the crown piece and the throat latch can be undone, allowing for more convenience in putting on and removing the halter, but also providing an opportunity for abuse if the halter is dragged over the horse's head in such a way that it hurts his ears. Because the strapping is wide, the English halter does not apply a particularly strong pressure on its own, so it is often used with a chain lead placed over the horse's nose.

Western halters are usually made of rope, only unfasten at the crown, and have only one ring, which is under the jaw. Natural horsemanship halters are similar, except they are made of two strands of narrower, softer rope and have no rings or metal fastenings. Because they are made of narrow rope, both halters are more severe than an English halter—overly so if the rope is stiff and hard.

Lead ropes vary mostly in length and in how they are fastened. The fastener should be strong but easy to undo. Some of the fasteners require two hands, which is not always possibly with a frightened horse. Eight feet of rope is comfortable for most leading and short-term tying, and twelve feet is right for basic training.

With the flat English halter many people use a chain lead for extra control. Chains present the opportunity for abuse, but when applied and used correctly they teach the horse to be responsive, not fearful. (The chain should be applied in the same way as the zephyr lead shown on page 23.)

The zephyr lead is a nice compromise, being a short piece of soft rope (about thirty inches) of the size and type used in natural horsemanship halters. It has a ring on one end to which the lead rope is attached, and a snap on the other. I first saw this in a TTeam book, so they can probably be purchased there (see appendix C), or you could make your own.

Chains and zephyr leads are only useful on a horse who tries to run past you or turn and pull away. Since they put additional pressure on the horse's nose, if you try to get the horse to come forward by pulling on these types of leads, it sends the opposite signal and you get a confused, and either frightened or angry horse. A natural horsemanship halter is a better answer because the pressure is placed on the poll and to some extent on the back of the jaw, thus asking the horse to drop his head and come forward.

Crossties often come with a quick-release snap on one end in case the horse pulls back. This snap should always be on the end of the tie closest to the wall. The last thing you want is to be grabbing at a frightened horse's head in an effort to unfasten him. Stretchy ties are good for a horse who tends to pull out of fear if he feels resistance, but might be dangerous for a horse who is a really determined puller, since there will be a great deal of pressure if they break.

So which one should you use? It depends on what you are planning to do and how much control you expect to need. And also what you are accustomed

When the zephyr lead is attached this way, most of the pressure on the nose is on the halter rather than the horse.

to. I grew up with English equipment and crosstying horses, so I generally use an English halter. But for ground training I like a soft natural horsemanship halter. However, if I had a very aggressive horse and lacked the time at that moment to improve his attitude, I think the English halter and a correctly applied chain, with a second lead attached under the jaw, would give me the most control. (See the photo on page 45.)

FIRST CONTACT

There are certain rules to keep in mind when you start working with any horse. To begin with, the horse by nature thinks of humans as predators. If he has always been well handled this reaction will be minimal, but even a small amount of clumsy handling will quickly bring it to the surface.

Good handling begins with the way you approach a horse, especially an unfamiliar one. It is important to approach the horse so that you are clearly visible but don't come across as threatening. This means you use soft eyes and approach at an angle from the front, where you can be seen but are at least risk of being kicked if the horse has any issues. And you *never* touch the horse anywhere until you are sure (by his turning at least his ears toward you) that he knows you are there.

The horse's personal space lies between the
dotted lines on the neck and the muzzle.

As with other humans, you don't invade the personal space of strangers. With another human, the only place you are allowed to touch at first, and then only if it is offered, is the hand. With a horse it is the muzzle. This is because both are used for the same purpose. After using the other nontactile senses—sight and hearing primarily, and probably smell more than we realize—the human uses her hand to touch a strange object if she wishes to explore it further. In a similar situation the horse touches with his muzzle, which in his case improves his ability to smell and enables him to taste quite easily as well. So the horse's muzzle serves as his "hand" when dealing with the unfamiliar, and therefore is acceptable as the first place for contact. But just as if you reached out to touch something and it suddenly reached out at you, you would recoil, so you must offer your hand but wait and allow the horse to reach out and touch you, not the other way around. Once he has done so, you can show your intentions by gently rubbing him in the muzzle area—sort of the equivalent of the squeeze you give during a handshake.

The horse's personal space extends from above his nostrils all the way back to the area just in front of his shoulder. Many people feel the horse should willingly accept touching anywhere. Yes, once he gets to know you he should, but that should be a result of his learning to trust you, not out of compulsion. And certainly it should not be demanded in a first encounter.

After the horse accepts your touch on his muzzle, you can proceed to his shoulder and then to the rest of his body. If the horse shows any signs of fear or resistance, such as moving away or raising his head, accept them as signs that he needs work in these areas, and some sort of advance-retreat exercise is in order to start creating a safe, trusting relationship.

Tidbits & Supplements

There are a number of ground training systems that are of great help in developing a good relationship with your horse through ground work. These are described in my book *What Your Horse Wants You to Know: What Horses' "Bad" Behavior Means and How to Correct It.* Or see appendix C for some suggestions.

COMMUNICATING WITH THE HORSE

Of course, besides the general messages your body sends, you need to send specific messages. Even more essential, you need to listen to the messages the horse is sending you. If the horse is tense or worried about something, you have to deal with that before you can expect to hold his attention in such a way that he is ready to learn or to take suggestions from you.

Some Subtle Messages from the Horse

We are all familiar with the obvious messages: ears forward or back, head high or low, tail quiet or swishing angrily. But there are more subtle messages that tell you, for example, whether the horse is listening or ignoring you. Here are some ways horses communicate what they are feeling. Just for fun, try doing each of these things yourself and see how they make you feel!

- Wrinkles around the mouth and eyes indicate tension and worry.

- Hard eyes indicate annoyance and unwillingness to listen. Soft eyes, by contrast, indicate acceptance and mental processing. This one takes a while to learn to see, but horses' eyes in general are very expressive and, like people's, are often a truer indicator of the underlying emotions.

- Licking and chewing indicate the horse is thinking about something that just happened, and processing it.

- Giving or not giving you his eye is an indication of his attention and willingness to listen. The best way to describe this one is to think of a teenager who is getting a lecture from his parents. He looks up, off to the side, anywhere except at the speaker. The message is, "I don't want to hear it!" That's why you'll often hear a parent say, "Look at me when I'm talking to you!" A horse in hand who is not giving you his eye—usually by raising his head and looking over you—can potentially be dangerous. He has taken over and is ignoring you, trying to take control. (Dealing with this is covered in Chapter 2.) If something spooks him he may jump right on top of you. Conversely, looking at you attentively indicates he accepts your guidance and will listen.

● Invading your space includes pushing on you, stepping or almost stepping on you, or forcing you to move out of his way. This is a dominance game. In herd dynamics, the lower-ranked horse moves out of the way of the higher-ranked one. If the horse can get you to move, that means he's in charge. Not the way you want it to be!

We'll learn more about understanding the horse's signals in later chapters, and the ground training disciplines listed in appendix C have a good deal of material on this subject.

Making Yourself Understood

At this stage, while you're working with the horse in the stable, you don't need a great many commands. The big secret to communicating is found in positive reinforcement, given at the correct moment. How often have you seen someone with a dog who jumps up? The dog jumps up and the owner says "down!" The dog gets down. The owner says, "bad dog!" What does that tell the dog? That getting down is wrong! Very confusing. The correct response would have been "good dog," said at the moment the dog started to get down.

Other than leading, which is covered in the next chapter, when you're working in the barn you want the horse to stand still, and move forward, back, and sideways a few steps with both front and hind feet. You also would like him to pick up and hold up his feet. These are all covered in depth in the disciplines listed in appendix C, but we will touch on them here as well.

Standing Quietly

This is mostly a function of age, feed, and exercise. With nothing going on to disturb him, the average horse is more than happy to stand still. However, a young horse getting too much grain who is asked to stand quietly while all his buddies are going out to play is not going to be very good about it. Other than cutting his grain, a good project to help his overall training would be to teach him, using positive reinforcement as much as possible, that if he stands quietly, at first only for a few seconds, he will then be let out. He learns a little useful self-discipline, which can then be applied in other areas. More

extended standing, as for grooming, should wait until he comes in
from playtime.

Gentle grooming and TTeam
touches encourage quiet behavior.
Overly vigorous grooming, as well
as noisy or overstimulating surroundings, tend to make the horse
nervous and fidgety. But it does
make sense to gradually accustom

Tidbits & Supplements

Positive reinforcement is used in
many training systems, but the
easiest way to learn about it is
through clicker training. (See
appendix C.)

the horse to unusual sights and sounds, while asking for quiet behavior. All the
ground disciplines have some system for teaching this. I have found Parelli's the
most useful, but what you use depends on the nature and experience of both
horse and handler.

Moving Over

The best way to teach the horse to move around in small increments on the
ground, I think, is Parelli's porcupine game, especially when combined with
positive reinforcement. If you use the four levels of pressure, being very careful
to observe the slightest reaction, you will soon have a horse who moves easily
with minimum effort from you. The important trick here is never to allow yourself to think in terms of *pushing* the horse, or *making* him move through your
efforts. Instead, you think of applying the pressure and *letting him move himself*
away from it.

When moving the horse's front legs to the side, one of your hands asks
his head to move over first, usually about thirty degrees, then the other hand
asks for the feet to move. Similarly, when moving his hindquarters, one
hand brings the head around gently about seventy-five degrees, then the
other hand, placed in the hollow above and behind the stifle, asks the feet
to move.

These exercises should usually be practiced in the following order, which
is best for most horses in terms of the way they bend most easily (see page 128
for more on crookedness in the horse).

1. Step the front feet to the right.

2. Step the hind feet to the left.

3. Step the front feet to the left.

4. Step the hind feet to the right.

Voice Commands and Rewards

In the barn, about the only voice commands you need are the cluck and the whoa. It's your tone of voice that is the more important factor in getting the result you want, and that depends on the circumstances and the horse. Shouting "whoa" at a horse who is frightened is, of course, only going to frighten him more. On the other hand, a horse who keeps wandering away when he is ground tied needs a firm, authoritative voice to get his attention. Again, it is essential to recognize the moment when the horse *begins* to respond and praise immediately. Praise can take the form of a "good boy," or a pat, a scratch, or a treat.

Many people believe using treats makes the horse pushy and distracts him from the work, but I find that this depends on two factors. One is your ability to teach the horse that treats only appear when *he* performs some desired action. That is, a treat is a reward, not a bribe. One of the first things you teach a horse is that pushing or begging *never* results in a treat.

The second factor might be called the piggy factor. Some horses are simply extremely greedy, perhaps from having been chased away from their feed as youngsters by larger, older horses, or from malnourishment, or just their natural inclination. In any case, piggy horses are usually better off not being offered treats, because they tend to focus on them too much. On the other hand, with such horses sometimes you can use treats to get a very quick behavior change, because food is so important to them.

HALTERING, TYING, AND GROOMING

Putting on and taking off the halter is something you do every day, often several times. It is just as easy to do it considerately as it is to do it roughly. Many horses learn to throw their heads or pull away because of clumsy handling during haltering. The main things to remember are:

• Stand behind the horse's head, rather than pushing the halter at the front of his face where he can't see it well.

• Always point the ears forward gently when putting them under the crownpiece. Don't pull the crownpiece backward, crushing the ears.

• When putting the halter on or removing it, always do so one ear at a time. If the halter is safely and properly fitted, forcing both ears through it will be quite uncomfortable.

• Adjust the halter so the nosepiece lies about two fingers under the cheek bone and is loose enough so the horse can open his mouth comfortably, but not so loose that he or another horse could catch a foot in it. The throat latch should lie close to his throttle, but not be tight.

Some people are very much against tying a horse at all, while others expect the horse to stand quietly either tied by a single line or crosstied. Most professional stables expect that horses can be crosstied, since with many people taking horses in and out, the idea of having horses left ground tied only is not acceptable.

However, being confined by a rope in an exposed position is threatening to some horses, and they start fighting the ties. This can, of course, be extremely dangerous to both horse and bystanders. There are a number of ways to deal with this problem (see the references in appendix C), but one quick and easy solution is to attach a strand of knitting yarn between the ties and the horse's halter. The fight reflex is triggered when the horse steps back and feels the pull against his head. If he is tied with something that instantly breaks, he never really reaches the panicky stage. Of course, it is necessary for you to be there at all times so he doesn't find out that pulling back is followed by freedom to trot out the door and into the pasture!

Tying the horse by a single line, usually to a trailer or fence, has a couple of caveats.

• Never tie a rope to a board or rail that could possibly be slid out or pulled off. A loose horse with a ten-foot rail attached to his halter is a danger to himself and anyone nearby.

• Adjust the rope so the horse can reach the ground with his muzzle, but not so he can get a leg caught in it. Conversely, you occasionally see horses left tied with a very short rope. I consider this cruel and unnecessary, since it forces the horse to keep his head and neck in one position.

Grooming tools should be chosen to suit the particular horse's sensitivity. Grooming is intended not only to clean the horse, but to get him relaxed and comfortable before the ride. If the tools are too rough for the horse he will be tense and angry, which will carry over into the ride. A clipped Thoroughbred in the winter is going to have a very different reaction to a stiff brush than would a furry Shetland Pony.

As with everything you do, pay attention to how the horse responds to your grooming. If something seems to bother him, try to understand why and help him to be comfortable with it. The last thing you want to do is make him unhappy and afraid of you every time you get ready to ride. Softer grooming tools, less vigorous application, and time spent teaching him to accept and like being touched and groomed all over will all pay dividends in a more comfortable and trusting mount.

Picking out the horse's feet, which needs to be done regularly, can be a quick, simple task or a tedious and lengthy chore, depending on whether the horse is properly trained. It is well worth spending the necessary time teaching the horse to lift his hoof high enough to make cleaning easy for you, and holding it up rather than expecting *you* to hold *him* up. Most ground training disciplines offer guides to training to horse to do this, but I especially like the Parelli method of pinching the chestnut in front and the cap of the hock behind to get the initial lift. Then you can shape the behavior using a clicker. This simply means that at first you praise and reward the horse just for lifting the foot, then gradually withhold the praise and treat for longer and longer periods until the horse will hold the foot up as high and as long as needed. Using the clicker to mark the behavior you want is more effective, since it is so precise, but with patience you can teach the behavior with your voice alone.

It is important, especially at first, that you have the horse standing square and balanced before you ask him to lift a foot. Many horses have one foot that they have more difficulty holding up, so you will need a bit of patience. Obviously, hurrying or pressuring the horse will only make it more difficult for him to find his balance.

I'm preparing to spiral the hoof down to the ground. A few minutes ago this horse wouldn't hold up her foot at all.

Tidbits & Supplements

You can quite easily cause a well-trained horse to lose all desire to give you his foot if you use painful medications to treat ailments such as thrush. A few sessions of having his foot subjected to acute pain will soon teach the horse exactly the lesson you didn't want him to learn. Always be aware of how the horse is responding. If something is obviously very painful, try to find a friendlier product or treatment. If you have to use a painful treatment, be very generous with praise and treats so the horse understands that you are not *deliberately* causing him pain.

If the horse finds holding his feet up very difficult, the TTeam exercises for the feet are usually helpful. This involves holding the raised foot in both hands and gently circling it and spiraling it down to the ground. You will find that at first as the horse lowers his foot he tenses up, snatches the foot away, and plants it on the ground. By repeating the exercise until you get some improvement, the horse begins to learn how to release the tensions that are causing his problem.

As a rider, you have the option: If you are considerate and caring, you can make the ordinary daily routine of preparing your horse for riding a learning, bonding, and generally pleasurable time. If you think that's a waste of time and too much trouble, then you cannot be surprised if the horse doesn't give you one hundred percent when you ride him. The choice is yours. And the benefits of choosing the first option far outweigh any extra time spent.

2

The Following Horse

Moving Around the Farm

I was at a horse show many years ago and happened to be walking by when a horse was being loaded into a van. I knew the handler, Marie, to be an experienced professional, and was quite startled to see that even before she and her horse approached the ramp she had taken a heavy hold of the line and was more or less dragging the horse along by the head. As the horse reached the unstable footing of the ramp, he naturally resisted and pulled back. A fight ensued and the horse eventually loaded, but as I walked away I thought to myself how much trouble could have been avoided if Marie had been a better leader.

∽

Leading, like other ground work, should be a bonding exercise, as well as a useful skill. A horse who will follow you willingly and quietly wherever you go is pleasant to have around, and in a situation where riding is not possible it can make a difference to whether you reach your goal or not.

We all know that an average horse weighs about a thousand pounds, or, to make it even more impressive, half a ton. Why we ever think that we can muscle them around escapes me. Leading is probably the easiest action for the horse to resist, because his power can be so effortlessly engaged to pull back. Rearing and spinning are also easy options for him. The wonder is that more horses aren't running around loose at any given moment!

Luckily, horses, being herd animals, have an instinct to follow and move in groups, especially with those they trust and respect, so the concept of following, or at least staying near someone, is hardwired into them.

TEACHING YOURSELF TO LEAD

People who have learned to lead incorrectly find that their bad habits are extremely difficult to break. Some of these habits are based on instinct, such as getting behind the horse's head and pulling to stop him, while others are based

To learn more about this topic, read Chapter 5 of the companion volume to this book, *How Your Horse Wants You to Ride: Starting Out—Starting Over.*

on fear, such as keeping the leading arm stiff. Be prepared to spend a fair amount of time relearning your leading skills. When they are correct, you will meet with virtually no resistance or tension in your horse's responses.

The directions here will be for leading from the left, which is the normal position. But in addition to teaching you to handle the horse correctly on the ground, leading also teaches you the feel of using your hands when riding, so you will want to practice leading from both sides so that you learn to use both hands correctly. And of course, the horse needs to learn to be led from either side as well.

When you start working on your leading skills, your first task is to learn to keep your leading arm relaxed, no matter how sluggish or aggressive the horse may be. Try to remember that the more pressure you put on the line, the more resistance you create. As you prepare for leading, go through the first five of the Seven Steps frequently, especially the shakeout. Shoulder squeezes and releases (page 119) are helpful, too. Also try imagining that the rope is made of rotten string that will break easily.

In the previous chapter we talked about muscular telepathy, which is a way of saying that the horse copies whatever you do with your body. One of the ways he does this is by following your line of sight. Looking where you want the horse to go seems to direct his eyes to the same area. So to begin leading, you need to be facing the direction you expect to go. (Nothing is more self-defeating than standing in front of the horse, facing him, and trying to pull him along.)

If you stand beside and slightly in front of the horse's head, in a "leader" position, facing forward and looking at the ground about ten feet in front of you, you have already given the horse a pretty clear message about your intentions. With a horse who is accustomed to being with you, simply moving off from that position is often enough to bring the horse along. In fact, I have to be careful if I walk away from one of my school horses when a new student is holding him, because the horse is very likely to start following me!

If the horse is new to you, or is distracted, there is an escalating scale of reminders you can give him to get him started. From your starting position, shift your weight and start to take a small step, making sure you let your leading arm dangle loosely behind you with the line slack. If you are in the habit of holding the line tightly, do a good shakeout of your leading arm so that you release the tensions all the way up to your neck and jaw.

As you start to pick up your foot, if you don't sense the horse starting to move, give a firm little cluck. Be sure *not* to walk away if you don't feel him

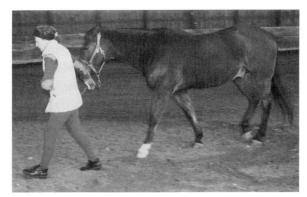

Starting up: My arm and the lead are
both soft and my gaze is ahead.

coming along. If the cluck doesn't work and you can keep your arm really relaxed, you can give a soft tug forward on the lead. Think of tugging on some-one's hand or arm to get their attention—which is really what you're trying to do, since we all know the lead is not going to pull the horse along.

Another method that frequently works is to use the same sort of tug a bit off to one side. Correctly done, this will cause the horse to turn his head, which will cause him to step sideways with his front foot to rebalance, which puts him in motion. A quick word of praise as you start to walk off in front of him in the new direction—still without pulling—should be sufficient.

If the horse is really determined not to follow, back off a little for the moment and see if you can figure out why. Generally speaking, especially if you and the horse are comparative strangers, you really want to avoid getting con-frontational. If the horse seems very tense, head up, looking around and not at you, then perhaps you should spend some time with a friendly game or some clicker work, to try to bring his attention back to you while establishing some trust. If he appears totally *in*attentive, you would probably do best to go right to work with the stick, using a lot of smiles and praise to get some attention and response. (See the photo on page 58.) When you're working with the stick, remember not to lose track of your body and eye positions. Also remember that the stick is intended as a signal, not a punishment. To keep your message clear and nonthreatening, begin with a light tap on top of the horse's croup. Look carefully for any sort of response—a little tensing of the buttock muscles, a flick of the ear, anything that shows the horse "heard" your signal. Wait three sec-onds before asking again and use the same degree of force as before if the horse responded at all. Repeat this several times, adding a cluck and a rein signal to help clarify your objective.

If the horse starts to ignore the signal, increase the pressure to the next level. Sometimes a horse confuses your wish to have him move with the friendly game, in which he is expected *not* to move when light touches are applied. This is where your intent has to be made clear. Even though you are not being physically aggressive, the horse has to sense that you are very determined that he should move, as opposed to your intent during the friendly game, which is that he should ignore what you are doing and during which your whole demeanor is more relaxed. This is a concept that both novice riders and novice horses find difficult at first, and it requires some practice. Be ready to praise the slightest move, even a shift of weight, in the desired direction.

On the other end of the scale from the horse who won't go is the horse who wants to take over and either lead you or drag you around. Again, your relative positions are very important. In the horse world, the one who is in front is the one who is in charge of the herd. Horses spend a lot of time working on their place in the herd hierarchy. Once you are no longer perceived as the predator, the next step for the horse is to make sure he has a higher standing in the herd than you—which, of course, you can't allow.

There are two techniques you use to teach the horse that he must give you precedence, and you can use them more or less simultaneously. As soon as he starts moving, the horse will usually move forward quickly so that his head is in front of your shoulder. He is now, in his mind, the leader. The usual

I am trying to block Lily at the shoulder.
She has turned her head away, and if she decides
to leave I won't be able to stop her.

Tidbits & Supplements

Even though the horse thinks he wants to be in charge, very often this makes him more, rather than less, insecure. In a world where he is frequently faced with situations he doesn't fully understand, if he is in charge it forces him to try to make decisions without sufficient data. So his solution is to turn and run, which, of course, is not acceptable to his rider. Everyone gets upset and no one wins.

If, instead, the horse has learned to turn over control to his rider or handler in a difficult situation, he feels comfortable knowing someone is in charge who understands what to do and he waits for a signal from the handler about how to handle the situation. If the handler is calm, the horse remains calm and everyone feels more secure.

---

reaction of the handler is to try to control the horse by stepping in close to his shoulder to block him, while hauling on the lead. The horse may or may not respond to this by slowing down a little, but it doesn't make any difference, because as long as his body is in front he feels that he is the one in control. So if you meet with any difficulties he is unlikely to submit to your authority.

Rather than stepping back as the horse steps forward, your move should be to step firmly *forward*, while at the same time applying a quick, firm tug on the lead to set the horse back (also see the active hand on page 167), so that you end up with your shoulder in front of the horse's head again. Circling quickly and sharply to the left, away from the horse, will give you the same result. With a determined horse you may have to do this a number of times before he finally decides he can't win. Here again, your intent is very important. If *you* are determined that, while you have no intention of hurting him, you are not going to allow the horse to dominate you, he will give up a good deal sooner.

In addition to the way you use your body, the stick is a very valuable aid here. Holding your stick in your left hand, reach across and swing it up and down vertically in front of the horse's face to form a barrier. If the horse decides after a few minutes that you really aren't going to use the stick and he can push by it, turn it so that the butt end is sticking up a few inches above your fist and give him a firm tap on the nose as he pushes forward. He will not perceive this as punishment, but rather that he walked into the stick and he needs to be

Setting back an overeager horse. I am showing Peg how
to step forward while pulling back.

more careful. If you can keep your eyes soft while doing so, it becomes even more impersonal.

Just as it was incorrect to try to keep the horse coming forward by dragging on the line, it is equally incorrect to try to keep him back with a tight line. The active hand action sets him back and is followed by an immediate release as soon as you feel resistance. Eventually the horse learns that if he follows quietly, neither hanging back nor barging forward, his head will be left alone.

Holding the stick to use as a swinging barrier.

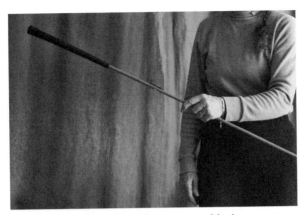

Holding the stick to use as a block.

TEACHING THE HORSE TO LOWER HIS HEAD

One exercise closely associated with leading is teaching the horse to drop his head on command. Raising his head is one of the ways the horse indicates that he is trying to take control. And it's not just horses; if you see a person with her head up and tilted back a little, looking down her nose, you automatically think, "arrogant; wants to take over." Conversely, someone who carries her head very low, looking out from under her eyebrows, seems overly weak and timid.

In a horse, a relaxed head and neck, with the poll slightly lower than the withers, indicates a willingness to listen and be respectful, but without fear. This is more of that emotion-muscle interaction we talked about in the previous chapter. That is, by putting the horse's body in the right configuration, you help to create the attitude you want.

As with everything, trying to force the horse's head down will simply create the very resistance you are trying to avoid. Instead, think of creating pressure that is just uncomfortable enough that the horse will want to move away from it, in this case on the top of the horse's neck, usually near the poll. When you feel the *beginning* of a yield to the pressure—which can be applied either with downward pressure on a halter or with your fingers or fingernails—you instantly remove the pressure and praise the horse. If you have already begun building a warm and caring relationship with this horse, he will quickly learn not only to drop his head, but that the feeling of giving up control to you is very relaxing and builds confidence. Later he can be taught to respond to neck pressure while being ridden.

Tidbits & Supplements

At one time I owned a really wonderful horse who had been abused and had a lot of trouble giving up control to his rider in difficult situations. I taught him to drop his head, so if we were out on the trail, for example, and he became upset and flustered for some reason, I would simply dismount. Then I would spend a few minutes walking him in hand and getting him to drop his head. Once he had done that, within a very short time he softened and relaxed and I could remount and continue. In his case I had to dismount because his reaction when he was very upset was to buck violently—a pattern I was trying to break. On a less violent horse I would have remained mounted and asked for the head drop from there.

RELATED GROUND SKILLS

When you are with the horse on the ground, there are things you do with him regularly in addition to leading. You may want to stop and have a conversation with someone and you certainly want him to stand quietly while you do so. You will also want to graze him in hand. At most stables there is better grass available in the areas where horses are not regularly turned out, such as along the edge of the driveway. Finally, you will probably want to be able to turn him loose in the field and catch him safely.

Standing Quietly

You have been walking your horse out after a ride and you spot a friend you would like to talk to. While you are doing so, you want your horse to simply stand still and wait politely. But horses can be very much like small children—they want you to pay attention to them! Every parent has had the experience of being in the room with a child who is playing happily by himself. Then the phone rings and the parent answers it. Within seconds the child is interrupting, asking questions, wanting help, and generally trying to get the parent to focus on him rather than on the phone. Horses tend to walk into your space, nudge at you, try to walk away—anything to keep your attention, just like the child. Spending a little time on ground training helps the horse become secure and comfortable even when he feels left out.

The Parelli yo-yo game is the model for this work. Essentially, you ask the horse to back out of your space, at first only a few feet. Then you insist that he wait there for a short period. Only after he does so is he allowed back into your space. Gradually you increase the distance and the length of time, until the horse finally says, "Oh, okay, I might as well relax and stand over here. It doesn't hurt, I'm not succeeding in pulling her chain, and she isn't giving in." Adding positive reinforcement in the way of smiles and praise will give you the best results. What is really interesting about this training is that when done correctly, the horse becomes far more relaxed and secure.

Grazing in Hand

You've had a good lesson with your horse, or perhaps you've come in from a long trail ride or even a hunter pace, or maybe you just want to spend a little quality time with him. So you decide to take him over to where there's some nice grass and let him graze. This can be a very pleasant bonding experience or it can end up as a series of arguments, depending on what sort of grazing manners your horse has.

If you have done your ground work, your horse will walk politely behind your shoulder as you take him over to the grazing area. But once you get there, he should not snatch the rope out of your hand without asking and stuff his muzzle into the grass as though he hadn't had a square meal in a year. Nor should he drag you from one place to another as he spots a patch of grass more appealing than the current one. And when you are ready to take him back to his stall, he should leave the grass without an argument.

Unless you are very much against the use of treats (in which case you can substitute verbal praise and patting or scratching), they are the most effective for teaching grazing manners. By substituting an even more appealing food item for the grass, you give the horse a concrete reason to listen to you in the face of all that temptation.

To teach him not to instantly put his head down when grass is available, begin in an area with no grass. Have him walk, then halt and wait with his head in normal position, then give him a treat. Once he figures out that he will get a treat when he stops and stands, the next thing that will probably happen is that he will start nudging for the treat. At this point you must be very attentive, patient, and firm, and not give him the treat until he stops all begging and stands quietly, waiting.

When he has learned that lesson well, move him to a place where the grass is nearby, such as the edge of the driveway. At first, repeat the stop-and-stand lesson with the grass out of reach, say five feet away. When you're sure you have his attention, move to where he can reach the grass easily. Once you're sure he understands that even with the grass there he must wait with his head up, you can use some verbal signal such as "okay!" to indicate that it is all right for him to graze. You will probably have to show him at first by reaching down and plucking some grass and using it to lead his head down. Continue to practice each time you lead him to graze, until he is confirmed in the polite behavior.

This behavior can easily be translated into a riding situation, so that you can, if you want, allow your horse to graze if you are sitting on him waiting for an extended period (but not long enough to make it sensible to dismount).

If at all possible, when the horse is grazing try to give him at least twenty minutes, which is about how long he requires to satisfy his nutritional need for fresh grass. But whatever the length of time you can give, at the end of it he should come up and follow you immediately. To get his head up, stand a little in front of his muzzle but not directly in front of his head, cluck, and give a firm, quick tug on the lead line. Don't try to haul his head up—he can outpull you every time and you may be teaching him to break away. Instead, if he doesn't respond after you have asked a couple of times, and assuming you have hard shoes on, tap him firmly on the side of the muzzle with your toe. This will almost always bring his head up momentarily, and if you are quick with the praise and the treat he will soon come up willingly—especially if you start the training after he has had adequate grazing time.

Another way to get his head up is to catch him as he is starting to move from one patch of grass to another nearby and raises his own head slightly. If your timing is right, the cluck and active tug will work to raise his head the rest of the way, and then you can praise and give him a treat.

Like the shoulder block, holding the horse this way
is asking for trouble. Lily has turned her head
and already taken a step away.

This is the correct way to holding a grazing horse. From this position I can quickly move either way to control Lily.

During grazing, if you allow your horse to move into a position where the line is running *back* from his head to where you are standing, you are setting yourself up for trouble. All he has to do is turn his head a little the other way and then march off whenever he feels like it. This is how horses, and more especially ponies being handled by children, learn to break away, which is one of the more unpleasant and difficult habits to eliminate.

Of course, as he grazes, the horse is constantly moving and it is easy to slip into the wrong position. However, if you teach yourself to always let your horse graze from a place almost directly in front of him, you will always have him under control, unless he has learned to break away. That is a whole separate problem, and requires that you simply never graze him in hand until and unless you cure him of this bad habit.

Turning Out

Turning the horse out is a time when many otherwise experienced horsemen risk injury through carelessness. Many horses—especially those who have to spend a good deal of time confined or who are getting large amounts of grain—get very excited at turnout time. They may explode out into the field with a series of bucks, kicking out behind not in any desire to hurt, but just as a way of releasing tension. However, they can very easily break your arm or your jaw. So your turnout pattern should be carefully programmed to avoid this. Anyone who handles your horse should also be taught safe turnout technique.

When you reach the turn out area, take the horse through the gate and turn him *all the way around* so that he is facing the gate. His head should only be about a step away from the gate. Unless he is very mouthy, it is good practice to give him a treat of some sort at this point, so he is in the habit of waiting. Then, depending on whether or not you turn out with the halter on, either carefully remove the halter (page 28) or unsnap the rope. An additional treat at this point is also a good idea. In any case, when the horse is free, step back into the gate yourself and allow him to move away on his own.

If other horses are waiting and your loose horse is blocking the gate and needs to be moved, swing the lead rope at him from a distance, bring a longe whip with you, or toss a small rock or sand at him. What you want to avoid is being within range of a loose horse's heels and then chasing him aggressively, because he is very likely to kick out in what he perceives as self-defense. And that's how you get hurt!

Catching

For our purposes here, we will assume the horse is not unwilling to be caught. (Catching a horse who doesn't *want* to be caught is a separate problem and has to do with trust and relationships.) When you go out to catch your horse, the first thing to remember is that if you pin him with your hard eye and walk purposefully toward him, you are setting yourself up as a hungry predator and thus triggering his defenses. Instead, allow yourself a little extra time and stroll out quietly, looking around with soft eyes. Work yourself around so that you are approaching at an angle from the front.

Your lead rope should be held casually in your hand or perhaps hung over your shoulder, but be sure you remove it from there before attaching it so there's no chance it could get wrapped around your neck. Talk to the horse as you come closer. You would like him to pick up his head as you approach. If you have treats in your pocket you can rattle them, or bite on a carrot to let him know that you have something good coming. If you have nothing to give him, rubbing the palms of your hands together makes an interesting sound that most horses respond to.

When he is within reach, put out your hand to let him sniff it, just as you do for an introduction. Then quietly slide your hand around to take the halter by the back of the noseband, equally quietly bring the snap over, and fasten it. Avoid quick, grabby movements or holding the front of the halter, both of which may be interpreted as aggressive. Also be careful not to hook your fingers into the rings of the halter, where they could get caught if the horse throws his head suddenly.

Once you have him, try to spend an extra thirty seconds or so just talking to him or scratching him, so that being caught is not always associated in his mind with immediately going to work. Although, if you're working him properly, he should look forward to his rides!

LEADING WITH A CHAIN OR A ZEPHYR STRING

A chain—or a zephyr string, which is applied like a chain but made of thin rope— is used with an English halter if the horse tends to get heavy and tries to drag you around. First, look at chapter 1 to see how to attach the chain to the halter correctly. This arrangement gives you more control in several ways than just the halter and lead alone. Running the chain through the ring and out to your hand gives you extra leverage because of the pulley effect. Running the chain up to the upper ring creates a head-lowering action. The correct way the chain crosses the noseband concentrates pressure on the horse's nose without being abusive. If you run the chain directly across the horse's nose instead, it can cause too much discomfort, perhaps causing the horse to become fearful or stubborn.

If the horse wants to run past you, simply use your active hand to apply pressure with the chain in the same way you used the regular lead on page 38. The chain will increase his discomfort enough to get his attention and thus give you extra control. It must be used carefully and not allowed to cause steady pressure, which could either frighten the horse or make him dull to the discomfort.

Here I'm using a zephyr string and a separate lead. If the horse was very difficult I could use a chain instead.

If you find yourself in a situation where the horse doesn't want to come forward but also tries to evade you by wheeling and breaking away, you will need a chain and a lead. The chain is attached as described above, and the lead is attached to the jaw ring in the normal way. You then use the lead to bring the horse forward and hold the chain lead in the other hand, ready to use it quickly if the horse attempts to pull away. It is very important in this situation to stay well ahead of the horse so he can't get the line into a position where he can easily pull against it.

LEADING WITH A BRIDLE

The same general rules apply to leading with a bridle as to using the halter and lead. The only difference is in what you do with the reins. If you are leading for a long distance or a long time, or in any situation where the horse might try to pull away, take the reins over his head and hold and use them exactly as you did the lead line. Just keep in mind that if you pull back you are pulling on the bars of his mouth, which are, of course, more sensitive than his nose.

For short distances in controlled situations, such as leading the horse out just before riding, the preferred method is to leave the reins over the horse's neck and lead with your hand on the near rein. Keep your fingers relaxed and open, so that if the horse moves his head suddenly the rein can slide through and neither one of you will be hurt by a sudden pull. The advantage of this method is that the reins are where they will need to be for riding. Many people are careless about the way they pull the reins over the horse's head in either direction when they mount. Shorter riders especially have a tendency to try to fling the reins over the horse's head, often cracking him in the face in the process, so if the reins are already there the horse is spared any possible discomfort.

This is also a good method for novice riders who are not ready to control a fractious horse. With the reins on his neck, if the horse gets away he is somewhat less likely to break his bridle before the instructor can catch him.

Leading is an integral part of working with the horse. If you perfect your skills, it will affect all aspects of your relationship with your horse. A horse who is accustomed to being polite and respectful on the ground will carry those behaviors over into riding. A horse who is accustomed to having his own way or lacks trust in his handler is going to be more difficult to ride. It certainly makes sense to solve these problems under the safest possible conditions!

3

The Floating Horse
Playing in the Arena

About fifteen years ago I had a mature horse to train whose carriage and atti-tude both needed a lot of work. In many ways, Shamus's poor attitude—tense and frequently angry—was a direct result of his high-headed, short-gaited way of going, which made balancing, especially on turns, very difficult for him. I was working with Ellen, his owner, at the same time, and would begin each riding lesson with an extensive free-longeing session—that is, I would work Shamus loose in the arena. During these sessions, by using praise I was able to mark for Shamus the moments when he began to move more correctly and freely. I also taught him to pace himself better so that he no longer came to the corners totally out of control. Over time he learned the most efficient ways to work off his tensions, so the sessions became shorter. He found better balance and began his riding sessions with a much more positive attitude. He and I and Ellen all benefited.

∾

Free-longeing is just what it sounds like: working the horse around you using an enclosure rather than a longe line to restrain him. While less disciplined than working a horse on a line, it should not be a totally uncontrolled exercise. **The objective of free-longeing is to help your horse find out how to work off his tensions effectively and safely, to improve his coordination and his abil-ity to handle himself in a confined space, and to teach him to listen to you in spite of having very little physical restraint.** From the point of view of the ground person, it takes far less skill than working the horse correctly on a longe-line, and therefore is more suitable for the novice. It's also a good way to learn the other skills of longeing before adding the line.

Free-longeing is extremely useful if your horse lives in a stall or compara-tively small space, or doesn't exercise himself when turned out in the field. Unlike line-longeing, you can encourage the horse to buck and run to loosen himself up with far less risk of him hurting either himself or you. If you are trying to hold the other end of a longe line and the horse makes a sudden big move, the resulting jerk on the line can easily cause injury to one or both of you.

To be effective, the enclosure for free-longeing must be large enough for the horse to be able to stretch as he moves. I have found that trying to get rid of stall tensions by using line longeing or turnout in a small space *where the horse cannot move freely* can result in a situation where the horse has to be longed for longer and longer periods each day before his muscles relax. A horse who is free-longed before riding, in a space large enough to allow for extension and free movement, quickly gets rid of his tensions so that he can be ridden safely and effectively, with better responses than if you rode him immediately.

Last but certainly not least, you will be improving your communication with him as well as observing his movement in freedom, which is always a valuable learning experience.

Let's begin by discussing some of the tools you will need. First we'll look at what they are and the theory behind their use. Later on in the chapter we will learn how to apply them.

YOUR CENTER

During free-longeing, since the horse is working at a distance and unfettered by lines, most of your control of him depends on understanding how to use your center. Throughout this book, I will talk extensively about this concept. It is difficult to define, because it has to do not only with your physical center (which is just in front of your spine and a little below your navel) but also with your center of energy. If you have ever done any tai chi, or yoga, or one of the Asian martial arts, you will be familiar with this idea. Since you will be using your center extensively for control during riding, learning to use it on the ground first will help you understand it and make you more adept.

How It Works

In everyday life you use your center in physical interaction with others by adjusting your moves relative to others' personal space. In some instances you want to stay out of their personal space or keep them out of yours; in other cases you want to allow them to move into your space, or you simply want to stay close to them as they move around. Most of this movement is unconscious and is referred to as *body language*. If you are seated next to a person, crossing your legs—turning your center—toward her indicates that you are comfortable with her in your space, while crossing your legs—turning your center—away from her means you would like to move away. She will unconsciously respond to these signals, as well.

Horses, as prey animals, have a strong sense of personal space. If the horse perceives another creature as threatening, his personal space enlarges—that is, he will not let the other creature get very close before he moves away. This sense of personal space is also directional, as in the game of tag. So if the perceived threat comes from in front, the horse stops; if it comes from the left, he turns right, and so on.

It does not require a serious threat to activate this sense of enlarging personal space; horses running in a group will move as necessary to keep from interfering with the horses next to them. It is this sense that you use to direct the horse during free-longeing. Most of the control you have over the loose horse comes from his unwillingness to run into your personal space, of which your center is an essential part.

We might say that your personal space is an expansion of your center. The more energetic and aggressive your center, the larger your personal space becomes, keeping others out. As your center becomes less aggressive and more passive, your personal space diminishes, allowing others in. This is a subtle but effective form of communication both between humans and between horses. Because it is more or less hard-wired in both, it is equally effective between human and horse. In other words, you can communicate with your horse by the way you place your body's center relative to his. Or, to put it still another way, you can communicate through the interaction of yours and the horse's personal space.

Many novices, faced with the thought of controlling such a large animal, find it threatening. Their feeling is that the horse, being large, will not pay any attention to commands given by little bitty me. But size has little to do with authority. In many herds, a pony half the size of the other animals will be bossing them around! You can probably also remember in school that there were some teachers whom you wouldn't dream of talking back to, and others for whom you had little respect, and it had nothing to do with size or strength. A little later we will discuss how to increase your feeling and appearance of authority.

Active and Passive Center

There are two ways you can use your center to interact physically: either keeping others out of your space or inviting them in. I call them the active center and the passive center.

Games that involve chasing another person are games in which we use our center to control the other person's moves. This is using the active center. That is, you make an active, even aggressive move with your center to drive the other person in the direction you want. As you run after someone in a game of tag, if she runs to the left you run even more to the left to cut her off and send her back to the right, perhaps into an area where she will be blocked by a wall and can be caught.

Games such as follow the leader involve using the passive center. The leader simply moves away and the others have the option of following or not, as they wish. If the leader chooses to perform a stunt that the followers find too threatening—or too silly—they can decide not to follow. On the ground with the horse, the passive center is used primarily in leading but is also an important aid when you are longeing or free-longeing.

INTENT

Intent is one of those very subtle tools that are totally invisible in one way but very clear in another. It can be either active or passive. Active intent says, "I'm going to do this and you'd better get out of my way!" Passive intent says, "I understand your need and I'm going to step aside and allow you to do your thing."

Many years ago I was attending the National Horse Show in New York. One of the classes was the Puissance. If you're not familiar with the show jumper world, the Puissance is a competition in which, as the class progresses, the jumps are reduced in number and increased in height until it ends with a spread (wide) fence and the Puissance wall (a wooden structure shaped and painted like a stone wall, with additional wooden blocks so it can be made higher). The wall is raised higher and higher until finally only one horse clears it successfully. It's a very exciting competition, and the horses are stretched to their utmost. (I should add that you cannot *force* a horse to jump high fences. He has to love it!) William (Bill) Steinkraus, the first U.S. civilian ever to win an Olympic gold medal in Grand Prix jumpers, was riding a not very large gray horse. The two of them jumped clean for several rounds. On the next-to-last round, when the wall was, as I remember, set at six feet nine inches, the horse put out a tremendous effort and barely cleared the obstacle. I said to my husband, "I don't think that horse can jump any higher than that." He agreed, and, as we found out later, so did Bill.

A second horse had also gone clean, so there was one more jump-off. The first horse came in and was unable to clear the fence. Then it was Bill's turn. He started out, jumped the spread fence, as was required, then turned and pointed his horse at the wall. He gathered him together and set him up in the proper impulsion, and then, about three strides away from the wall, he became totally passive. You could see in his whole posture and way of riding that he was saying to the horse, "It's up to you. If you think you can make it and want to try, go right ahead. I'm just going to stay out of your way and let you make the decision." His center was saying, "keep going if you can," but his intent was entirely passive. The horse set himself, sailed into the air, and cleared the wall! It was one of the most memorable rides I have ever seen.

Many years later I used the same trick with a novice horse in a class where I felt he was overfaced, with equally successful results. It was very satisfying!

At the other end of the scale, during the years I was actively teaching, there were many, many occasions when I asked a rider to do something that, at some level, she wasn't really sure she wanted to do. She would try, and fail, and try, and fail. Finally I would say to her, "You have to *make up your mind* that you really want to do this. When you do, the horse will do it." At the same time, if I was quite sure she could do it, I would make *my* intention quite clear by looking as if I was prepared to wait all day, if necessary, for her to make up her mind. Sure enough, an expression of determination would come over her face and the horse would say, "Oh, you want me to canter [or whatever]? Of course. No problem!" And he would canter blithely away as though he had just been waiting for her to tell him. Which, of course, he had.

Intent is a very important element in getting the horse to cooperate and do his best for you. We all have the ability to convey our intent. It just takes self-awareness and practice.

YOUR EYES AND POSTURE

Your eyes have a major effect on directing the horse because they indicate to him where you plan to go next. The horse, being a prey animal, is very sensitive to the eye focus of the predator, since it predicts both if and how the predator is going to try to trap him. But, because of muscular telepathy, he is also aware of the leading focus of the rider. That is, if the rider, or in the case of free-longeing the ground person, *looks* at the point at which the horse would look as he moves forward, the horse reads this and follows the handler's eye.

The Passive Eye and Posture

Your passive eye is generally a soft eye (page 14) and is usually used in conjunction with a passive center. At the same time, you also incorporate a passive posture. This is not the same as a weak or humble posture, which might encourage the horse to take advantage of you. The best way I can describe it is to think of standing back to allow someone to go ahead of you through a doorway. You are not being weak, you are simply choosing to allow the other person to go first; it shows in the way you stand and indicates intent. You stand erect, with your neck a little rounded so that your head is slightly bowed—a gesture of acquiescence. Your center is turned away a bit, indicating that you do not intend to move into the available empty space, but are allowing the other person to do so.

The Active Eye and Posture

The active eye is used in a more commanding way, especially if the horse starts to become aggressive. It is a focused, fairly hard eye. The accompanying posture is very erect and grounded. It says, "Pay attention. I'm talking to you!" Facial expression is also a part of it. Parelli calls it the "mother-in-law" look.

Your gaze is directed at the part of the horse you want to control at that moment. For example, if you want the horse to turn away from you, look firmly at the side of his neck just in front of the shoulder. If you want him to face you, look at his hindquarters so that he will swing them away, bringing his head toward you. If you want a stop, place yourself so that you are more or less facing the horse as he comes toward you and look directly at his face.

OTHER TOOLS

Enclosures

To work with the horse on the ground, you need a midsize space. A round pen will work if that's all you have, but for learning your moves in free-longeing, round pens are a little small. Plus, the lack of any straightaway limits the horse's ability to loosen up and makes him tire more quickly without necessarily becoming more relaxed. A sixty-by-eighty-foot rectangle is a fairly good size to start the horse in. You want enough space for the horse to move around, but not too much. The long side gives him room to run a bit; the short side slows him down and brings him back within reach.

If the space is too small the horse will be unable to really stretch out, which is the main point of the exercise. If the space is too big *you* have to walk a lot and it is almost impossible to keep the horse going at a steady pace, because you constantly lose contact with him. You may want to start the horse in a smaller space to give him the idea, then move him to a larger one.

Some horses need more space than others, depending on their size, length of stride, and coordination, among other things. If your horse tends to run to the other end of the enclosure and stop in a corner, try a smaller space. If he seems to have a problem handling the turns and shows signs of liking to really stretch out, you may need something larger.

Tidbits & Supplements

You can create different-size spaces in an arena using posts and some sort of clearly visible horizontal barrier. Jump poles or heavy tape are two options. The barrier should be about four feet high, lower for ponies. Two strands of tape—one at two and one at four feet—is the best arrangement. However, if the horse is likely to try to jump out, tape could be dangerous if he gets caught up in it.

Driving Tools

For most horses, you also need something to initiate movement if the horse does not respond to a cluck or your voice. This can be a longe whip, a long rope, or a stick with a plastic bag tied to it—anything you can swing and the horse will respect but not fear. Whatever tool you use should always be held in your following hand, that is, the one away from the direction in which the horse is moving.

Sometimes you find a timid or nervous horse who has had the longe whip used too aggressively. If your horse tends to run too much and seems unwilling to walk or trot quietly even after being out for a while, try working without anything in your hand. With these horses just a gesture with your hand will get the desired response, or perhaps tossing a little sand from the arena floor once he gains confidence.

Most of the time, when gesturing with your hand, whip, or rope, the gesture should be almost horizontal, not up and down. The exception is when you are asking the horse to turn away, especially with his forehand, that you use the tool vertically to point at the area where you want the horse to move.

APPLYING THE TOOLS

Horseless Work

Although you rarely hear it mentioned, the active center is one of the major aids used in free-longeing work. I suspect many novices who fail in round pen or other free-longeing work do so because they send messages to the horse with their center that directly conflict with their other signals.

The easiest way to get a feel for the active center is to start on the ground with another person working with you. You don't need any equipment for this exercise. All you need is a small, restricted space such as a room or a small pad-dock, and a goal, which can be the other side of the room.

1. Stand facing your partner, about an arm's length away. Her back is to one wall. She is the "horse." Her aim is to get to the goal, which she is facing across the room. Your aim is to prevent her from doing so. The only rule is that you may not touch each other in any way. As she moves, simply move as necessary so that your body is always between her and the goal.

2. She may persist for a while and speed up her moves, but unless you are very unequal physically she will fail. After a while she will simply give up!

3. Change places and be the "horse" yourself.

This exercise demonstrates that you can block the "horse's" movement by placing your body, which is your energized center, between your partner and her goal. Because all your signals are nonthreatening, the "horse" is not provoked or frightened into aggressive behavior to "win" the encounter. (With a real horse who is aggressive for other reasons, adding a rope or longe whip will add the necessary energy to control him, probably without having to actually strike him with it.)

For the next exercise you need a space large enough for the "horse" to walk around the perimeter. This exercise is free-longeing your "horse." The rules are:

1. The "horse" should try to cooperate. That is, she should try to interpret what you are asking for. She should watch you carefully and try to respond to your body movements as promptly as she can.

2. You may not use verbal directions, except for gait changes. Use only your center to ask for direction and a cluck to ask for movement, and the word "good" or the equivalent to indicate that the "horse" has made the right response.

3. You may, if necessary, take the "horse" by the hand to position her, but only when she is standing still.

Once you both understand the rules, it's time to start the exercise.

1. To start the "horse" moving, place yourself so that you are a little behind and to one side of her, facing the direction you wish her to go. Then cluck to start.

2. To keep her going, walk a smaller circle inside of hers, always aiming a little behind her. As you step around, try to cross one leg in *front* of the other so that you are always moving slightly forward. Move so that an extension of your path would take you behind her, not in front of her. Use a soft eye, aimed at the "horse's tail."

A crossover step; the horse is just
out of the picture on the left.

3. To change her gait, try changing your own gait in addition to the other commands or movements. Once she is in the gait you want, you can return to a walk.

4. To stop her, walk across the circle and face the way she is coming. Look directly at her as she approaches, and if necessary block her as you did in the first exercise.

5. To turn her, if she is in the middle of the space, step to the side away from where you want her to go, and then move to keep blocking her until she turns in the direction you want. If she is out on the "rail," you have to first block her by getting out on the rail in front of her, as you did when you were asking for the stop, to indicate that you don't want her to go by. This is where it takes a little experimenting, because different people—and different horses—respond in different ways. One person might stop and just stand there, another might try to cut past you, another might turn and go back. Use praise to cue your "horse" that she's doing the right thing.

Your goal is to get the "horse" walking and jogging around the "rail," stopping, and executing direction changes. (Hint: Using soft eyes will help with your awareness of the "horse" relative to the space, and will also help her understand where you want her to go. Hard eyes directed at the "horse" will demand attention.) After you have succeeded, discuss with your partner how she felt about your commands, then take a turn as the "horse."

Depending on how responsive and sensitive your "horse" is, you should begin to have a feeling of how quickly you can get a response to a movement of your center. One of the things you should have noticed is that to get the "horse" moving you need to get *behind* her center. If you stand in front of her and look at her, she has no place to go. This is one of the most common mistakes made by people trying to work a horse on the ground.

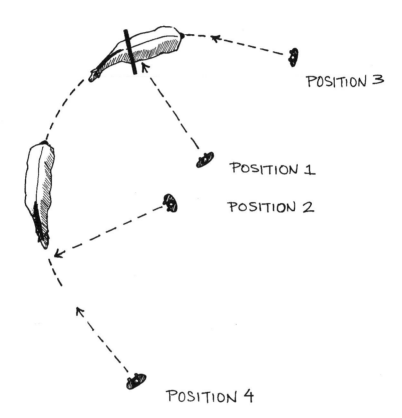

POSITION 3

POSITION 1

POSITION 2

POSITION 4

POSITION OF CENTER DURING LONGEING AND FREE-LONGEING.

Position 1: Correct position for maintaining the horse's gait.
The projected path is toward a point slightly behind the horse's center.
Position 2: Most common mistake. The handler's body is turned so that
the projected path is ahead of the horse's center, blocking his forward movement.
Position 3: Position for sending the horse strongly forward when free-longeing.
Positions between 1 and 3 will send the horse forward less or more,
depending on the angle.
Position 4: Position for blocking, to stop or prepare for a turn. Positions between 2 and
4 will block the horse less or more, depending on the angle.

Working with the Horse

When turned loose in a large space, some horses will immediately start to move around by themselves. Others will just stand and stare at you. The hardest part then is getting them started. There are two ways to approach this problem. One is more passive and is used with the horse who seems tense; if, for example, he is facing you with his head up. The second, active method is used with a horse who seems more lethargic; wandering around with his head down looking for bits of hay. In either situation, *without looking directly at him*, walk past him about five feet away until you are behind him, off to one side. You are thus placing yourself so that your center is a little behind his, and you are facing in the same direction as he. Be ready to praise the moment you see any signs of moving away (as opposed to turning to face you).

Begin with the passive method:

1. Direct your passive, soft, eye to a point ten or fifteen feet in front of the horse, that is, the point at which he will be looking as he moves forward.

2. Cluck and move your feet as if you were starting to walk, perhaps turning slightly away as if you were opening a door for him to go through.

If he doesn't move, you will need to gradually become more active. Begin by pointing the hand farthest from him toward his head to keep him from turning to face you again, and at the same time swing the other arm in a forward sweeping motion toward his tail from behind. (Many horses have had the whip used too aggressively in longeing or free-longeing situations, and respond more calmly to arm signals.)

If the horse keeps spinning around to face you, first check to make sure your gestures that ask him to move are directed *behind* his tail and are coming forward horizontally, not vertically or toward the side of his hindquarters. If you are doing this correctly and the horse is not responding, you need to use a different approach.

1. Lead the horse to the rail and stand him next to it, facing left hand around (counter-clockwise).

2. Place your left hand lightly on his halter just above his chin and stand so that you are facing his body near his shoulder.

3. Take your hand off his halter but keep it fairly close to his head, pointing at it with your fingers and looking at him. Ask him to stand or whoa.

4. If you are carrying a longe whip place it in your right hand, holding it by the middle, parallel with the horse's body. The butt should be pointing toward the front and the lash toward the rear of the horse.

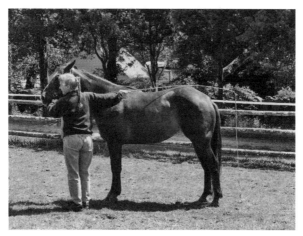

Preparing to start a reluctant horse.

5. When he stands, keep pointing at his head and slowly turn and step back so that you are *facing the way you want him to go* and standing just oppo-site where his saddle would be (just behind his center) about an arm's length away, leaving the whip parallel to the horse. **Caution:** If you do not know the horse, or if he seems at all tense or likely to kick, position yourself at least six feet away.

6. Look away from him toward where you want him to go, but keep your left hand or the butt of the whip pointing toward his head. Then cluck and ges-ture quietly with your right hand or the lash end of the whip to ask him to move. If he tries to face you, get more active with your left hand or the whip butt to chase his head away. Praise any movement in the desired direction.

Since free-longeing is not a disciplinary procedure, it is important for the horse to learn to move quietly away from you without fear, rather than feeling

---

Tidbits & Supplements

Another, and very easy, way to get a horse to move is to put the horse out with another horse who moves around willingly, as long as they won't fight. The horse soon learns he is out there to move around and begins to do so easily on his own. We used this method to exercise horses before using them in my school; they had a wonderful time rac-ing and playing together.

he is being driven away, which can result in tense rushing around rather than movement that helps him relax. Your goal is to help the horse find out what kind of "exercises" he needs to do to loosen up his body. Some horses need to walk for quite a while at first before they feel loose enough to move faster. Others like to get out and run and buck right away, then settle down to a brisk trot or canter to finish up.

> ### Tidbits & Supplements
>
> Rolling also is good, vigorous exercise. If I have a horse who likes to roll, I turn him out with no tack and allow him to do so. Some horses like to roll right when they are turned out; others like to run first and roll later. (This means, of course, that if your horse likes to roll there is no point in grooming him until after you've free-longed!)

You use your voice to encourage good movements or discourage unsafe ones. Good movements are head shaking, safe bucking, and running at safe speeds. If the horse looks like he's "driving too fast for conditions" use words such as "whoa" and "steady," followed by "good" when he slows down a bit. It takes some skill and practice, and an eye for movement, to figure out when you should ask for more movement and when you should encourage the horse to slow down.

If the horse does not trot or canter right away but walks around quietly, after a few minutes ask him to move along in the same way you asked him to move in the beginning, that is, by getting a little behind him, facing the way he is going, and clucking or otherwise signaling him to speed up. Try for a quiet trot at first. If he is voice trained you can use the word "trot," or you can start to jog a little yourself, swing your arm, rope, or stick at him, or whatever works. Just remember that you want to *encourage* him to do what comes naturally, not get him running out of fear. Keep him trotting until his head begins to stay down and his gait to smooth out. If he is really out of shape he may need to catch his breath a couple of times before he loosens up.

Next, ask for canter and let him move around at a more vigorous pace. This is when most horses will play if they're going to, but if not, and if you think he has that little glint in his eye that says he's feeling good, after a while you can clap your hands or chase him a little more aggressively to see if he gives a couple of good loosening bucks and runs. After that, I look for the gait to level out again and then encourage him to stop.

Some horses will fool you by acting as if they don't want to do anything at all except walk and jog reluctantly. Not infrequently, these are the really tense ones who take a long time to loosen up to the point where they feel able to buck and play safely. Be especially suspicious if the horse has been confined for a while.

You do, of course, want to work him in both directions, but to some extent you need to listen to what he has to say on the matter. Most horses are more comfortable warming up in one direction and will resist going the other way. If this is so, go along with it for a while. Then, as the horse warms up, insist that he work the other way at least at the walk for a little while, then reverse and work his good direction, then back to the difficult one, and so on. If you insist that he work at speed in his difficult direction, you will only make him tense about it and there is a risk he may fall.

You also need to consider what kind of shape the horse is in. A fit horse will probably take a bit longer to loosen up than a horse who hasn't been working much. The stiffer horse is also more prone to strain injuries so he shouldn't be encouraged to do too much. If you're planning a fairly hard ride you don't want to wear the horse out before you start, but if you're planning a short ride or don't have time to ride at all, you can work the horse longer.

I realize some of this sounds a bit vague, but every horse is different and you just have to watch and learn what works for each one. And of course, it's fun to watch!

THE ACTIVE AIDS

Many people find it difficult to keep the horse moving around the arena at a steady pace. He seems to constantly stop and turn without being asked, or to go tearing around. Part of this problem often relates to the horse's natural tendency to want to hurry toward the gate, which he perceives as safe, and get away from the far end, which he perceives as a trap. However, at least some of it is often the result of the handler positioning her center or using it in ways that confuse the horse.

To begin with, check to make sure at all times that the hand that is away from the direction in which the horse is moving is the hand that asks for forward movement. Now review step 4 of free-longeing a person (page 55). Then check your moves carefully and try to figure out what you may be doing to place your body in a way that prevents the horse from continuing. Very often it is something as minor as looking at the horse as he comes around the corner.

To learn something about a particular horse's response to your active center, as he moves around the arena, position yourself on the side of the arena from which he will be approaching the gate. Stand about fifteen feet from the wall facing the horse as he comes down, moving almost directly at you. Without moving, look directly at him and watch his reaction as he comes toward you.

Through your body language, placing yourself firmly in the horse's way, and looking directly at him, you use your center as a block. Since you are standing still, it is not a very aggressive block. Thus you will get one of a few responses. He may hesitate, or even stop and reverse direction. A horse who feels very threatened and trapped may run into your space momentarily to get past you and away, rushing through the small space between you and the wall. He may even accompany this with threatening gestures in hopes of scaring you off long enough to let him "escape." Unless he decides to make a habit of charging in this manner, it's best to ignore this behavior except as an indicator that he feels unsure.

If the horse seems to rush around too fast, even after he has worked off his initial energy, you may be sending aggressive signals. Walking briskly behind the horse may be perceived as chasing. Carrying the whip so that it is pointing toward or just behind the horse, or even having a whip at all, may be interpreted as aggressive by some horses. When you are not trying to send the horse, the whip should be held in your following hand, turned around and held so that the lash is dragging behind you. *It is particularly important not to chase a horse who is running fast. It is too easy to distract him so that he runs into something and injures himself.* (Also see the passive center, page 49.)

Many horses will move rather reluctantly to the far end of the arena—away from the gate—and then race home and stop. After a while you can start to control this by positioning yourself near the home end of the ring, about

Trailing the whip. The horse would be off to my left,
and going to the left.

twenty feet from the wall along which the horse will be running home and facing it so you can see the horse coming without blocking him. As he approaches the far end, use a whoa command *before* he starts his bolt for home, and be prepared to block him firmly if he tries to rush anyway.

Sometimes you need to set up a partial barrier with jump standards and poles so that you can control him better. When he slows down to a sensible pace or stops, step aside and become passive and allow him to come back home, being ready to check him again if necessary. He soon learns that he *will* be allowed to return home, but *only* if he does so slowly and sensibly. This will help you with control when you start trail riding.

This pattern of slowly leaving home and rushing to return is very common and interferes with training in many ways, since the horse is tense. If you can teach the horse, without being threatening, that he can and should maintain a more even pace around the arena, it will be helpful for later training.

Horses who want to stand and rear should be gently encouraged to move forward. Rearing is often a result of conflict of interest. The horse wants to run, but either he is a little frightened of the space, or perhaps his neck and shoulder muscles are tense so that he gets in his own way. In either case, if you chase too aggressively you may make things worse. Rearing can also occur if you try to chase the horse when he is facing you, because you block him. Always be sure to get behind a rearing horse before you ask him to move. If he continues, put a lead rope on him and lead him quietly and carefully until he seems comfortable. As for teaching him not to rear, rather than yelling at him for rearing, watch carefully and as soon as he comes down, praise him effusively.

The center can be such a nonthreatening aid that the horse may decide he can ignore it. This is especially likely to happen to a novice rider. Experienced horsemen have many tools to work with, so they know they can get a response with one of them. This gives their body a confidence and power that the horse recognizes. Some trainers speak of this as energy. Energy can also be derived in other ways—Centered Riding (see appendix C) offers some wonderful thoughts on finding and creating energy in yourself.

The most common way of increasing your energy is by using some sort of tool, such as a whip, but you should leave this as your last option. If your energy is a bit low the horse will often ignore you by becoming sluggish. To correct this, first let your eye focus on the horse's hindquarters as you ask for more movement by clucking. If you get no response, step aggressively toward his hindquarters, pushing your hip at him as if you were going to swing and kick like a horse. (Be careful to stay out of his range!) Throwing a small handful of sand from the arena floor in the direction of his hindquarters very often gets a good response. If not, swing the whip or rope at him or whack it hard on the ground—but some horses figure out that you aren't really going to hurt them with it.

If you feel the horse is ignoring you or not giving you sufficient respect, consider being somewhat more obvious. Wave your arms, or throw the rope, or run at the horse (carefully), or throw sand at him, followed by effusive praise when he stops, or moves away from you, or does whatever you wanted.

You can be positive about what you want even when you're not quite sure how to get it. Pretend that, instead of being a large horse he is a rather small dog who is your pet, but is about to lift his leg on your upholstered chair! You would yell and run at him quite aggressively to get him away from the chair, but once he backed off you would want to reassure him; so you'd wait a second, then walk toward him reassuringly. You can use the same techniques to get the horse to move around the ring, being as aggressive as necessary until he starts to move away, then becoming passive and reassuring when you want to come up to him. However, when being aggressive **never** come closer than about ten feet. A horse who feels trapped and threatened will very often kick in self-defense.

Be sure you praise any effort on the horse's part to respond. (This is a good time for clicker training techniques.) As a final resort, if you are absolutely sure you are not making any mistakes and the horse is not in any pain or discomfort, you can pop him once with the rope or whip, just enough to make him sit up and pay attention. Think of it as taking TV privileges away from your spoiled child who has decided you aren't going to be able to stand up to his demands. The contact needn't be very hard, but should smart a little. It should be aimed just below his buttock point with particular care taken to make sure the lash or rope end doesn't go *between* his hind legs, where it could cut the tender skin.

It is easy for the novice to get into the trap of overusing the whip. You just have to avoid the temptation to get too aggressive and make the horse fearful or angry. If you can't get a response without using the whip a lot, then either your signals are unclear to the horse or he has a physical or emotional problem that you haven't recognized.

Occasionally an animal has been exposed to this or similar work in a way that either confused, frustrated, or hurt him, and he developed a serious anger about it. If the horse is really hostile about free-longeing, it's best to skip it until you can get some help, especially in building trust and relationships.

Stops and Turns with the Active Aids

Once the horse is moving around the ring fairly easily, you can begin to ask for other responses. The next one should be the stop. Use the same techniques you used to practice with the person, but add some voice commands and suggestions such as "whoa," "steady," and "good." Be sure to allow plenty of time for the greater size and speed of the horse. If he is trotting or cantering, give him a voice command to stop when he is on the opposite side of the ring from where you actually want him to stop. At first, ask for the stop as he is moving away from the gate. If you realize he isn't going to stop in time, step politely out of the way and ask again the next time.

Giving the horse a treat when he stops the first time or two will ensure his cooperation. However, do not let him come to you to get the treat, since this tends to teach him to beg. Make him wait for you to come to him, if necessary leading him back to where he was before you give him the treat.

When you can control his speed, then you can ask for direction changes. This is where it gets interesting, since you have to figure out where to position your body so that he turns and still keeps moving. It is easy to confuse him at this stage if you make a mistake, so don't be impatient if you don't get the right results immediately.

Begin by asking for a stop. When he is stopped, or nearly so, walk over close to the fence and then walk toward him, look past him on the outside, and cluck. Look for any tendency to turn away from you into the center and praise it. Then walk parallel to him and a little behind him so he has to walk across the ring or back to the wall in the opposite direction. If he just doesn't get it and stops and stands there, walk up to him quietly and lead him around until he is facing the other way, praise and reward him, and start him up again as before.

Turning toward the fence to reverse is trickier. You stop him as before, but then, instead of walking toward a point *outside* him to get him to turn to the inside, you walk toward a point just *inside* of his head to encourage him to turn to the outside. However, he may feel trapped between you and the wall, especially if he stopped close to the wall, because there is no place for his head to go if he turns to the outside. You have to leave him a little space to back up a tad and swing his quarters toward you. Again, you may need to lead him into the reverse a few times until he starts to get the idea.

Another method is to walk toward him (while he is walking), staying close to the rail, so that he veers away from the rail. Then cut across to get on his other side and send him back toward the rail in the new direction.

The main thing is not to become impatient or judgmental either with him or yourself while you're both figuring it out. Once he understands what you're after, you should be able to get direction changes with little effort or loss of forward motion.

THE PASSIVE AIDS

If the horse is at all unsure about you, he will be hesitant about going past you in a confined area. By becoming passive with your center, you can become less threatening and invite him into the space you want. It is very similar to inviting someone to pass through a doorway in front of you.

1. Have the horse loose in a moderate-size area such as an arena—big enough so that you won't keep blocking the horse because it's hard to stay out of his way. Using the techniques described in the section on getting the horse started (page 57), get him moving around the rail at a slow trot.

2. Use your active center to get a stop by positioning yourself about halfway down a long side when the horse is on the opposite side. Stand about ten feet from the rail, facing the direction the horse is coming from and looking at him as he approaches you. He is most likely to stop, but as we have seen, occasionally a horse will rush past you.

3. Now send the horse around again and position yourself in about the same place but another step or so away from the wall.

4. Instead of facing the horse as he approaches, turn your back and drop your head so you assume a very passive position. Do not turn your head to look at the horse. At this point, he will probably accept your invitation to go past you through the "door" you have opened for him. If he is timid he may still be suspicious, and perhaps will either stop again or hesitate and rush past.

5. Experiment with the amount of passivity you need to offer to get the horse to pass you quietly and with confidence. You become more passive by moving farther away, thus allowing the horse more room for his personal space. Breathing and not allowing yourself to consider whether you are "winning" the encounter are also important.

6. Once you have found a formula the horse is comfortable with, you can increase his confidence in you by gradually becoming a little less passive without becoming aggressive. Slowly turn around, a little at a time, and move a bit closer to the wall again. If the horse refuses to go by, you have done too much too soon and you will need to become more passive again. At no time should you stand directly in his way or look directly at him.

This is a useful way to develop trust between you and a timid horse, and also to increase your awareness of the horse's responses.

Transitions and Turns with the Passive Aids

While you can use your active center as described in "Stops and Turns with the Active Aids" to block the horse and cause him to stop, the resulting transition is often very abrupt. You can get a much smoother downward transition by using your center passively. This is also more like what you use for downward transitions when riding.

1. Get the horse moving around the arena at the trot. Use your active center to maintain his gait. If the horse is very responsive to voice commands or clucks, try to *avoid* using them as much as possible until you get a feel for working the passive center.

2. When you are ready for the horse to slow down, while still staying a little behind his center start making your movements less energetic and smaller. Move more slowly, put your hands behind your back, drop your eyes, breathe, and generally allow your body to indicate that you are no longer asking the horse to keep trotting.

3. Look for the first sign of slowing down and praise. When the horse comes to the walk, approach him and praise and reward effusively.

4. If the horse stops abruptly, praise but then ask him to trot again and keep your center a little less passive as you ask for the downward transition, so that he maintains forward movement and balance instead of stopping abruptly. Think of gradually allowing your car to slow down as you approach a red light, as opposed to driving right up to it and then jamming on the brakes.

Many tense horses have been taught that stopping is not acceptable, even when there is no signal to keep going. The horse learns that he must wait for a positive signal before stopping. The trainer wants the horse to learn not to break gait, so he does not permit it even when the horse feels awkward and unbalanced and wants to stop to regroup. Thus the horse is forced to keep going no matter what. This may cause a horse to resort to bucking or running when he feels unsure.

By teaching him that it is all right to stop if there is no signal to keep going, we give him an option that is much safer for all concerned. Then, if horse and rider get into a situation where the rider is too unbalanced to give a stopping signal, the horse at least knows that stopping is an option.

When you have become quite skillful at using your passive center for slowing down, you can experiment with using the passive center for turning. There are two ways that are easiest for you and the horse. One is to place yourself in front of the horse as he is walking so you are walking in front of him, and then turn yourself, praising him for following. At first, make your turns *toward* the

---

Tidbits & Supplements

Now that you understand something of how your center works, you might want to return to Chapter 2 on leading and think about how your center works in that relationship. Because you are using a lead line the horse can't wander away, so he learns to follow your passive center. If he becomes aggressive, your center becomes momentarily active as you step ahead of him, then passive as you ask him to follow. If you need to be able to longe him on a line at shows, you can combine your knowledge of leading and free-longeing to teach the horse to work around you without either one of you fighting the longe line.

---

gate—that is, get in front of him as he is walking away from the gate, then turn in a half circle back toward the gate. The second way is to observe the horse beginning to turn and consciously allow and encourage it by stepping out of his way—the "after you" behavior.

There are other times when the passive aids are useful. For example, if you accidentally find yourself in a position where your center might block the horse from continuing on the track, allow your eyes to become passive and look along the path you want him to take. Being passive, your eyes ask the horse to follow and are a subtle, nonthreatening indicator of your wishes.

If the horse becomes frightened or overexcited and starts running in a way that could be dangerous, and you are not in a position to block him with an active center, adding a passive eye and center to quiet voice commands will help keep him safe until you can stop him.

Passive control is most useful for encouraging the horse to do something that he wants to do anyway. In that sense it tends to go with clicker training.

Once you have worked out the moves for free-longeing, you can work in a larger space with two people, passing the horse from one of you to the other as he moves around a space where one person would have trouble staying with the horse. You can also work with two or more congenial horses in the same space, focusing on first one and then the other as you ask for transitions and direction changes. This is the basis for the "liberty horses" one sees in a circus.

With practice, you can move the horse easily around the ring, stopping and changing direction with very little effort and very few commands. Your horse will be paying attention to you and doing as you ask, without the two of you being physically connected. That's fun for both of you. If you are a novice, it will give you quite a feeling of power. You can actually ask the horse to do something and have him do it! Wow!

Part II

Riding So Your Horse Likes It Too

4

Clothing, Tack, and Mounting
Starting Out Right Is the Key

Many years ago I had a student who was having an unusually difficult time learning to sit the trot. I had given her a horse with a very slow, gentle jog, but even then she wasn't doing too well. Then one day she casually mentioned something about her panty girdle! I asked her if she was wearing one and she said yes, she wore it to avoid chafing. "Well, no wonder she can't sit!" I thought to myself. Then I explained that the girdle compressed all the muscles and flesh in her seat and upper thigh, so that her seat was hard and pinching no matter how much she tried to relax it. Thereafter she left the girdle home and the sitting problem soon solved itself.

∾

Riding is difficult enough without problems created by wrong or ill-fitting equipment, whether on you or on the horse. There are plenty of options to choose from, but here are some fairly simple guides to follow.

CLOTHING

Let's start from the top.

Your Head

The horse world is full of people who think you only need to wear a safety helmet if you are jumping. I have personally known three people who died of head injuries falling off horses, and none of them was jumping at the time. I didn't wear a helmet for years, for all the same reasons—or excuses—that everyone else gives, but when it was pointed out to me that I was setting a bad example for my junior students, I started wearing one. Thereafter it saved me from serious injury several times, and now I feel as uncomfortable riding without a helmet as I do driving without a seatbelt. Don't take the chance; new helmets are

71

To learn more about this topic, read Chapters 4 and 6 of the companion volume to this book, *How Your Horse Wants You to Ride: Starting Out—Starting Over.*

comfortable and well designed. Get one and wear it every time you get on a horse. Save your cute hats for ground work.

Less apparent, but still dangerous: Women should avoid long, dangly earrings that can get caught on parts of the horse or his clothing. Having an earring ripped out is no joke. Very long, free-swinging hair can also be a hazard. I have long hair and a couple of times have come a little closer than I liked to having some of it pulled out by the roots.

Your Neck, Arms, and Upper Body

Along with the dangly earrings, stay away from things around your neck that could get caught. That includes long scarves in winter and long neck chains that are exposed in summer.

All clothing should be comfortable and follow your body movements—in other words, stretchy knits or fairly loose-fitting fabrics. For winter, wear the obvious layering and choose a fabric for next to the skin that wicks away moisture. In the hot weather, be a little cautious about baring your upper arms and shoulders, especially if you have a mouthy horse.

For lessons, try to wear tops that fit fairly close so that your instructor can see clearly what your upper body is doing. Big, baggy sweatshirts can cover up a lot of serious mistakes.

Your Lower Body and Legs

Again, there are lots of choices. The main thing is comfort and freedom of movement. Breeches, jodhpurs, or riding tights are all comfortable in moderate weather. Jeans or slacks tend not to be comfortable in an English saddle because the stirrup leathers can chafe. Sometimes you can get away with it once and the next time they rub your legs raw. Tight-fitting nonstretch trousers of any sort are a disaster, just like the panty girdle.

I have seen people ride in shorts in hot weather and I don't know how they do it. Chaps over shorts will work if the chaps are cut high and the shorts are not too short. That's something you might do if you had to work around the barn as well and didn't care too much what you looked like. Otherwise, cotton-blend riding tights are just as cool and a lot more comfortable.

Chaps are useful in cool weather to keep you clean and fairly warm. Of course, they also tend to cling to the saddle more than fabric, but that is not always an advantage (as you will see in later chapters). They're easy to throw on over slacks or jeans to protect your legs.

If you plan to ride regularly in very cold weather, invest in insulated riding pants. (I ride in ski warm-ups, but they're rather slippery if you aren't well centered.) You lose a tremendous amount of warmth through your legs, which also leads to cold feet. Riding when you are cold is one of the more dangerous things you can do. Cold muscles and joints are stiff, so you are far more likely to fall if the horse spooks—and far more likely to fall hard!

If you show in cold weather in breeches and boots, keeping warm can be a serious problem. You can add long underwear; buy below-the-knee length if you can find it. If not, cut a full-length pair off below the knee—mark the length when you are sitting with your knee bent—and use knee-high panty hose to hold them in place. These will fit under your boots and add a little additional warmth, but you should have something available to throw over yourself when you aren't actually in the ring.

This is just my opinion, but I think that breeches, which are intended to be worn under high boots and so have a somewhat unfinished look at the bottom, look pretty silly with short boots. That's what jodhpurs or riding tights are for. If you want to wear the breeches, some sort of half chaps will be more comfortable and better looking with short boots.

Another prejudice of mine: If the pants, whatever they are, have belt loops, there should be a belt as well.

Your Lower Legs and Feet

Whatever you wear on your feet must allow your ankles to flex freely and your feet to relax and spread out on the stirrups. Without that you cannot ground, and unless you are grounded you will never ride really well, nor will your horse go well. In addition, if you are riding for long periods in an English saddle you will probably want the protection and support for your leg that is supplied by high boots or boot-leather half-chaps.

High Boots

High boots are the ultimate in lower leg and footwear, but they are certainly not for everyone. In the first place, they have to be cut extremely well in order to fit and look well. Second, they have to be broken in correctly from day one. When you first flex your ankles in them, they form the beginnings of wrinkles and will ever after wrinkle in the same way. A good saddle shop knows how to start the first wrinkle that determines the others and will guide you in placing the boots on your leg correctly.

Tidbits & Supplements

It looks very sloppy to wear field boots with the laces sticking out and flapping around. The most attractive and traditional lacing is done this way.

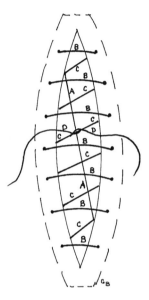

Lacing a field boot.

At the bottom, thread one end of the lace through one of the holes from inside to outside, across to the matching hole and through from outside to inside. Now take the end diagonally up to the top hole on the opposite side and thread it from inside to outside, across to the matching

They come unlined, fully lined, or cuff lined. I prefer cuff lined, because the upper part, which is lined, tends to hold its shape and stay up better, while the unlined area around the ankle breaks in faster and is more flexible. They should have smooth soles, which are safer in the stirrup, but rubber heels, which give more grip when walking.

There are some other options you can consider, depending on how you intend to use the boots. Many people like the closer and more flexible ankle fit hole and through from outside to inside (A). Adjust the two ends of the lace, one at the bottom and one at the top, so they are about even. Now, starting from both top and bottom, run the laces through the rest of the holes as follows: diagonally across to the opposite hole in the next set of holes (B, C), through from inside to outside, across and down through the matching hole from outside to inside. The knot will be tied where the laces meet in the middle (D) and then tucked neatly under the lacing. The immediate impression is of no knot at all.

A properly laced and tied field boot.

you can get with a field boot. It has lacing at the ankle, enabling you to loosen it to get your foot in—especially useful if you have very high insteps. Once on, the laces can be tightened to keep the boot fairly snug around the ankle without loss of ankle movement.

The dress boot, which is required wear in certain disciplines, has no lacing and is thus a bit harder to break in. But it is the classic boot, and when well made, it is attractive and comfortable for long periods.

Tidbits & Supplements

If you haven't worn your boots for a fairly long time, such as over the winter, even though you haven't gained weight you may have trouble getting them on, because leather seems to shrink a bit if left to its own devices. I have found this to be an inexpensive safeguard and solution.

A week or so before I plan to wear them, I try the boots on over whatever legwear I expect to use. If I have difficulty, and more especially if I can't get them on at all, I do as follows: I begin by putting on a pair of full-length panty hose, and if I expect company a pair of trousers with loose legs. (**Never** put boots on your bare legs! The dampness will create suction and you may have to cut the boots off to remove them.) Then, using a little talcum powder if necessary, I put the boots on directly over the panty hose. (If they won't go on even then, they may need to be professionally stretched or even have a gusset inserted on the back seam. Are you *sure* you didn't put on weight?) Once they are on, I use a spray bottle filled with warm water to dampen the tight areas. Then I walk around in them for as long as possible, and at least until they are dry. The next day, in addition to the panty hose I put on some knee socks and go through the same routine with the spray bottle. The next day I should be able to put them on over my breeches, and again repeat the spray and walk routine. Then they're ready for another season.

The zipper-back boot is convenient and is acceptable in all but very formal situations. If you have a heavy calf and are narrow below the knee you can get a better fit with the zipper. If you have a problem that makes the effort of pulling on a regular boot difficult or potentially dangerous, the zipper solves that problem as well. The difficulty with a zipper is that it is almost impossible to keep the ring dust out of the teeth, so it has to be carefully cleaned after every use! Best also to zip it up and down a few times and make sure it is working smoothly before you try to put the boot on.

Rubber boots, lined or unlined, are not good for novices or people who have trouble relaxing their ankles. Rubber has no "memory," that is, it does not form wrinkles in the flexing areas that thereafter enable you to flex more easily. Rubber boots are only really useful if you have to ride in very wet weather. They are especially bad for children, who do not have the weight to force flexion.

Any kind of footwear made from artificial materials has to be fitted very carefully. Leather will stretch and mold itself to your foot and leg, but artificial materials will not. What you buy is what you get.

Short Boots

Short boots are the most comfortable and most commonly worn footwear for English riding. I find that the fashionable high laced paddock boot, which reaches four or five inches above the ankle, is a serious barrier to ankle flexion. It is mostly used in England, where riding with the feet pushed well forward is permissible. When the feet are forward the heel will go down even though the ankle isn't flexed. However, when you try to ride with your feet underneath you, the tight lacing and the height of the boot act almost like a splint to keep your ankle rigid. I can't count the hundreds of times I have started a new student with previous experience in the saddle and had her tell me that she just couldn't keep her heels down. After I unlaced and loosened her boot down as far as the ankle, as soon as she rested her weight on the stirrup, her heel went right down and a surprised smile came over her face! These boots only work if your ankles are supple to begin with, the boots are soft and well broken in, and are not laced too tightly across the front of the ankle where it flexes.

A number of laced short boots are available now that just cover the ankle bone, thus supporting the ankle laterally while still permitting maximum longitudinal flexion. There are also slightly higher jodhpur boots, some with zipper closures, that have elastic inserts on the sides. They give a nice look but not quite the freedom of the shorter boot. The elastic does tend to lose its stretch after a while, too, so the fit becomes sloppy.

An option that combines the advantages of short and tall boots is the short boot worn in conjunction with leggings. Traditional leggings are made of either canvas and boot leather or plain boot leather. The canvas ones lace snugly from above the ankle to just below the knee. The leather ones have a zipper, elastic under the instep, and a "spat" effect that covers the instep and boot laces. The look from a distance is that of a high boot, and they give you protection and support with far more comfort and far less expense. They are, of course, not suitable for very formal occasions.

Even less formal is the half chap, leggings made of soft chap leather reinforced at top and bottom to maintain their shape. They do not give any support but do afford protection from chafing.

Other Useful Information About Footwear

Try to clean and polish your boots *after* you use them, especially if you don't use them often. Dirty leather will crack and split. Also, always use shoe and boot trees. If the soles are allowed to curl up they don't stay in the stirrup as well, and the wrinkles in the leg invite cracking.

If your laced short boots constantly come untied, here is a very useful knot that will stay until you pull both ends. Tie the bow knot as usual, but after you wrap the second loop around and tuck it through, instead of pulling it tight, wrap it around and tuck it through a second time, then pull it tight. Unlike the knot where you tie the two loops in a second knot, this knot can be undone easily by pulling both ends, but won't come undone by itself.

If you ever have some sort of injury when you are wearing high boots and the boot must be cut off your leg, there is an easy way to do it without permanently damaging the boot. Tell the person cutting it off to run the knife or razor under the thin strap that runs up the back of the boot, cutting the stitching on both sides of the strap and also the cross stitching at the top that holds the turned-under end of the strap. Pulling the thin strap away will expose a row of stitches that holds the back of the boot together, and they can be easily cut as well. Unfortunately, if the boot foot has to be cut as well, the boot will not survive.

TACK

I have an oft-told story of a horse I was asked to train because of his erratic and sometimes violent behavior. I discovered in the first five minutes of free-longeing under tack that the horse had a very sensitive midline. If the saddle slid back the least bit, so that the girth lay on the cartilage rather than on his breastbone, the horse reacted with intense bucking and bolting. We put on a breastplate and made sure the breast strap was snug. Problem solved.

One of the more satisfying and permanent ways to solve a behavioral problem is to relate it to the tack, as in the example above. And it is surprising how often this is the case. (This is not going to be a discussion of bitting or the use of artificial devices such as martingales and tie-downs—it's just about fit and application.)

Bridles

Bridles per se are not usually the cause of severe problems—those are usually caused by whoever is at the other end of the reins! But there are a few things that can cause the horse discomfort and that are easily remedied.

Particularly with the larger breeds, it is important to make sure the brow band is long enough. The crown piece should not be pulled up against the backs of the horse's ears. Not only do you risk causing a sore, but the discomfort will make the horse's ear muscles tense. And tense ears, believe it or not, are related to tense backs. Of course, the discomfort also distracts the horse from the business at hand.

The throat latch should be adjusted so that it crosses just above the middle of the horse's cheek. If it hangs too low, it flaps around sloppily and also

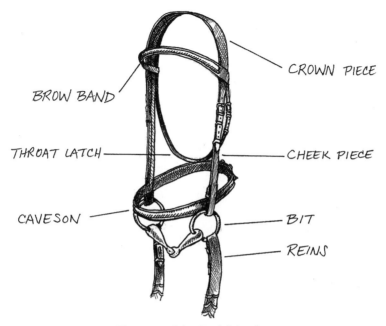

CROWN PIECE

BROW BAND

THROAT LATCH

CHEEK PIECE

CAVESON

BIT

REINS

The parts of the English bridle.

won't keep the bridle on. If it is up in the groove above the cheek bone, it will press on the salivary glands and interfere with flexion.

Cheek straps are often too long, so the buckle rides too high on the crown piece, forcing the brow band up as well. Often, as the bridle breaks in and stretches it cannot be adjusted short enough for a good fit, especially if you change from, say, a small to a large ring snaffle. Cheek straps are quite easy and inexpensive to have shortened at a good tack shop. A little advantage of having them shorter, so they are not adjusted so high on the crown piece, is that if the horse steps on his reins and breaks the bridle, there are still holes left in the crown piece. That means you at least have a shot at putting the bridle together again, even if temporarily and a little tight, so you can get home.

The caveson length should be adjusted so it hangs about two fingers below the horse's cheek bone. It also tends to have an overlong cheek strap, which may require shortening. It should be adjusted snugly but not tightly around the horse's nose. He should be able to chew the bit (or a bite of carrot) comfortably.

Drop and figure-8 nosebands should be adjusted the same way. They are intended to have a curb effect on the horse's chin, not to force his mouth shut. If he is opening his mouth to evade the bit, look for the cause. Nosebands, whether part of a bridle, a halter, or a hackamore, should never rest on the unsupported nose bone on the lower part of the horse's face. If you put your finger and thumb on either side of the horse's nose just below the cheek bone, then run your hand down, you will feel the nasal passages begin as hollows on either side. From that point on, the nose bone is not attached to anything on either side and pressure on it is very painful.

Snaffle bits should be fitted to gently pull on the corners of the mouth. Two or three wrinkles is the basic rule. Curbs can hang slightly lower. If you are using a full bridle, the snaffle hangs above and in front of the curb. The mouthpiece should be wide enough so the side rings don't pinch. Thicker bits are less severe than thinner ones, but the bit should not be too fat to fit comfortably between the horse's bars. With a gelding or stallion, check to make sure the bit doesn't rest against his upper tushes.

If your horse seems very fussy about the bit, have the veterinary or dentist check for concealed wolf teeth—small, rudimentary teeth in front of the first premolars. When the dentist is floating the horse's teeth he should be particularly careful with the premolars, because as pressure is put on the bit so that wrinkles are formed, they will rub against those teeth. Any roughness on the teeth will cause discomfort and fussiness.

Curb chains should always be free of even the smallest twist. If you hold the untangled curb chain out straight, the front side of the chain goes down on the off-side curb hook, while the back side goes down on the near side to keep the chain flat.

Another one of my pet peeves: Modern reins are too short. To develop his back properly and stretch himself out well before serious work, the horse needs to be able to reach nearly all the way to the ground with his nose. Most reins will not allow this, so the rider is constantly getting jerked out of position as the horse snatches and hangs on the bit in his efforts to lengthen. The other possible scenario has the horse going with a compressed neck and back, which interferes with proper movement and thus with performance and soundness. When the horse has his nose on the ground, you should be able to sit up straight and hold the reins so they form a straight line from elbow to bit.

If your reins are this length, there is no question that when the horse brings his head up and starts carrying himself and you so that his poll is about level with his withers, you are going to have a lot of reins left over. This is a possible safety issue if the reins get caught on your toe or the stirrup. There are several potential solutions to this, depending on circumstances.

The simplest one, if you're not showing, is to tie an overhand knot (see appendix B) in the end of the reins after the horse has warmed up and is carrying his head level. The advantage of this is that at the end of the ride when he's a bit tired and wants to stretch down again, all you have to do is undo the knot.

Looping a long rein. It can be pulled out of the left hand
or gathered up as necessary.

I prefer the second solution. It takes a little practice, but is easy to learn if you ride fairly frequently. You simply loop the extra rein around your left hand. The extra rein is thus immediately available if you need it. This is especially useful if you work with a horse who is in the process of learning to carry himself and the rider, since at this stage he is constantly lengthening and shortening his neck as he tries to adjust his balance—similar to what you do with your hands when you're trying to learn to ice skate.

The third solution is one you would probably use for showing. You either make, or have made using leather or rope and snaps, a pair of extenders of the necessary length, which you use for warm-ups. You then remove them before entering the show ring. The extenders must be attached at the bit end of the reins; otherwise the join would be on the hand part of the reins and would get in your way as you tried to adjust the reins.

Saddles

The importance of the saddle fitting the horse comfortably cannot be overestimated, especially if you're riding the horse for long periods at a stretch. However, for the average rider I find that the importance of having the saddle fit the rider is all too frequently *under*estimated. It is really impossible for even a good rider to be properly balanced and grounded in an ill-fitting saddle. The resulting unsteadiness throws the horse off balance, while causing the rider's aids, especially her hands, to be tense and interfering. This one of the major reasons why school horses are so often called ring sour or stubborn. They just get so tired of fighting a losing battle that they quit.

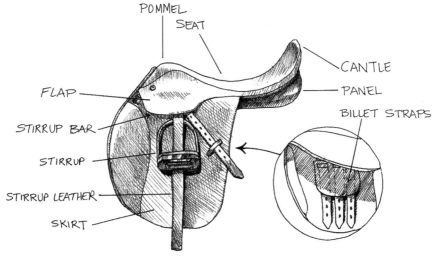

Parts of the English saddle.

When I had a riding school, I assigned the saddle to the rider rather than the horse. I bought good quality saddles with a medium tree and used appropriate padding and careful placement, with the addition of a breastplate or crupper if necessary, to fit each saddle to the horse as riders were changed from lesson to lesson. I *never* had a horse with a sore back or one who was "mysteriously" cranky or lame due to saddle fit. My school string was as obedient and good-tempered as any group of horses could be.

Of course, as you will see, I was pretty strict about not letting my students do things that they weren't ready to do, with the resulting unfair demands on the horse!

I also strongly recommend to my students that, once they feel committed to riding, their first major purchase should be a saddle.

Fitting the Saddle to the Rider

Unless you are very experienced, if it is at all possible take your instructor with you when you are shopping for saddles. You will have to pay for her time, but, given how expensive saddles are, it will be worth the small extra expense. Decide on the type of saddle you want, then look at a number of different ones in your price range. It's best to spend a little extra to get what you want. A well-maintained saddle will outlast you by many years!

First sit in each saddle to check for comfort. It should feel *very* comfortable. If it doesn't when you are sitting still in the tack shop, it is going to be impossible on a long ride. Before "mounting," check to make sure the saddle is sitting absolutely level on the "horse," that is, that the exact center of the seat is the lowest point. The relative heights of cantle and pommel are a result of design and should not be used to determine whether the saddle is sitting level.

Ask an observer to look and make sure your pelvis is not tipped either way, which would affect how the saddle feels under your seat bones and crotch. Your sacrum should be vertical. (Men should check page 117 about the importance of the proper underwear.) If you are unable to find a saddle that feels comfortable under your seat bones, it is possible they are spaced far apart so that you are sitting on the arms of the tree rather than on the supporting "hammock" in between. Some brands of saddles are made to accommodate this problem. There are also saddles designed specifically for the male or female pelvis.

The saddle should be long enough in the seat so that you can fit four fingers between your buttocks and the end of the cantle. Much smaller and there won't be room for the movement you must make as the horse moves. Much larger and you will tend to slide around too much.

With your feet in the stirrups, try the different positions you will be riding in, especially if you ride cross country or jump more than very small fences, to make sure there is room for pelvic rotation as your hip angle changes (see Chapter 9).

The next thing to look at is stirrup placement. The stirrup bar must be placed on the saddle so that, in full seat with the stirrup leather hanging vertically and your foot correctly placed in the stirrup (page 185), for all-purpose riding the back of your heel is lined up with your trouser side seam at the hip. For dressage it should be slightly farther back.

If the back of your heel comes well in front of your pants seam, you may be a candidate for adjustable stirrup bars. Very tall people, and people with long

This adjustable stirrup bar is easily adjustable while riding, for different conditions or horses.

This adjustable bar is designed to adapt the saddle for rider conformation and must be adjusted on the ground.

thighs and short calves, are the most likely to need them. If you have a lot of trouble finding your balance in half seat, being able to move your stirrups back an inch or two can create an instant miracle.

I happen to be a strong advocate of the adjustable stirrup bar. With a simple adjustment that can be performed while sitting on the horse, you can move the stirrup forward or back as much as four inches. Besides being an aid to people with conformation or size problems, this enables you to ride in balance with your center quite far back on a badly balanced horse or one who is having trouble going forward, or quite far forward if you are riding on a very forward-going horse or jumping high fences. Saddles are made with the adjustable stirrup bars as part of the package or, in some cases, can be retrofitted by a competent saddler (see appendix C).

However, if you are only doing one kind of work on a fairly well-trained horse, you can probably get along just fine with a fixed bar. Once you understand how centering and grounding over your feet should feel, you can adapt quite well.

With your feet in the correct position (as I have just defined), check the knee roll. Except for a very small amount of padding inside your knee bone (which is actually the end of your femur) if you are sensitive there, the knee roll should be entirely in *front* of your knee. I prefer a knee roll that is narrow from front to back but triangular in cross section so it forms a pretty good barrier.

Contrary to common belief, the knee roll is not there for you to rest against all the time. If you are doing so, it means you are out of longitudinal balance,

A practical knee roll.

with your center in front of your base. Rather, the knee roll is your emergency brake. I was once on a hunter pace with a young horse who was out for the first time. He had been going extremely well, and about three-quarters of the way through the ride we were galloping freely down a wooded road. A large puddle appeared and although my horse was not afraid of water, he was looking ahead and didn't see the puddle until he was right on it. He stopped dead in his tracks, dropping his head to do so, and I found myself with my crotch somewhere in the neighborhood of the base of his neck, just in front of his withers. Fortunately, my knees were still behind the knee rolls so I was able to struggle back into the saddle instead of ending up ignominiously in the puddle! Conversely, I once watched a very competent professional in the same situation, but without knee rolls, end up with his feet still in the stirrups but trapped head down on the horse's neck with his chin on the horse's poll, the horse's chin on the ground, and neither one able to move! He had to be rescued by a friendly spectator, who helped him to dismount.

The saddle skirt should be shaped so that it supports your leg no matter what your stirrup length. You should be able to shorten and lengthen your stirrups as much as you plan to—longer for flat work, smooth-gaited horses, and horses wide in the barrel; shorter for jumping and cross country, rough-gaited horses, and horses narrow in the barrel. No matter what the length of the stirrup, your knee should be about the same distance from the knee roll and always in the "pocket" that will eventually form in the saddle with wear.

Fitting the Saddle to the Horse

Fitting the saddle to a horse who is being used for some high-performance discipline such as endurance riding is an art and a science, and is not covered in this short chapter. The same applies to horses with difficult conformation or soundness problems. But for the average horse, being given light exercise—that is, an hour a day or less—making him comfortable is usually not difficult.

When you're shopping for a saddle, besides choosing the right tree width (which would be medium if you don't own or ride a particular horse), you should also inspect the panels. They should be wide at the cantle, projecting outside the saddle seat on each side. The distance between the two panels—the channel—should be a good three fingers wide. The panels should also be comparatively flat both lengthwise and sideways. If you look at a well-developed horse's back on either side of the spine behind the shoulder blades, which is where the panels rest, the overall surface is fairly flat (allowing for the downward slope) and the panels should be, too. Also look at the saddle from the back to make sure the panels are centered on the saddle, not off to one side. Saddles are all handmade, and a certain number are bound to be made by less-experienced saddlemakers!

Having chosen a saddle that should be a reasonable fit, your next issue is to put the saddle in the correct place on the horse. A surprising number of riders, even professionals, place the saddle incorrectly—usually too far forward. Everyone is so afraid of putting the saddle too far back in case the horse's loins, and thus his kidneys, are affected, that they tend to overcorrect.

To maintain his longitudinal balance under all conditions, the horse must have freedom of movement of his front legs. We all hear about the horse using his head for balance, which is perfectly true, but he must have free movement of his front legs as well so that he can throw them forward as necessary, in much the same way as you throw your hands forward if you trip. Only then can he recover his balance if he loses it badly, or at least not risk serious injury from back strain.

To use his front legs freely, he must have maximum use of his shoulder, which includes his shoulder blade. If, as is so often the case, the saddle is placed on top of the shoulder blade rather than behind it, shoulder movement is severely restricted. In addition, the rider is placed further forward relative to the horse's center, so he has to cope with that as well.

Putting the saddle up onto the horse's shoulder also lifts the front of the saddle, thus lowering the back. This defeats the purpose of putting the saddle forward in the first place, since the backward tilt of the saddle throws the rider's weight toward the cantle, especially during the posting trot, so the horse's loins take far more abuse than they would if the saddle was properly placed and level.

Because of differences in conformation, the *only* way you can tell if the saddle is in the right place is to slide your hand over the horse's shoulder blade, under the panel of the saddle. The tree point should be resting behind the

This saddle is placed too far forward. Notice where the
lowest point of the seat is.

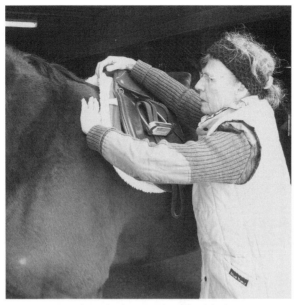

Finding the horse's shoulder blade.

entire shoulder blade. Ideally, this should place the center of the saddle, where your weight will rest, over the lowest point of the horse's back, which also happens to be the strongest.

I was using a student's horse for a demonstration recently. Before mounting I glanced at the saddle and it appeared to be in the correct position relative to the horse's withers. However, after I mounted I realized there was a slight backward tilt that I hadn't expected in a fairly new and well-designed saddle. I dismounted and looked around for something to lift the back of the saddle with. I undid the girth and then, looking more closely, noticed that the pommel was sitting distinctly higher on the horse than the cantle. When I ran my hand under the panel I found that the horse's shoulder muscle ran much further back than one would expect. I slid the saddle back a good two inches and refastened the girth, which was now two inches further back as well. Looking at the horse's withers one might think the saddle was too far back, but when I remounted the saddle was sitting level and I had a very successful ride. The horse also had a reputation for being rather sticky, which was probably due at least in part to the saddle placement affecting his balance.

Now that the saddle is sitting in the correct place, the next thing to look at is how well the fork of the tree follows the horse's conformation from the front. That is, the angle of the tree points should approximate the slope of the horse's back on either side. If the tree is a little wide the saddle will come too close to the horse's withers. (You should be able to fit four fingers vertically between the withers and the underside of the pommel when you are dismounted.) If this is the case, it is easy to fix, unless it is very close, by adding a thicker saddle pad, which will fill up the space on either side, making the tree effectively narrower. However, if the tree itself is too narrow, the saddle should not be used unless the rider is very light and the ride very short. No padding is sufficient to keep the tree points from digging straight down into the horse's back muscles, quickly creating severe soreness.

Now you have to see whether the saddle is sitting level, just as you did when you were trying it out in the store. This is especially important with a new saddle. The webbed seat will break in wherever you sit during your early rides. If you are to ride successfully you *must* be seated in the center of the seat, so that *must* be the lowest point—since gravity will carry your seat to the lowest point, wherever that may be.

In most cases, if the saddle is tipped at all it will be tipped back. In a new saddle the saddlemaker adds additional padding in the front, knowing it will pack down fairly quickly, bringing the front of the saddle lower and thus making it more level. But until this happens you will have to add some sort of lift to the back of the saddle. The usual soft foam that is found in so-called lift back pads is totally worthless because it compresses to nothing as soon as you sit on it. Closed cell foam can be used because compression is minimal. There are also pads with sections that can be filled with as much air as is needed and pads that will accept shims. Towels—folded carefully so there are no lumps—can be inserted into the pocket of a liftback pad after you have thrown away the foam, or you can simply place them under the saddle if you are not concerned about appearance.

If the saddle is tilted back you will find yourself constantly leaning forward trying to get your center over your feet, which will tend to push out in front of you. If the saddle is tilted forward it will create uncomfortable pressure under your crotch so you will tend to round your back and sit on your tail bone instead. A forward tilt can be the result of the saddle sitting too low on the horse's withers, which is dealt with as I've just described, adding a pommel pad if necessary. But a saddle may also tilt forward if the horse's back is short and the saddle is long, so that the cantle sits farther up the slope of the back. This happens with breeds such as Icelandic horses—small horses often being ridden by large riders—and they have saddles specifically designed to deal with the problem. The only way I know of to deal with it otherwise is to use the thinnest possible pad under the whole saddle, and then add a pommel pad to bring the front of the saddle higher. You do need to be careful that you don't lift and narrow the front of the saddle too much and either make it unstable or create pressure points under the tree.

Occasionally you get horses who, due to poor training or injury, are very crooked and throw the saddle to one side. This happens because one shoulder is farther back than the other, and since the saddle rests against the shoulder blades one tree point is pushed back. This pushes the cantle—and the rider— off to the opposite side. After a while the horse's whole back on that side becomes weakened and lowered and the horse becomes more and more crooked. I used to use towels on one side to lift the saddle up to level, and a strap similar to a side saddle balance strap to keep the cantle from turning. The towels are still a good idea, but pads are now made with a wedge or pocket that goes in front of the skirt and keeps that side of the saddle back, and thus even with the other side.

The last problem I'll cover is the saddle that won't stay in place longitudinally—that is, it slides either forward or back. Sliding back is more common, because of most horses' shape and because of the grain of the hair. A breastplate is the obvious solution to this problem, but breastplates have their problems and limitations. The hunt breastplate is the one most commonly used, but if it is snug enough to keep the saddle in place then the shoulder straps dig into the horse's trapezius muscle along the front of his shoulder, causing discomfort and limiting forward leg movement, especially if the breastplate is made of very narrow leather. Begin by making the strap that goes down to the girth quite snug, so that some of the pressure is taken by the girth. You can also put sheepskin fuzzies on the shoulder straps to make them more comfortable.

A better solution, though not appropriate for showing in some divisions, is the jumping breastplate, which attaches to the D-rings on the tree points. It is made of wide elastic, covered with a fuzzy, and you can add a chest strap as well, if you like. It runs across the shoulder rather than down it, so it doesn't cut. Western breastplates fasten in the same areas and so don't cause any problems. Polo and race breastplates also work well for some horses, since they attach at the girth on the sides, and go in front of the shoulder. They have to be carefully adjusted and attached so that they neither cut into the horse's gullet nor slide down below his shoulder points.

The danger in not using a breastplate when it is needed is that the saddle can slide so far back that it either turns over or becomes a bucking strap. I had a very bad accident as a child on a horse who should have been wearing a breastplate and wasn't.

The effect of not using a crupper when it is needed is usually more subtle. I remember taking a group of junior students fox hunting. One of them was on her own pony, and very shortly into the hunt the pony began to stop at fences. Since he hadn't shown this behavior before, I wasn't sure what to do. Fortunately, I was riding a quiet horse myself, and since I am small enough to ride a large pony, we traded. It only took me a few minutes to realize that the saddle was too far forward. Not much, but just enough to move the rider's center too far forward, making the unfamiliar jumps too much for the pony. I tried readjusting it and tightening the girth, but as soon as we went down a hill it slid forward again. So I shoved my feet forward and rode in the "back seat" and managed to get us both home safely. The next week we introduced the pony to a crupper and he improved immediately.

Most people think only ponies need cruppers, and usually only the small ponies. But it is not uncommon to find a large pony or a horse whose shoulder isn't angled back very far, or perhaps is so fleshy that the saddle rides up over it instead of tucking in behind. Any time you see a horse under tack who appears to have a very long back and a very short neck, you are looking at a horse who needs a crupper. And since having the saddle too far forward puts the rider too far forward relative to the horse's center, the horse will inevitably have balance problems that affect his performance.

For some reason, although breastplates are perfectly acceptable, cruppers are frowned upon, especially in the Hunter ring. But my students have won very good ribbons at some top shows on horses or large ponies wearing cruppers. Apparently the judges were too busy to notice, or didn't really care. Of course, both breastplate and crupper would be inappropriate in a conformation class, because of the inference of a flaw in conformation.

You do have to get a horse accustomed to the crupper. Having something under his tail is inclined to make the horse clamp his tail on it and buck. He needs to be introduced to it gradually, and then, if possible, rigged out in a surcingle with both a breastplate and a crupper attached and left in his stall with some hay to get him dropping and raising his head so he gets used to the pressure. The crupper should be adjusted to be snug but not tight with his head in the normal position.

One serious difficulty is attaching the crupper securely to the saddle. The metal or leather crupper tees that fit under the panels will pull out when the horse flexes his back strongly. I had a piece of harness made that attached to the billets on either side and ended behind the saddle in a ring that the crupper was attached to, but it tended to chafe the horse's back. The best answer is a large, heavy D-ring, installed by the saddler as low on the tree at the cantle as it will go. Since the crupper will tend to pull the cantle downward, extra lift under the cantle may be needed. I also believe inserting a short piece of girth elastic in the crupper strap allows for more flexibility.

If you really don't want to use the crupper, there is another device called a foregirth, often used on Warmbloods, some of whom tend to have a conformation that allows the saddle to slide forward. A foregirth is a surcingle that goes in front of the saddle. It has a tree shape in front to keep it off the horse's withers, and thick wedges mounted on either side. These wedges hold the saddle back, so the

---

Tidbits & Supplements

A tip if you are not sure whether you have chosen the right size girth for an unfamiliar horse: Unless the horse is very fat for his length of leg, a girth buckled or held to the bottom hole on the billets will reach just about the top of the horse's hoof if it is the correct size. Again, this saves you a lot of running back and forth.

---

back, so the foregirth can be placed against the horse's shoulders and the saddle will be forced back into the proper position relative to the horse's center. This will work for the horse whose shoulder doesn't extend back far enough, but not for the horse whose shoulder is too flat, since the foregirth will slide up over the shoulder.

Another solution is to have an extra billet placed on the tree point, in front of the regular billets. The front of the saddle is then held down more firmly, so it is less likely to ride up over the shoulder. However, it also means a tighter girth, and not all horses will or should accept this.

Girths should be wide and soft, especially where they cross the horse's midline. They should be positioned so that they rest against the horse's sternum, rather than against the cartilage that lies directly behind it.

When putting the girth on, it is most efficient to attach it on the left side first, fastened at the bottom hole of the billet straps. Then walk around to the off side and fasten the girth as high as it will comfortably go; about the way you would fasten your own belt. When you go to tighten the girth preparatory to mounting, you will have left yourself the maximum number of adjustments to work with on the near side, as the horse loosens up. This saves you a lot of walking back and forth from one side to the other.

Even though custom has us use the first and third billet straps, all saddles and most girths are designed to have the girth fastened to the front two billets. If you use a tight breastplate, using the first and third might be preferable to keep the cantle from tipping up if the horse drops his head. Never use the back two billets alone. The front one is attached to the saddle on separate webbing from the other two, so if one webbing breaks you have a chance that the other will hold long enough to get you off the horse safely.

One of the most common sources of horse abuse is overtightening the girth. *The girth should only be tight enough to hold the saddle down over the withers.* The saddle is kept in place by the withers (which keep the saddle from slipping sideways), the shoulders (which keep it from sliding forward), and the spring of the ribs (which keeps it from sliding back). If the horse lacks the proper conformation in any of these areas, then breastplates, cruppers, special pads, or girth covers, and *centered riding* are the correct ways to deal with the problem. Overtightening the girth is *not* a viable solution. It creates tension, which can cause anything from shortness of gait to unsoundness to dangerous behavior such as bucking, bolting, and throwing himself on the ground. And it is, as I said, abusive.

When you're checking the tightness of the girth, slide your fingers in under the saddle itself at the widest point on the horse's barrel. (Sliding your hand in below the saddle flap will always give a false reading.) The saddle should feel snug but not extremely tight. When tightening the girth, first pull down on the billet, and then take up the slack and insert the buckle tongue in the appropriate hole. For safety reasons, only tighten one strap at a time. Only tighten as much as the horse will give you without resistance. Using TTeam in the girth area will help to desensitize a horse who is overreactive to the girth.

Expect to adjust the girth at least four times: when saddling, immediately before mounting, immediately after mounting, and after about fifteen minutes of riding when the horse's muscles have loosened and stretched. The girth should, of course, be checked any time the saddle feels unstable.

If you ride western, so that checking the cinch when mounted is not an option, the horse should be walked for five minutes or so and the cinch checked and adjusted several times. If the horse is also young or sensitive, dismounting after fifteen minutes or so of warm-up for a final adjustment is a safe and humane way to make sure the cinch is not overtight.

RIDING BAREBACK

Riding bareback, that is, with nothing on the horse's back at all except you, is a lot of fun. It's a lot easier in terms of preparation, too. Just grab a lead rope, fasten it to the halter, and hop on. Of course it can get more complicated than that, but it can also be that easy. However, the nature of the human seat bones is such that long periods of riding the horse with no protection for his back can be very painful and tiring for him. Not to mention the sweat and hair marks it leaves on the seat of your pants!

I find that most of the bareback pads you can buy offer minimal protection, have too narrow a girth (which creates pressure over the horse's withers), and don't fit the rider very well. For those reasons I recommend using a well-padded "bareback" arrangement. It consists of an easily washable liner pad; a thick, square fleece pad; possibly a closed-cell foam pad if either horse or rider is exceptionally bony or sensitive; and finally, a saddle-shaped pad with billet loops.

You can buy a surcingle (the strap that replaces a girth) at most tack shops. Don't get one that is padded around the horse's spine; it's too uncomfortable

Tidbits & Supplements

This is just a funny story with no educational value except perhaps for honesty. One of my students brought her boyfriend up to see her horse, and after a few minutes they took the horse for a walk in hand out on the trail. For insurance reasons I had a rule that no one was allowed on a horse who wasn't signed up in our riding program. After they returned I took one look at them and called them over. "Sally," I said, "you know perfectly well that you're not allowed to put anyone on your horse, and I know that John was on him." She stared at me as if I was some sort of magician and apologized in a very flustered way, saying that at least she had made him wear her helmet. As they turned to walk away, the telltale marks on the seat of his khakis stood out clearly. I suspect they figured it out later!

to sit on. The all-elastic ones are too stretchy to hold the pads securely. Be sure to measure your horse first and allow for both stretch and the padding. You can also make a surcingle using your girth and two stirrup leathers. Lace the stirrup leathers through the off-side buckles of the girth until the buckles of each are

Creating a surcingle with your girth and
stirrup leathers.

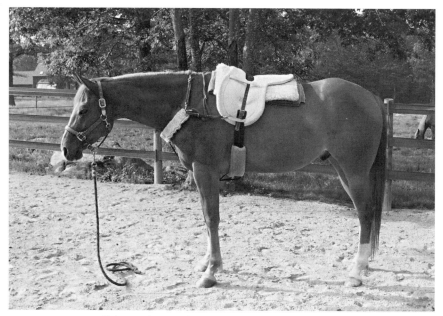

All dressed up and ready to go for a bareback ride.

touching. Then place the leathers across the top of the horse's back—and the pads—and fasten to the girth on the near side.

Since bareback pads have no tree to keep them in place I strongly recommend a breastplate as well. The photo above shows a horse in bareback attire.

MOUNTING

After you put everything else on the horse, the last thing on is yourself. And that's the most important thing to put on him correctly. Statistically, mounting is the most dangerous part of riding. That is, more accidents occur during mounting than at any other time.

This is partly because many riders do not take the time to establish some sort of relationship with the horse before mounting. Jane, a horse lover with limited experience, has a horse at home, Blackie, whom she has had for a long time and who is perfectly quiet with her. She decides to ask her friend Sue to ride on good old Blackie, while Jane rides her new horse. Nobody takes into account that Blackie has had only one rider for many years, so when a total stranger walks up and starts to mount, Blackie is startled and wheels away suddenly. Sue, not being very experienced, comes off before she ever really got on. She is frightened, Blackie is frightened, and Jane is upset and confused.

Making good use of the concepts and skills explained in this chapter will solve many riding problems before they start. It's well worth the effort to learn them.

Mounting Made Easy

The officially recognized method of mounting in an English saddle—that is, beginning the mount facing the rear of the horse—is not easy for either rider or horse. It is intended to avoid the possibility of the horse kicking the rider. But as many horses bite as kick during mounting, and the method is so awkward and difficult that most riders don't do it correctly. Also, many horses will not stand quietly because it is so hard for them to maintain balance when you mount this way.

Mounting from the front forces the rider to do a complete 180-degree turn while in the process of scrambling up. All the while she is hanging on one side of the horse, thus putting all her weight over the horse's one front leg. It should be obvious that lack of balance of both horse and rider is dangerous, and also unnecessary.

A much safer and more efficient way of mounting is to mount facing the front of the horse, which, after all, is the direction you want to end up in once you're mounted. While you should be able to mount from the ground if necessary, use a mounting block whenever possible. It is much less strain on both you and the horse. Using the method I will describe, I, who am five-foot-four and no longer young, can mount a 16.2-hand horse from the ground without difficulty!

1. Take the reins in your right hand and place your hand on the pommel.

2. Stand by the cantle, facing forward. Use your left hand to hold the stirrup.

3. Place your left foot in the stirrup, then take firm hold of a good hank of mane with your left hand. *Do not place both hands on the saddle.*

4. Push off with your right foot and pull strongly at the same time with your left hand. Go straight up until you are standing in the left stirrup with both legs straight and side by side. Do not try to swing your right leg over as you are coming up. If you are quick you can reach over to the off-side saddle flap with your right hand, pushing down on it to help prevent the saddle from turning (see the box on page 98).

5. Swing your right leg over, turning your upper body to face forward at the same time.

6. Keeping your balance, put your right toe in the stirrup.

7. Sit down gently.

Preparing to mount from the rear.

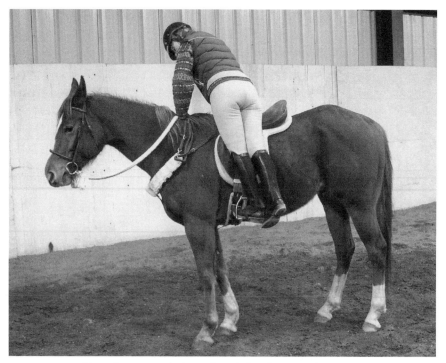

Mounting, second phase. I am balancing over the center
of the horse before swinging my right leg over.

Mounting, third phase.

Mounting When Fear Is a Factor

Another cause of mounting problems occurs as the result of a recent bad experience. When a rider has a scary fall, even though she is not hurt, gets back on again, and continues successfully, the problem is not over. The next time she comes to ride the fear returns, and she needs to be helped with mounting and resuming riding, usually with a person nearby on the ground for five or ten minutes, until her body realizes it will be all right.

If the bad experience is more serious, or the horse or rider is more timid, they may have to try a different approach. I call this "baby step" mounting, and it involves going through the whole procedure one step at a time. It is best done using a mounting block, as that is less strenuous for both horse and rider. Read the previous section on correct mounting before you try this. The baby steps are:

1. With your reins in your right hand, on the pommel, place your left foot in the stirrup.

2. Remove your foot and come back to the block again. When you are completely relaxed with this step, and not before, proceed to the next step.

Tidbits & Supplements

The main reason most riders overtighten the girth is that the saddle turns during mounting. If the horse has really good withers this is not a problem, but many horses do not. The best solution is to have someone hold the other stirrup. Using a mounting block also makes it easy for you to place your right hand on the off-side skirt and push down on it as you mount. Failing these, take a lead rope and snap it to the stirrup on the off side. Pass the rope under the horse's barrel, so it lies on the girth, and bring it up so you can wrap it around the fingers of your left hand as you mount. Now the saddle cannot turn more than an inch or so. After you are mounted, drop the rope, lift up the stirrup, and unfasten the snap. You should practice these steps with the horse on the ground first, so he gets used to feeling the rope drop and drag along. If you are going trail riding, you can take the rope along in case you need it.

Keeping the saddle from turning while mounting. The white rope is attached to the stirrup on the far side of the horse.

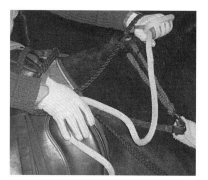

In addition to the rope, my right hand is pressing down on the off-side saddle flap, always a good practice.

3. After placing your foot in the stirrup, stand up on the stirrup so your legs are side by side but do not start to swing your right leg over the horse.

4. Bring your right leg back to the ground or block again. Take your left foot out and return it to the block as well. Continue in the same way with the remainder of the steps, each time working on a step until you and the horse feel totally relaxed about it before going on to the next. Be sure to return to the start position each time, at least until you feel really comfortable.

5. After standing in the stirrup, swing your leg over but don't sit down or place your foot in the other stirrup.

6. Place your foot in the other stirrup.

7. Sit down, continuing to hold the pommel with one hand.

8. Go through the seven steps several times.

Dismounting

Dismounting, while not as dangerous as mounting, also must be done with some consideration for the balance of both horse and rider. There are two acceptable methods. The first is more conservative, and should be used on young, nervous, or poorly balanced horses. It is also the best method for an unathletic rider or any time you want to come down slowly, such as during very cold weather.

1. Place your left hand on the horse's withers and your right hand on the right side of the pommel with the fingers pointing down.

2. Stand up in both stirrups.

3. Take your right foot out of the stirrup, and, keeping your center over the horse's midline and lined up vertically with your left foot, swing your right leg over the horse's croup. Keep your left leg straight and vertical and finish this step with your legs side by side (see the photo on the bottom of page 96).

4. Resting on your hands, take your left foot out of the stirrup.

5. Turn your head to the left so you are looking forward. Keep your body straight and roll over onto your right hip so your whole body faces forward, then allow yourself to slide slowly down the horse's side.

6. Wiggle your toes a little as you slide down, so that you land softly with relaxed feet and ankles.

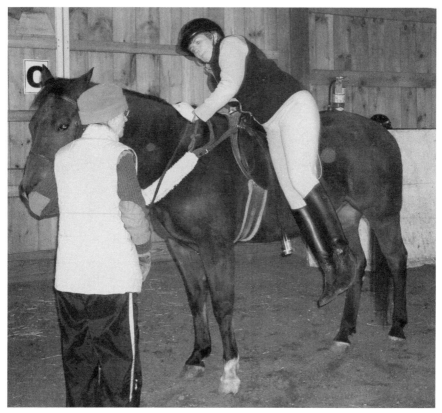

The final step of dismounting.

The second method is slightly different and does affect the horse's balance somewhat, so some of them don't like it.

1. Remove both feet from your stirrups.

2. Lean forward, grasp the mane with both hands, keeping your thumbs parallel with your fingers and perpendicular to the horse's neck. At the same time, kick back and up with your right leg so it clears the horse's croup and comes down on the left side. The faster you do this, the easier it is.

3. Turn your head and torso to face forward, and slide down the horse's side, relaxing your feet and ankles as above, to hit the ground softly.

The correct hand position for a quick dismount. This is shown bareback, but it would be the same in the saddle.

This second method can easily be adapted to become an emergency dismount. Steps 1 and 2 are the same as the previous method. Then:

3. As your right leg clears the croup, use your arms to push your body *away* from the saddle and at the same time turn to face forward.

4. As you hit the ground, take a step forward.

Practice this first at the walk, then at the trot. It gets easier as the horse's gait becomes springier, lifting you out of the saddle. Don't forget to turn forward—that's what will keep you from breaking your leg if you ever have to do it at speed.

You have to mount and dismount every time you ride, and they mark the beginning and end of each ride—framing it, as it were. For that reason, as well as for safety, mounting and dismounting should be made as pleasant for the horse as possible. Happy horses give you better rides.

5

Make Yourselves Comfortable

Sitting on the Horse Without Stirrups

Beth and Marty, two of my "e-students" (riders who belong to my e-group and sometimes ask my advice), took a challenge from me last fall to do some work without stirrups. They were to help each other by taking turns being the ground person, so that control would not be an issue. After much grumbling and complaining they finally did start to do it, and actually worked very hard at it for awhile. Then other things came up, they went back to the saddle, and I heard no more. More recently Beth wrote about some other riding she was doing, and commented with some surprise that it was far easier than it had been last fall. The only explanation she could find was that the dreaded bareback work had actually helped, improving her seat immensely. My immediate thought was, "Why am I not surprised?"

∾

People who have always ridden with stirrups have the misconception that it is much harder to ride without them. It is true that fast work, especially if it involves a lot of turning, is easier with stirrups. However, if you want to use the stirrups effectively you must be able to ground on them, and grounding on stirrups is much easier said than done, especially for the novice. The strangeness of the movement, and the height, and the slippery saddle—and for most novices, far too many things to think about—all create tension. So much so that any sort of grounding is impossible. In addition, because the stirrups are wobbly and small, it is against every instinct to commit any sort of weight to them. In an effort to do so anyway, the rider uses her leg muscles to press against them, thus preventing herself from grounding on her seat as well.

If you take away the stirrups until the student has learned to relax and ground into her seat, when you add the stirrups later the stability already

To learn more about this topic, read Chapters 6, 7, and 9 of the companion volume to this book, *How Your Horse Wants You to Ride: Starting Out—Starting Over.*

created makes grounding on the stirrups far easier. The only exception to this might be a student with a very high center of gravity, who just couldn't cope without the lateral assistance of the stirrups. But it would take her quite a bit longer to attain any degree of security, and at some point she would still benefit from the work without stirrups.

BAREBACK ADVANTAGES

I recommend strongly that if at all possible you spend some time on a bareback pad (page 92), rather than a saddle with the stirrups crossed or removed. Lateral stability is the principal challenge without the support of the stirrups, but saddles are flat and slippery, increasing the tendency to slide off to the side. Bareback pads, on the other hand, follow the contour of the horse—which is more like a flat gable roof or an upside-down V—with his spine denoting the midpoint for your center. Pads are also fuzzy, and thus not slippery at all. (You can make the saddle less slippery, though no less flat, by using some sort of saddle cover, preferably of sheepskin or fleece.)

Another advantage of riding bareback is that in the cold weather it is *much* warmer, especially for your feet, which don't have to rest in those cold stirrups.

If you are just starting out and don't want to do any fast work, it is also a good idea in cold weather to dress your horse for warmth. Since stables are warmer than the riding area, if you take all the horse's warm clothes off in the barn and then expect him to walk and jog around quietly in the freezing cold ring, you are being very unfair. My practice in the New England winters was to have everyone ride bareback (on pads) and remove only as much of the horse's clothing as was necessary for him not to overheat. If the class was only walking and jogging, the horse just wore his barn clothes with the pads and related equipment on top. Not very elegant, perhaps, but before I figured out the necessity of this my students fell off the cold, tense horses with frightening regularity. Once we started keeping blankets on, the horses behaved the same in the winter as in the summer. Toasty warm horses don't need to run around and buck!

PREPARING TO RIDE

Decide whether you are going to ride on bareback pads or a saddle without stirrups. If you are on a bareback pad you will need a neck strap (appendix A), adjusted so you can hold it comfortably without leaning forward. If you are riding in the saddle, holding the pommel works very well. If you are going to use an uncovered saddle, wear chaps or full seat breeches if you have them, since they will keep you from slipping around quite so much. You probably *don't* want to wear them with a bareback pad, because then you would find it hard to adjust your center at all.

Next, decide if you will be comfortable and relaxed on your horse riding alone, or whether you would feel more secure if you had a ground person. You shouldn't have to be worrying, or even thinking, about controlling the horse at first, since you will need to concentrate on your position. (Contrary to the popular concept of multitasking, the reality is that nobody can *concentrate* on more than one thing at a time.) You will also probably have more fun if you can find someone to join you, and then you can take turns riding and leading. If you decide to ride without a ground person, try to at least be riding in a space by yourself, with no obstacles that could get you or the horse in serious trouble.

A major goal of bareback riding is to learn to adjust your lateral balance as the horse changes from straight lines to turning and back again. For that reason, a good choice of space is a small paddock that will allow you to ride in straight lines at least part of the time while discouraging the horse from wanting to go fast. A round pen or a longe line is not as good because you are constantly turning, which is harder and also doesn't teach you to adapt to change.

MOUNTING

If you are riding bareback you use a different mounting technique, since you have no stirrups. There are three mounting methods to choose from. The first two require a mounting block; the third requires the assistance of a reasonably strong person.

Method 1

Use this method if, when you are ready to mount you are standing high enough (on the mounting block) relative to the horse's back that jumping up will only require a short hop. That is, your crotch is nearly level with the horse's back.

You might want to practice the hop on the fence a couple of times to coordinate the movements of your leg and hands.

1. With your reins in your left hand, place your hands about eight inches apart on either side of the high point of the withers.

2. Keeping your back as straight as possible and your eyes up, lift up your right leg, bending the knee at the same time. Your knee should be almost as high as the horse's topline or higher. (Think of a dog lifting his leg at a hydrant.)

3. Bend your left knee a little, then push off with your left foot and your hands at the same time to hop up. *Don't* try to throw your body across the horse.

4. As you jump, turn your head to face forward. Your body will follow and you can bring your right leg across the horse's back to the other side.

5. Use your arms to keep yourself from coming down too hard, which would be uncomfortable for both you and the horse.

Bareback mount, method 1,
from the high mounting block; step 1.

Bareback mount, method 1, step 2.

Bareback mount, method 1, step 3.

Method 2

Use this method if the horse is too high for method 1. Again, you might want to practice the hop on a fence before you try it on the horse.

1. Place your hands as in step 1 of method 1.

2. *Keeping your legs side by side* and your eyes up, bend your knees. Then, using your hands to help, spring *straight up*. Do not allow yourself to jump toward the horse. You won't get up high enough, and you'll get stuck halfway up.

3. At the *top* of your spring, allow your upper body to go over the horse's back. Do *not* try to swing your right leg over at the same time. Again, you will just get stuck. You should end up with both hands still on the withers and your body lying across the horse about at your diaphragm. Keep your back and hip joints as straight as possible. Try not to collapse over the horse.

4. *Do not move your hands.* There is no handle on the horse's off side. It is a little awkward having your right hand underneath you, but that's where it belongs. If necessary, wiggle up a little bit further over the horse, using your right elbow to pull against, until the tops of your hips are almost on top of the horse.

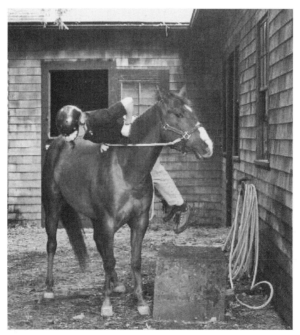

Bareback mount, method 2, step 1.

Bareback mount, method 2, step 2.

5. Turn your head to face forward and at the same time reach up and across with your right knee and hook it on the horse's spine. Then using your knee and your hands, turn and face forward, and sit up, allowing your right foot to drop as you do so. Don't try to put your right foot down until you are facing forward or you will dig the horse in the flank, which he may not like.

Method 3

This is simply getting a leg on from another person.

1. Stand facing the horse's left shoulder with your hands in the same position as in method 1. Keeping your knees together, bend your left knee.

2. The person helping you puts one hand under the base of your knee and the other under your ankle. If there is no one available to hold the horse, she should put her left arm through the left rein, as well.

3. Keep your eyes up and your hip joints locked open. Think about going *straight up*, **not** about getting on! Bend your right knee and, on the count of three, push off with your right foot, using your hands to help, at the same time as your helper lifts *straight up* (not out) on your left leg. Keep your knees together as you go up, going right past the horse until your crotch is level with the horse's back.

4. Then bend your right knee and swing your right leg over, turning to face forward at the same time.

Tidbits & Supplements

During a leg-up mount, it can be very dangerous if the horse walks off as the rider is halfway up. If the rider then lands behind the saddle or on the horse's loins, the horse will very likely take off bucking, and from that position the rider can only have a very nasty fall.

If you try to get *on* the horse before you are above him, you will get stuck. If you collapse your hip or bend over when your helper is trying to lift you up, she will have to drop you and start again.

PUTTING THE SEVEN STEPS TO WORK

Now that you are on the horse, take your reins in two hands. Immediately use the first two fingers of one hand, still holding the reins, to grasp the neck strap or pommel. If you have a ground person or a dependable horse, you can hold on with both hands, which will keep you more square. (For the moment, you should always have at least one hand holding on at all times, until your body fully accepts the situation and finds its balance.) At this point there should be no pull on the reins, the pommel, or the neck strap.

The next step is to use the Seven Steps (see Chapter 1) to ground yourself in your seat. Do each step very slowly and thoughtfully, observing how it affects your body. The first five steps are almost the same as they were on the ground, with some minor differences as follows.

In the shake out, you usually do one hand at a time on the horse, since the other is holding on. And when you shake out your legs you only go as far as the knee.

In the teeter-totter, let go of the neck strap and hold your hands out in front of you as if you were on a diving board. Keeping your back straight, bend forward at the hip joint very slowly, trying to feel when you start to grip with your thighs. The object is not to see how far you can bend forward but how aware you are of developing tension. Then rock back, still with a straight back, and look for tension in your lower back and buttocks. Repeat a couple of times, finishing up in the leaning back position. From there, come forward very slowly, being aware of the tension in your back. At the moment the tension disappears, stop. You should now be longitudinally centered with no tension. If you have a ground person, ask her to look at you from the side and see if you are vertical, with ear, shoulder, and hip all aligned.

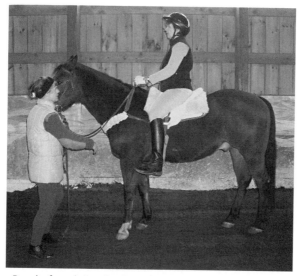

Peg *before* doing the Seven Steps. It looks pretty good until you compare it with the next photo.

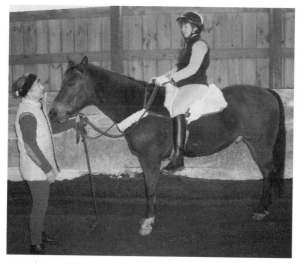

Looking at this, you can see how tense Peg was in the previous photo. She seems much more part of the horse, and even her slightly flat hand is softer.

Soft eyes are done the same on the horse as on the ground, but for riding you should have a little more understanding of their use. Your eyes tend to be hard when you lose control or balance. Soft eyes improve your awareness of yourself in space, making it easier for you to stay centered over the horse and maintain the desired relationship with objects around you. Hard eyes are linked to your left brain, which is verbal, linear (like reading numbered directions), and controlling. Soft eyes are linked to your right brain, which is nonverbal, holistic (like putting numbered directions together into a whole), and noncontrolling. Most of the time when you are riding, it is more desirable to be in right-brain mode, which helps you feel what's happening and better relate to it. If you deliberately make your eyes soft, you will go into right-brain mode automatically.

Moving Right Along

When you have gone through the first five steps, if possible at a standstill, it's time to start your horse walking so you can think about centering and the following seat. At this point your legs should be hanging softly from your hips with no tension anywhere. *What keeps you on is not grip, but gravity.* If you *allow* your legs to fall down on either side of the horse, they will hold your seat down against his back. However, do not force them down, which would lift you off your seat bones and make you tense.

If you squeeze, especially in your thighs and buttocks, you lift yourself away from the horse. (You can try this in a straight chair to see what I mean.) In addition, the tight muscles will make you bounce at the faster gaits.

The Horse's Center

Your goal with centering is to keep your center exactly over the horse's. **What keeps you from falling off the horse is having the horse underneath you.** When the horse is no longer underneath you, because of the law of gravity you hit the ground—as we all know to our sorrow. But what exactly constitutes the horse's center? It's more complex than you might think.

The horse's physical center is a point on his longitudinal midline, about on a line with the girth and level with the bottom of the saddle flap, so that's a little below the widest part of his barrel. Of course, it varies from horse to horse depending on his conformation, but an experienced horseman knows without question when she is in the wrong place relative to the horse's physical center. The horse also knows and will try whatever is necessary to feel balanced. Pokiness, rushing, and crow-hopping are examples of the horse's response to feeling unbalanced forward. Cutting in and spooking sideways are responses to a sideways imbalance. (Unless he is rearing, a horse cannot be unbalanced to the rear, because his hind legs support him.)

You might almost think the horse was designed to be ridden, because the low point on his back, where your weight naturally comes to rest, is not only the strongest point but also places you conveniently a little behind the horse's center, making it easy for him to balance you if you don't allow yourself to be thrown forward. At the same time, unless he is very plump, his spine gives you a clear awareness of his lateral center, so that if you keep one bun on one side and one on the other—as I like to describe it—you will be centered laterally over the horse's physical center.

Sounds easy. And it would be, if it weren't for the laws of motion, in particular the law of inertia. That law says that objects in motion tend to continue in the same direction at the same speed until something interferes to stop them. That's just a fancy way of saying that if the horse is galloping along at twenty miles an hour, sees something scary, stops, and spins left, you, not being a part of him, will continue the way you were going, still at twenty miles an hour, until you hit the ground—which will effectively stop you!

The way experienced horsemen refer to this observable fact is to speak of the horse's "center of motion." We mean that as the horse moves faster or slower or changes direction, he exerts a force on your body—about which you have to do something if you want to stay with him. What you have to do is to learn how to adjust your center effectively and quickly to compensate for his motion.

There is also something I call the center of force. This comes into play when the horse is *trying* to change direction or speed, and so is, in essence, pushing against you, trying to get past you. If you think of a loose horse and how you have to keep moving your center around if you want to block him from running past you, or how you have to stay behind him to keep him going, that is a somewhat clearer example of the center of force. Neither of you is touching or trying to physically push the other, but your centers are interacting. This must be taken into account when you are riding, as well.

Longitudinal Centering

For the most part, longitudinal centering means learning not to tip forward when the horse slows down or stops. You tip forward either because your hip joints close or your upper back collapses. In both cases the solution is to be aware of the correct position of your upper body, which results from the growing exercise and is refined by the other four of the first five steps.

The easiest way to begin to work on your longitudinal centering is with a ground person leading the horse, although if the horse will slow down or stop on a voice command that would be almost as good. You should avoid using the reins at first, since that will tend to pull you forward until you find the knack of holding your position.

Either use a voice command to stop the horse, or ask the ground leader to stop him, at first fairly gradually. Think about how your seat feels on the saddle. It should stay wide and soft, and the pressure on your seat bones should not

Tidbits & Supplements

There is a useful ground exercise to teach you the basic feel of resisting a forward thrust. You only need a straight chair, or better yet an office chair with wheels, a rope, and the leg of another heavy chair or table to attach the rope to. Put the rope around the table or chair leg so that you can hold both ends. Sit in your chair facing the rope, which you are holding. Your pull on the rope represents the force that thrusts you forward when the horse slows down. Tuck your feet back so you can't use them to brace with. Be very conscious of how your seat feels on the chair. Keeping your elbows in front of your ribs, begin to pull on the rope but don't allow yourself to tip forward *at all*. At the same time, don't allow your buttocks or thighs to tense. The pull on the rope flows through your body and into your seat bones, which sink into the chair. None of the angles of your body should change. If your chair has wheels it will roll toward the rope. If your chair starts to tip at all, you know your center has moved forward.

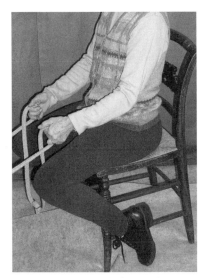

Pulling correctly leaves the
chair firmly grounded.

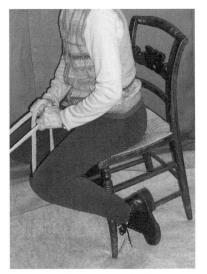

Collapsing your back
causes the chair to tip.

move around from one place to another, which would indicate that your center is moving around. Pulling on the neck strap or pommel in the same way you pulled on the rope in the ground exercise (see the box above) will help you ground and remain still. Be careful not to pull just with your arms, but allow the pull to go all the way down to your soft seat. Don't pull so hard that you create tension. Remind yourself of the first five steps frequently.

Many problems with keeping the horse coming forward are caused by an unstable longitudinal center in the rider. Developing your awareness of this will enable you to use all of your aids more subtly.

Lateral Centering

Riders, even advanced riders, seem to have more trouble with lateral centering than with almost any other position problem. It is subtle much of the time, but sometimes needs to be very drastic, as when a horse does a sudden leap sideways to escape an imaginary bear. It requires a lot of thought and practice in the beginning to instill lateral centering firmly in your muscle memory.

You might well say, "Why bother? I can always grab with my legs if he does something that extreme. Or even grab the saddle. Besides, my horse doesn't do stuff like that!" You wish! You never know what will set a horse off. My oldest and safest pony once bolted with me because I took a piece of paper out of my pocket and unfolded it. The only way you can save yourself in such situations is if your body already knows exactly what to do. Hence the need for instilling skills into your muscle memory so that your reflexes can do the work for you.

If you have someone on the ground to help you with this you can get a good feel for it, or you can just envision it. When the horse turns, your body tends to keep going straight, so if the horse is turning left, your body will tend to slide to the right. The sharper and faster the turn, the farther and faster you will be moved. If you are thrown too far, the horse will no longer be underneath you and you will fall to the ground.

If you move your center to the left when the horse is standing still by sliding your seat off to that side, you will reach a point where you feel in danger of falling. If you go further, the horse will no longer be underneath you and you will fall. However, if you circle the horse sharply to the left just before you start to fall, *he will move back underneath you* and you will feel centered and secure. When he stops turning, again you will feel threatened.

About grabbing with your leg to save yourself: Just to see what happens, in the saddle slide your seat off to the left side until you are insecure (be sure you are holding the pommel). Now squeeze with your right thigh (don't use your lower leg) and try to use it to pull yourself back on. You will find that squeezing with your thigh brings it up the saddle and makes you even more insecure. This is why learning to grip is so unproductive. Besides the fact that it's tiring and can't be sustained for long periods, it simply doesn't make your seat more secure.

The move that works to recenter you laterally is the one you used in the Seven Steps on the ground to move your center from one side to the other. That is, you grow, then bend your upper body slightly in the opposite direction, which creates a space in your waist and enables you to move your center. When you are sitting without stirrups, you have to hike your seat up a little bit by lifting your shoulder on that side to move it over. You can practice this move in a straight chair with your feet tucked back under you. Be sure you move straight across from left to right or right to left—don't let yourself twist.

There *is* a way you can use your leg to stabilize yourself if the horse makes a sudden, violent move sideways. At the same time as you make the centering correction described above, push *down* hard with the leg you want to move toward. As the leg goes down around the horse, bring your calf in so that it is holding gently below the horse's midline. (You have to release your inner thighs to allow this to happen.) As you become centered, bring the other calf down as well. If you do this right, not only does it help to hold you down and stabilize you if the horse is still moving around, but the soft closing of the legs helps support and soothe the horse.

Because of natural crookedness (see pages 127 and 152), centering your body correctly to the right is quite difficult to learn, especially as you grow older and your body gets more set in its ways. Practicing in a chair in front of a mirror helps. On the horse (and standing still), after you go through the first five steps, raise both arms over your head to keep your body as stretched as possible. Then rock from one seat bone to the other, not allowing any twisting and keeping your shoulders level. You should feel that your hip projects beyond your shoulder as you move to each side.

The whole lateral centering movement needs to be practiced a great deal in slow repetitions until your body is very comfortable with it. At that point it will be able to deal with a surprisingly sudden movement without difficulty or even conscious thought.

If you have a ground person, she can lead your horse in bending lines and circles, or you can just let the horse wander freely. Think about the pressure on your seat bones, which should be the same on both sides. Move your center from side to side as necessary to keep the pressure even. Think of rolling a ball from side to side inside your pelvis. Review the first five steps often.

The Following Seat

The seventh step, which helps make the others flow together, is the following seat. Begin by sliding your left hand well in under your buttocks to locate your seat bone. Imagine it is glued to the saddle or pad. Go through the first five steps, focusing especially on growing, then start the horse moving. As he walks, be aware of the movement of his back under your left seat bone. You may perceive it as moving up and down or back and forth, but in any case think about letting your seat bone follow it wherever the movement takes it. Try to work in straight lines as much as possible at first, so you don't get confused with your lateral centering. When your left seat bone is following well, start thinking about your right seat bone too. You are looking for even pressure, both in the sense of being constant from one minute to the next and of each seat bone exerting the same pressure.

In addition to your seat bones moving alternately up and down as the horse's back moves, there is also a distinct forward and back movement. Place one hand so your little finger is just below your belt buckle. Now feel how the movement of the horse's gait pushes your hand forward and then allows it to come back. If you run your mental eye down to your seat bones you should become aware that you are rolling from your seat bones forward until the front of your crotch bone bumps gently against the back of the pommel, then back to your seat bones again. You should not feel that you are rolling back onto your tail bone, since that would create tension in your buttocks.

If you place your hand on the small of your back, you should feel that it goes from flat to hollow, not rounded. It is especially important to learn this whole following movement correctly, because sitting the canter (which is totally different from sitting the trot) involves the exact same movement and is much easier to learn if you already follow the walk really well.

SITTING WORK FOR MEN

Novice male riders, especially if their instructor is a young female, sometimes have trouble believing that men can be comfortable doing sitting work, especially bareback. When the Greeks and the Native Americans are pointed out as examples of success, I have had men tell me that they (the Greeks and Native Americans) must be made differently!

My information comes from my late husband, who was an excellent and experienced horseman. The secret, first of all, is to wear boxer shorts, not briefs. Second, sit straight up, not hunched over, and especially not with the pelvis tipped back—both of which limit the available space. Third, keep the pelvis wide and the thighs open (without allowing the knees to point outward significantly, which would indicate tension across the back of the pelvis).

The result of all this is to create the maximum amount of space and softness in the surrounding muscles, to permit comfort. You should also spend extra time at the walk on all aspects of centering, since it is when your center gets out of place that the whole area tenses, which is most likely to cause a problem.

POLISHING YOUR SKILLS

Once you have worked on the Seven Steps individually, you are ready to put them together, which you do by running through them in your mind as you allow the horse to walk around freely. Separating following seat and lateral centering is a tricky mental exercise, since both involve your seat and pelvis. It helps to realize that the following seat is a passive activity. That is, all you need to do is use the other steps to get yourself relaxed and sitting correctly, and *allow* the following seat to happen. Lateral centering, on the other hand is something you have to think about consciously, at least for quite awhile, until your body learns to do the thinking for you. It is an active movement, because instead of *giving* to the forces that are affecting you, you have to *resist* them.

It is perhaps easiest if you think about *keeping even pressure on the following seat bones*. So as you walk down the straightaway, your seat bones are lifting and dropping to keep even pressure on the horse's back as it lifts and drops. As you go around a corner, your seat bones continue to lift and drop, but unless you adjust your lateral center you will have *uneven* pressure—more on the outside seat bone than the inside one—which will create tensions that interfere with the following seat.

Troubleshooting at the Walk

The main problem most people have when riding without stirrups is the tendency to grip. They do it with stirrups, too, but it is worse without stirrups unless you work on it. And since relaxing the legs is the principal object of the exercise, you need to correct the tendency as soon as possible.

Wringing Out

The first exercise is the thigh and buttock squeeze. Sit as correctly as you can, then tighten all the muscles in your buttocks and thighs as hard as you can. Hold them tight until they begin to tire and hurt a little. Now you can easily identify the areas of tension.

The next part is to consciously release the tension, one section at a time. Before releasing each section, take a deep breath, then let it out slowly as you release. Begin with the small of your back, a few inches below the waist. Here there are a pair of muscles called piriformus that run crossways, which act to pull your thigh bones so that your knees turn outward. Think to release them outward from your spine toward your hip. Next is the gluteus maximus, the principal muscles in your buttocks. Tension in them lifts you off the saddle rather than allowing you to sit. They run diagonally. Think to release them from your spine down and out toward the top of your thigh.

The glutes attach to a long muscle running down the outside of your thigh, called the iliotibial tract. Releasing this helps release the glutes more fully and also allows your knees to drop down. Release straight down the outside of your thigh.

Finally focus on your inner thigh. There are several muscles here that run from your pelvis to various areas of the thigh bone, pulling it inward. Again,

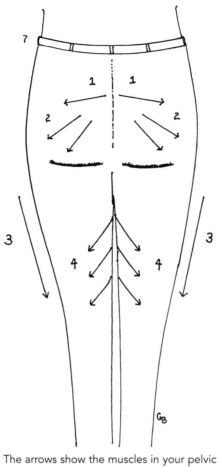

The arrows show the muscles in your pelvic
and thigh area that develop tension.

tension in them lifts you up and away from the horse. Don't forget that *gravity* is what keeps you on the horse; grip lifts you off. Release these muscles down-ward and outward from your inner pelvis along the whole thigh.

Practice these releases slowly and often. The tensions you are releasing are the same ones that arise when the horse does something sudden and frighten-ing. You can eventually teach your body to do the releases as soon as it senses you are beginning to tighten up. This will save you from falls and your horse from being scared by your tensions.

If shoulder tension is making your upper body cramped and your hands rough, you can perform a similar exercise (the shoulder squeeze) by drawing your shoulders up around your ears, then releasing downward and outward in four breaths.

Knees up. Douglas, who has only had a few lessons, is sitting very firmly and comfortably on his seat bones, with no tension.

Knees Up

This exercise should be done on a quiet horse with someone holding him. Knees up is easiest in the saddle, but it also works on a fairly thick pad on which your knees hook over the front. Both knees up and sidesaddle are much easier than they sound.

Lift your feet up, one at a time, until you can hang your knees over the tops of the saddle skirts with your feet hanging down the horse's shoulders. This exercise really helps you to discover where your seat bones are and forces you to sit on them. It is a real eye-opener for many riders.

Both exercises can be performed at the walk and the jog, and are often a good way to work on the sitting trot on a smooth-gaited horse.

Sidesaddle

This exercise, like knees up, should be performed on a quiet horse. It's best to have someone holding him the first time you try, just to make sure. Both this exercise and the previous one, knees up, have the same goal: to get your thighs to let go so that you can truly sit. But here you position yourself so that there is nothing for your thighs to hold on to.

For sidesaddle, place your left hand, *with the reins in it*, so that you are holding the pommel or on the withers holding the neck strap. Put your right hand behind you and hold the cantle, pad, or surcingle—whichever is easiest. Then quietly bring your right leg up across the horse's neck, over the reins, until your knee is directly over the horse's midline and your right calf and foot are hanging straight down his left shoulder. Once you're set, if you need the reins bring them out from underneath, but be sure to put them back before you try to bring your leg back over. *It is dangerously easy to get a toe caught if you try to bring your foot **under** the rein.*

Keep your pelvis straight across the horse *and your right shoulder back.* This will prevent you from falling off backward on the opposite side from your legs if the horse spooks. Shake your legs out as necessary to keep them from trying to hold on while you find your balance. Be especially careful not to pinch your buttocks. You might want to do a buttock squeeze before starting off.

Practice this on both sides of the horse.

Both exercises can be performed at the walk and the jog, and are another good way to work on the sitting trot on a smooth-gaited horse.

Sidesaddle. Douglas is sitting squarely across the horse,
with his left hand supporting his right leg.

SITTING THE TROT

Sitting the trot, or rather the jog, is far easier than you think, provided you have learned to sit the walk correctly. It requires a bit more shock absorption and thus more flexibility in your buttocks and lumbar spine, and more attention to lateral centering, since the speed, and thus the force when turning, is greater. If you approach it sensibly, however, you should have no difficulties.

Ground Work

After going through the Seven Steps, practice walking down stairs, and jogging in place on a hard floor, in both instances seeing if you can hit the ground very, very silently. The noisier you are, the less shock you are absorbing through your body. All the Seven Steps are important here, but growing and following are especially so.

On the Horse

If you have a horse who will maintain a slow jog and stop on a voice command even if you are not quite correct, you can work on your sitting without assistance. If not, try to get someone to lead him, at least in the beginning, because it will be much easier.

If there is no help available and you can post without stirrups (page 206), you can revert to that if the trot gets too fast to sit. Failing that, being able to do an emergency dismount easily (page 101) will keep you out of serious trouble.

One secret for learning to sit the faster gaits is to use your hand on the pommel or neck strap to help you ground more securely. It's the same technique you used to teach yourself how to resist being thrown forward when the horse stops suddenly, only now you focus on the grounding aspect.

Keeping your body erect but not tense, lift up against the pommel or neck strap as if you were trying to gently pull the horse up against your seat bones. Be careful not to pull your shoulders upward. You might want to do a shoulder squeeze as well as a buttock and thigh squeeze to make sure you have released all the tensions in both areas. Tense shoulders will create tension in your back. Your buttocks and thighs should feel very wide and soft. Your hip joints should be open, but don't lean back so far that you create tension in your lower back (see the photo on page 123).

Walk around for a little while, using the grounding lift with your hands but making sure you are still flexible. Walking down a slight incline or over ground poles will increase the springiness of the horse's gait without adding speed, which will help to prepare you for the trot.

The sitting trot. Pretty good for a first time! Notice how the pull on the neck strap, with no tension, is keeping Douglas well grounded.

Begin the trot as gradually as possible, on a straight line. Only trot a few steps at first, then walk, find another straight line, and start again. Your seat should stay right down on the saddle. If you start to bounce up at all and can't reground immediately, stop and start again.

As you begin to feel secure, begin to lengthen the time you trot and incorporate some turns. The increased speed, creating additional inertial force, plus the springiness of the trot, which lifts you up, combine to throw you to the outside on the turns quite a bit more than at the walk. Therefore you have to make an extra effort to maintain your lateral centering.

It is easier to center to the left, so it's best to begin left hand around. As you approach the turn, lift your left shoulder a little to open up that side and allow your center to move. The springiness that lifts you, making you bounce to the outside, also makes it easier for you to move your center—which is to say, your pelvis—to the inside. As you start the turn, keep your eyes soft and think about how the pressure on your seat bones is feeling, moving to the inside as much as you need to keep the pressure even on both sides. Be careful not to lean forward, which would unbalance the horse and make you grip.

If you feel yourself starting to bounce, your tendency may be to pull harder with your hand on the neck strap and push your legs down in an effort to sit deeper, but the pull will only make you tense and your legs will start to pinch, both of which will make you bounce worse. Try to think more about staying taller and looser in your upper body and wider in your seat and legs.

Many people find that trying the sit trot in sidesaddle or knees up position is much easier. It's best to try it with a helper on the ground at first, unless your horse is very dependable. If you are alone and get into difficulties while your knees are up, it is a simple matter to let them drop down again. If you are sidesaddle you can just let go of the pommel with your left hand and slip off. Don't forget to face the front of the horse as you slide down. Practice this a time or two at the walk before you try it at the trot.

Learning to sit the jog without stirrups prepares your body for all the rest of the sitting work. Learning to do it well improves your horse's comfort, confidence, and way of going. And besides, it's fun!

6

Making Conversation

Listening as Well as Talking

Mike enjoyed horses. As often as possible and when the weather was right, he went to the local hack stable and took an escorted trail ride. Mostly because of his youth and courage, he eventually progressed to the "fast ride," which involved cantering and even galloping when the trail permitted. So when his new friend Susan asked if he rode, he described himself as an experienced horseman. Susan then invited him to take a ride with her on the horses she kept at home.

Much to Mike's embarrassment and the dismay of both Susan and the horse Mike was riding, Mike found himself with very little control. The horse was accustomed to a moderately skilled rider and Mike's aids, such as they were, were rough and confusing, so the horse became more and more upset and difficult. They managed to return home safely, but no one had a very good time.

Without being aware of it, Mike had really only been a silent passenger, in the sense that although he may have used his aids, the horse was actually following the other horses and a routine that he knew.

∽

A total novice can go to a hack stable and take an escorted trail ride—and usually return safely without incident—precisely because although she may have been shown how to use her aids, as a practical matter she has no control whatsoever. Since the horse feels in control and is following an established routine, he doesn't feel threatened, so he doesn't do anything that would frighten his rider. Similarly, very young children can ride quite successfully on the lead line. It is when the rider starts trying to give directions that trouble, and usually failure and frustration, ensue. Though in a much more complex way, it's the difference between being the passenger in the car and being the driver.

Controlling the horse is far more complex and subtle than "kick to go, pull to stop." It's a good deal more like bringing up a child or maintaining a good relationship in a marriage or being a successful office manager.

125

To learn more about this topic, read Chapters 8, 16, and 19 of the companion volume to this book, *How Your Horse Wants You to Ride: Starting Out—Starting Over.*

To begin with, you never have "control" of the horse in the same way that you have control of, say, a bicycle. The horse can only do what his brain tells his body to do. Correct aids do work on the horse's reflexes, but if a horse is panicked the panic reflex will override any others. So the serious horseman accepts that he is actually a passenger on a vehicle controlled by the horse himself. **The rider's task is to make himself an informed passenger and trustworthy guide whom the horse listens to and turns to in time of trouble.**

So what are your concerns as you focus on "control"? First, if you ask someone to do something, you have to know what you want and you have to know how to ask for it. You also have to be sure the one you ask is listening and is willing and able to perform the task. And, if necessary, you must be ready to help him prepare for it.

WHAT YOUR HORSE IS TELLING YOU

We'll talk about the first part of the previous paragraph a little later. To begin with, we need to understand what part the horse plays in all this. First of all, is he listening to you? You can tell mostly by his ears, which tell you what his eyes are doing, which tells you what he is focusing on—which should be you! A horse who is listening and working has soft eyes, and his ears are soft as well—relaxed and turned slightly toward you, though they may flick away momentarily.

His head will be at whatever level is commensurate with the level of collection he is in. If he is not collected but his head is up, that's another sign that his attention is elsewhere.

"Willing" and "able" tend to go together, because a horse who does not feel able to perform a task is usually unwilling to try. The horse who trots faster and faster in a small arena, rather than picking up the canter, is a good example of that. In a space that is too small for him to be *able* to canter safely and easily, he is *unwilling* to try. The horse who doesn't want to leave the barn is in the same fix, but the problem is more psychological. He doesn't feel *able* to cope with being alone in the great outdoors—and doesn't perceive his rider as a partner—so he is *unwilling* to go there.

When it comes to preparing him for the task, this can be as simple as a half-halt to prepare him for a transition or as complex as a long-term balancing and muscling program to prepare him for cantering in the smaller space.

Tidbits & Supplements

I have taken some really nasty falls off horses who were loaned to me as "absolutely bombproof. All the beginners ride him!" In each case, when I asked the horse to listen to me rather than take charge himself, the horse became angry and resentful. I was not aggressive or cruel or even annoyed with the horse, but because his previous experience with capable riders was bad, he assumed I would be the same way. That is, capable riders who were bad horsemen had forced the horse to do things he wasn't comfortable with. The novice riders didn't and couldn't do so, so the horse, having control himself, felt comfortable with them. An experienced rider such as myself, merely by showing my ability to get the desired response from the horse, became such a threat that he had to get rid of me. Each of these horses waited until I relaxed and let the reins out, and then threw me—deliberately and hard. Not a nice experience for an old lady!

Psychologically, it means creating a feeling of trust in the rider. This must begin with an overall ground training program, ideally starting from birth, which conditions the horse to be comfortable with people. It can progress to a deep and intimate relationship where the horse will do things that are frightening or painful for him, to accommodate a rider whom he loves and trusts. At a simpler level, a horse who is comfortable with humans will allow anyone to ride him on short notice and will do those things that he already does well, just as two people who meet at a dance will enjoy dancing together even though they are relative strangers.

A good deal of the time, when a rider says her horse isn't "listening," if you question her in greater detail you find that it's more a question of the horse being unable, and thus unwilling. And that, in turn, is often a question of lack of preparation of one sort or another.

RESISTANCE AND NATURAL CROOKEDNESS

"Resistance," in the sense of not responding to the aids, is another much-misunderstood response on the part of the horse. It is usually equated with stubbornness or a "bad attitude." But resistance is much less complicated than that. It tells you very simply that the horse, for whatever reason, is not ready to respond to that aid at that moment. The cause could be physical, as in loss of balance; mental, in that he is confused about what you want; or emotional— he is afraid of something related to the task.

A major cause of resistance, especially lateral, is the phenomenon known as natural crookedness. One of the things no one ever tells you is that horses' bodies are not naturally entirely straight. Neither are people or dogs or anything else, as far as I know. When you read about the Spanish Riding School spending an entire year "riding the horse straight" before they begin serious training, they're not talking about straight lines, they're talking about teaching the horse how to keep his body truly straight, which is something like teaching a person to be ambidextrous.

This crookedness is consistent in its form in virtually all animals. You may observe that one horse is stiffer on the right side, another on the left. This does not mean their crookednesses are different. It simply means that, due to conformation or training, one horse is tenser than the other. The tension produces a secondary crookedness, but the primary crookedness is still there.

In other words, one factor in how crookedness develops is the degree of tension in the horse. The more he is compressed rather than stretched and rounded, the more crooked he becomes. Compression can occur as the result of bad riding, especially as it relates to the rider's hands; from working or keeping the horse in too small a space, so that he is never able to stretch and loosen himself; and from tension caused by any one of a number of outside influences, for example, overfacing him.

But let's get back to natural crookedness. The basic or primary crookedness manifests as a tendency to be bent to the right. **The left side of the horse is the longer, stiffer side. The right side is shorter and softer. The horse's left hind foot is the supporting foot and tends to step in under his body more, so**

Tidbits & Supplements

Although I have not experienced it myself, I have been told by an experienced horseman who trains racehorses that if a young horse, on the track where there is plenty of room, is allowed to go forward with a minimum of interference when he is first looking for his balance with the rider, he will develop very little crookedness.

Interestingly enough, when I was working with my young grandson, taking him along slowly so that he was not tense, he found lateral centering much easier than my adult students. So the combination of youth and optimum conditions seems to affect the degree of crookedness. Of course, if later "training" introduces tension and compression, the crookedness will return.

that the track of his left hind foot is to the right of the track of his left front foot. The right hind foot tends to hang off to the right as well.

One observable result of this is that the horse finds collection at the canter easier on the right lead, which comes off the left hind leg, which is naturally up under him to support him. The right hind leg, however, is the driving leg. Thus the horse's "speed lead" is the left lead, which comes off his right hind leg.

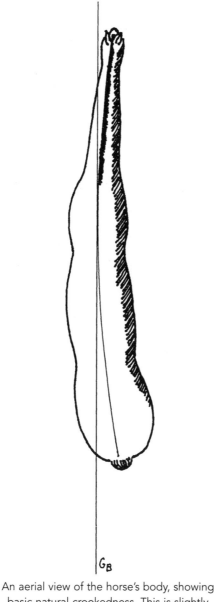

An aerial view of the horse's body, showing
basic natural crookedness. This is slightly
exaggerated for clarity.

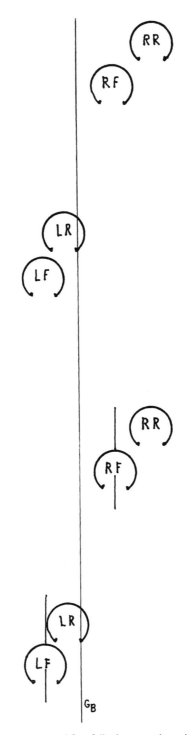

The basic natural footfall, showing the relative positions of the front and hind tracks.

Tidbits & Supplements

You can see the same "speed lead" pattern in humans. For example, racing blocks for foot races are nearly always set with the left leg forward and the right leg back, so the person stands over the left (supporting) foot and pushes off with the right (driving) leg. An experienced shoe store salesman will tell you that most people's left foot is larger than their right (from carrying the weight), while the right calf is heavier (from pushing off.)

Compression causes a change in the shape of the horse's body, when viewed from above. The basic crookedness, as I said, is a curve to the right. The horse tends to put more pressure on the left rein, to pop his left shoulder, to curl up to the right. The left front foot is free to move out easily to the left, so the horse goes more easily to the left but he remains bent to the right. When you ask for a turn to the left, the horse follows his left front foot and goes left, but since he doesn't bend to the left, his head and probably his hindquarters are carried to the outside. This, in turn, means his left hind leg, which he needs for balanced support on the turn, is too much to the outside, so he has to support himself with his left fore, and thus turns with his weight on his forehand. If he gets too much on his forehand he may not feel comfortable about the turn, so he will tense up and become even more crooked to the right.

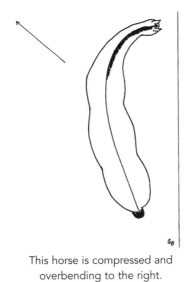

This horse is compressed and
overbending to the right.

The usual way to try to correct this is to demand left-hand flexion. However, because the left side is the stiffer side, if you force the horse to give on that side without first stretching it to eliminate the stiffness (which will take months rather than minutes), you will cause a new problem. When you try to correct by compressing him, instead of getting rid of the basic curve you create a secondary curve called an S curve. Now the horse tends to hang on or resist the right rein, and because the S curve prevents both his right legs from moving freely, he becomes extremely unwilling to turn to the right. Although he now bends his neck to the left, he still does not have his left hind leg where it will support him, so he remains somewhat on his forehand and does not step forward freely through the turn (see the diagram on page 134).

Unless you are working toward a high level of competition and are prepared to spend a great deal of time working on your horse, you probably will never get him very straight, at least not in the ring. However, you can allow for the crookedness in the way you ride him and the way you ask for responses. If you do so, you will meet with far less resistance, your horse will be a safer ride because he is better balanced, and he will stay sounder because you are not asking him to do things that he is not in a good position to do.

The overall answer to overcoming resistance to turning is twofold. First, *the horse must feel balanced over his feet to feel secure and thus relaxed and without tension*, which means you must think first of getting his feet in the right place, rather than worrying about his bend. For example, when turning left, if you ask the horse to leg-yield to your right leg so that his feet track properly, although his head will be to the outside while he is learning, he will relax and move freely forward. As he relaxes and stretches, the crookedness is diminished and eventually the horse is able to bend to the left correctly as well.

This brings us to the second point, which is that *if the horse is resisting the reins, the rider must be able to use her aids in whatever way is necessary to help him achieve balance again*. You will read more about this in Chapters 8 and 10.

Tidbits & Supplements

You can get a very good feeling about these problems in your own body by trying to bend over to pick something up off the floor beside you, in both correct and incorrect bends. Also review the lateral centering exercises to see how your body responds. Moving your center left, which involves bending to the right, is quite easy, but moving your center to the right requires additional stretching of the left side before it is soft enough to bend (see the photos on page 17).

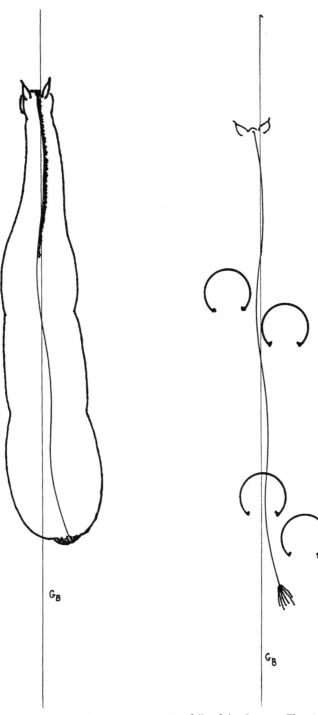

G_B

G_B

The S-curve. Notice that the curve in the neck is repeated in the loin.

Footfalls of the S-curve. The right hind leg is now blocked by the left hind leg.

Turning to the right, it's the horse's right front leg that is awkwardly placed, so that it cannot step out to the right easily. The horse then tends to pop his left shoulder and drift or even rush out to the left. The harder the rider pulls on the right rein, the more the horse's right front leg is trapped. In extreme cases the horse will start to skid uncontrollably out to the left, completely out of balance laterally and unable to go forward again.

Again, the horse must be asked to leg yield to your right leg, which now moves his hindquarters to the outside (left.) This opens up his right side, he is able to straighten his neck, and his right front leg is able to move to the right and begin the turn (see the diagram on page 135).

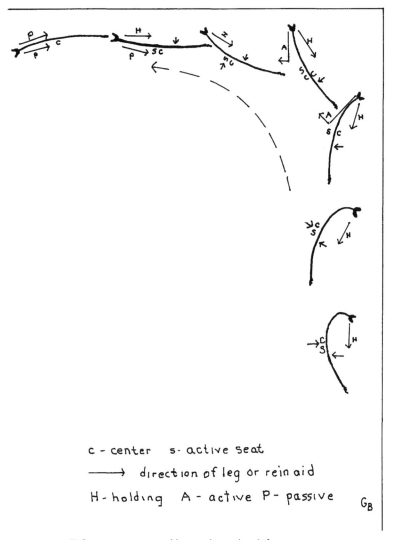

c - center   s - active seat

⟶ direction of leg or rein aid

H - holding   A - active   P - passive

G_B

Riding a compressed horse through a left turn . . .

It is easier to visualize this rather complex description if you think of riding left-hand turns as though they were turns on the hindquarters (in counter bend,) and right-hand turns as though they were turns on the forehand.

Another aspect of the crookedness is the way the horse takes the reins. As you will see in Chapter 8 on hand effects, when you take a steady contact on

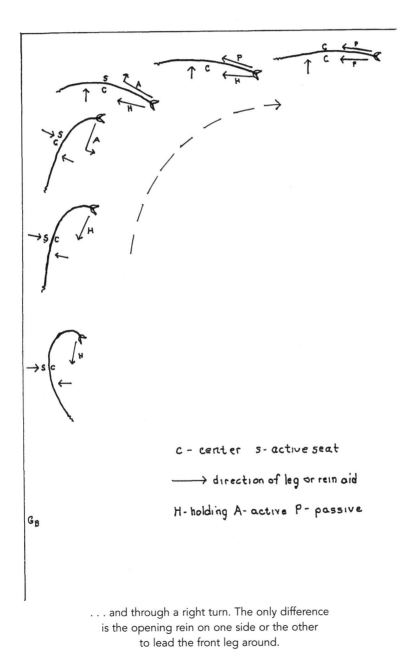

c - center   s - active seat

——→ direction of leg or rein aid

H- holding A- active P- passive

. . . and through a right turn. The only difference
is the opening rein on one side or the other
to lead the front leg around.

the reins, the horse should respond by taking a steady contact back, with the result (if done properly) that each of you is helping the other to ground.

When we ground, we ground diagonally. That is, in the case of the human, a push or pull on our right hand should be transmitted to grounding our left foot or seat bone, and vice versa. In the case of the horse, contact on the right rein should be transmitted to grounding on the left hind leg.

You can feel this in yourself by placing both hands on a heavy table or a windowsill, then backing away with your feet until you are leaning somewhat on your hands, but not heavily. Breathe and release as many tensions as possible so you feel well grounded on both feet and relaxed in your shoulders and hands. Now lift up your right hand and your left foot and see how that feels. Next, put your left foot down and lift up your right foot. You will immediately feel tense and unbalanced. Experiment a little with different combinations.

The simple natural crookedness pattern places the horse's feet so that his left hind is restricted by being too much under his body. As a result, he tends to have a problem grounding against the right rein, so he tends to overbend to the right and go behind the bit on that side. After stretching his left side, when you move his hindquarters to the left until his left hind foot is following in the track of his left front foot, he will be able to take the rein and start to lengthen his right side, which will eventually give you the left hand bend.

When the horse is in an S curve, his right hind leg is restricted because both the left hind and the right fore are in the way. The horse now goes behind the left rein (see the drawing on page 133). Because in the simple crookedness he is apparently resistant to the left rein, this yielding is usually seen as desirable. However, when you take contact and ask the horse to take contact in return, he is unable to do so and thus unable to ground. Now you have to go through a somewhat complicated procedure of riding him forward on both reins, while stretching the right side until he softens and returns to his basic crookedness. You then ride him as above until he begins to straighten out and track correctly.

Don't worry if you don't get this right away, or even for quite a while. As you begin to understand better how the horse should feel to your hands and how his movement should feel, especially in transitions and turns, you will be able to experiment and feel what works. Which is to say, when the horse responds willingly and fluidly because you have showed him the easiest, best way.

THE THREE ESSENTIALS

Now that you understand a little more about the problems of straightness—or at least understand that perhaps the problem is different from what you thought—we need to talk about the three essentials that the horse must present to perform his best and be his most responsive to the aids.

You often hear trainers talking about "forward," as in, "That horse really goes forward nicely," or, "You need to ride him more forward." Generally, when you hear remarks like these, you assume the speaker means the horse has to go faster, or at least cover more ground. But forward, in its deeper sense, is more than that. When you have a horse going forward in the best sense, what you feel is that you and he have got it all together. You feel that at any given moment you can ask for whatever the horse is able to do, and you will get it without resistance or difficulty. Forward in this sense is what keeps us riding. You might call it the Joy of Riding.

There are three essential factors involved for a horse to be going truly forward. They are usually presented as Calm, Forward, Straight. And this is where the confusion arises, I think. "Forward" in this context refers more to what is also called "impulsion": the energy and power the horse must have to perform his tasks. However, the adjective "impulsive" has a totally different meaning. For that reason, I have substituted the words "energetic/powerful" into the formula, so the three essentials are Calm, Energetic/Powerful, Straight. Not quite as concise and elegant as the classic formula, but I think it solves the problem of semantics.

Calm

Exploring this formula further, notice that the first word is *calm*. Before anything else can occur successfully, the horse must be calm, relaxed, self-confident, trusting, and secure. Not at all the same as lazy, or logy, or sticky, all of which are actually signs of tension. A horse who is truly calm is alert and attentive, both to his surroundings and to his rider.

Calmness is achieved as a result of training—especially trust-building ground training experience, good biochemistry, and, to some extent, natural proclivity. Calmness results in a minimum of both mental and physical tension, so the horse is able to easily handle whatever tasks are presented to him that are within the scope of his abilities. And that, in turn, means his rider doesn't have to exert a lot of effort to get results.

Energetic/Powerful

Physically, we value horses for their power and energy. Once we have created trust and the other factors necessary for the horse to be calm and attentive, then we can harness that power and energy. Historically, horses have served humanity with those qualities in innumerable ways, making life easier and safer for their owners. Now, of course, horses (at least in our culture) are used primarily for sport, but the same qualities of strength and the will and energy to apply it are still necessary. They arise first of all from heredity. You choose a horse who has the kind of strength and energy you need. A person looking to buy a winning racehorse has totally different requirements than an instructor of beginners who wants a quiet, dependable weight carrier.

Health and nutrition are the second requirements. I remember a horse, Rocky, who had a good build and temperament and should have worked out well in the school, but he was terminally "lazy," or so his riders believed. There were times when stick or leg had no effect on him at all! Personally, I do not believe that there is any such thing as "lazy." Horses—and people—who are so described are either in poor health or they hate what they're doing. Since all Rocky was being asked to do was walk and trot along with the other horses (and since I don't permit even my beginners to attempt things on a horse that would be abusive), I felt his problem must lie in poor health. Sure enough, when we explored further we found that he had a severe problem with dehydration, even in the cooler weather. That is, something was wrong with his ability to maintain a normal fluid-mineral balance. The result was that despite his healthy appearance, there were times he just didn't have the strength to move. If you've ever experienced heat prostration, you know just how he felt. We were able to improve him materially over time, and everyone was much happier.

Tidbits & Supplements

I had a program in my stable to address the problem of too little exercise, and it worked very well. I used the private horses part time in the school, with their board pro-rated based on the number of hours the horse worked. It worked because the owners knew that since I wouldn't allow *them* to abuse their own horses, I certainly wouldn't allow any one else to do so.

The horses got both mental and physical exercise, and since we never asked for more than they were comfortable with, their training and attitude improved as well. I didn't have to carry such a large string of horses of my own, and the owners had horses to ride who were fit and ready for the desired level of work.

Another solution can be a half-lease, so that someone else shares the time requirements. And, of course, you can always pay a professional to keep your horse legged up for you.

On the other side of the scale you have the horse with *too much* energy, which becomes a different kind of tension. Again, this is virtually always nutritional or biochemical—that is, too much grain or some sort of mineral imbalance. However, it can also be the result of pain and discomfort. A horse who is perfectly content to loll around his stall or paddock but is a very "spirited" ride is virtually always indicating discomfort of some sort in the only way he can. It is his cry for help.

The last element is training and exercise. This is where a lot of riders fail their horses, especially in the exercise department. A horse requires the same sort of regular, carefully graded exercise as any other athlete. And despite what you might think, horses who are turned out do not keep themselves fit. Wild horses are probably about the only group who can be said to do so. A horse *must* receive the amount and kind of exercise necessary for the physical challenges he is expected to meet. But a surprising number of otherwise caring owners think it is all right to ride only once a week, during which they go out for a three- or four-hour fast trail ride!

Straight

We have already discussed straightness at some length in the section on natural crookedness, earlier in this chapter. While straightness is given equal value with the other essential elements, it is rarely given the same consideration by riders. If your discipline is one that involves mostly straight-ahead unrestricted movement, such as racing, foxhunting in big country, or endurance riding, then straightness is, to a great extent, addressed by the nature of the work itself. But when you confine the horse to rings, lots of turns, and other work that tends to compress and shorten rather than open and lengthen him, straightness is going to become a consideration. You will have to deal with it or pay the consequences in "disobedience" and unsoundness.

The Three Combined

The three elements, Calm, Energetic/Powerful, and Straight, are generally shown as an equilateral triangle. This means they are of equal importance, and also that each one affects the others. For example, a crooked horse, because of how his feet are placed, isn't going to be able to use his power effectively; a horse who is lacking in the energy and power to cope with the tasks he faces is going to be tense; a tense horse is going to be compressed and thus crooked. So in looking at your horse's progress, you must look at it from the point of view of these three elements to determine what your next steps should be.

THE AIDS

We said early in the chapter that to get the horse to do what you want, you must first of all know what that is, and second know how to tell the horse about it. In the first case—knowing what you want—if you don't have a very clear picture of *exactly* what you want the horse to do with his body, your message is going to be less than clear and your results will be equally cloudy. This is one of the main reasons a beginner will struggle and struggle to make a circle or pick up the canter. However, an advanced rider on the same horse is able to perform those tasks with no trouble, simply because the advanced rider understands clearly what she wants the horse to do.

Telling the horse about it is what the aids are for. Communication with the horse is both simpler and more complicated than you thought. More complicated because you have to know how to use your aids in response to *all* the physical problems the horse runs into in his efforts to deal with the rider. Simpler, because **once you know those responses, you can ride any horse who is rideable.**

Many—if not most—riders think the aids work by causing the horse discomfort or pain, which ceases when the horse performs the desired action. This system is called "reward and punishment." You pull the rein, this hurts the horse's mouth; the horse stops, you stop pulling the rein, and the horse eventually learns to stop when he feels the pull of the rein.

It is true that the horse can be trained this way, in a limited fashion, but it is neither kind, nor effective, nor efficient! Imagine dancing with someone and every time he wanted a change of direction or rhythm he pinched you or poked you or pulled you, and you tried to guess what it was he wanted, knowing that if you guessed wrong you would be poked again! I doubt if those two great stars of the silver screen, Fred Astaire and Ginger Rogers, would have lasted long as a dance team on that basis!

This idea arises directly from the concept that horses don't want to be ridden and therefore don't want to cooperate, so they must be forced in some way. Which, in turn, arises from an attitude on the part of the rider that the horse is an unfeeling, unthinking slave who is only able to understand such treatment.

In reality, the primary aids work in the same way the leader in dancing influences his partner: **The aids have a physical effect on the horse's muscles or balance, which causes a reaction that results in the movement we want.** In essence the aids *help*, or "aid" the horse to perform the desired action.

The ideal result of your use of the aids is for the horse to do exactly as you ask, and do it willingly and easily. That is, **for him to move his feet in whatever direction at whatever speed you designate, while still maintaining his balance and confidence.** This can only happen if you understand the horse's needs and learn to communicate with him in ways that he can understand and respond to.

Part of this is planning. Frequently the rider waits until she reaches the place where she wants the horse to turn or stop, applies the aid, then is frustrated because the horse doesn't respond immediately. So she escalates the aid, making the horse tense and angry. Instead, she must realize that **the horse is the one "driving the car." That is, his brain controls his body, and the rider is sitting in the passenger seat giving directions.**

Think of what is involved when the driver of a car wants to make a turn at an intersection. First he has to be in the correct lane, then he has to put on his turn signal, then he has to slow down, look for other cars, and finally, turn the wheel. If the passenger waits until the driver reaches the intersection before she says, "Turn left here," the answer she will probably get is, "You've got to be kidding!" How much lead time she needs to give depends on the driver, the road, and the traffic. In the case of the horse, it depends on the footing and his pace, balance, and experience. Taking these into consideration makes a big difference in the effectiveness of your aids.

Something else to consider is how much strength and skill it takes for the horse to perform an action. Moving from a walk to a slow trot is comparatively easy for the horse—although the footwork is far more complicated than you might think—but coming from the canter to the halt takes a lot of strength, balance, and agility. Riders in cold climates often get frustrated in the winter because the horses seem so unresponsive, especially to downward transitions. What is really happening is that the horse's cold muscles are slow to loosen up and function well, so the horse *can't* stop quickly. Even under normal conditions, asking for "sharp" responses before the horse is strong enough to do them can result in joint and muscle strain. The assumption that the horse is just being lazy or unresponsive is a dangerous one.

One of the most important things to consider in getting the horse to do what you want is what we call "intent"—in this case as it applies to the horse. As we have seen, the aids work by affecting the horse's body in such a way that the desired result becomes the easiest, most obvious thing for the horse to do. Therefore, if the horse has no agenda of his own, you apply the aid *correctly* and the horse does what you ask. Once you have developed a good relationship with him, he is looking to please you and be cooperative, and you have made it easy, so why not?

When it gets difficult is when the horse *does* have an agenda—an intent. He wants to go back to the barn, or he doesn't want to leave the other horses, or he doesn't want to go by the funny-looking rock. All these problems are fear-based, and a horse who is even a little unsure can be hard to control, especially if you are unsure as well. In this instance, rather than the horse thinking about doing what *you* want, figuring out the aid, and cooperating, he is thinking about ways to *evade* the aid to solve his own emotional difficulties. Unless you are pretty advanced and very quick at changing your plan, it becomes almost impossible to figure out the right aids to use. Therefore, your concern should be to practice new skills in a situation where the horse feels secure and relaxed, and so is most likely to try to please you.

Forcing the horse and/or focusing on his failure through punishment result in creating fear. **Fear is the greatest barrier to learning.** I was riding Kim, a horse who had come from a demanding training stable. We were in the field and I decided to leave by a different gateway from the one through which I had entered. There was a single bar lying on the ground and I walked Kim up to it. When he reached it he stopped and began to shake. It was very apparent that he was afraid to try to step over the bar. I patted him for a moment, then turned him away and rode him toward it again, keeping my body completely passive and saying to him in my head, "I think you can walk over this bar, but if you can't, that's okay too." He hesitated briefly, then stepped over the bar and breathed a sigh of relief as I patted and praised him. Here was a horse who was so fearful of failure and punishment that he was afraid to even try!

So rather than thinking of the aids as a way to *make* the horse do your bidding, think of them as a way of *showing* him what you want, and also *how* to do it. And to do that, you must understand what the different aids are and how they affect the horse.

Defining the Aids

Aids are usually classified as natural, that is, part of your body, and artificial, that is, manmade. Your leg is an example of a natural aid; the whip is considered an artificial aid. I prefer to classify aids as either physical or learned. A physical aid is one that causes a physical knee-jerk type of response in the horse, and a learned aid is one in which the horse is taught that responding in a certain way to a specific signal results in a reward. While some aids are more physical and some more learned, most of them involve both aspects.

A horse can learn to respond to almost any kind of signal. Teaching the horse to stop when he hears the word "whoa" and go when he hears a cluck are the most common examples of learned aids, but horses have also been taught to stop, go, and turn in response to taps on the neck or tugs on the mane, which often bear little relation to the action being performed. By contrast, a physical aid causes a physical response that is directly related to the aid, which will be covered in detail below. Of course, like any physical skill the horse does learn to respond more quickly with practice. And under certain conditions, especially extreme fear, the horse may not respond to any aids at all. Which is one of the reasons why the first requirement for any well-trained horse is to be calm.

Although a learned aid isn't an aid in the sense that it *helps* the horse perform the action, since most people use the term "aid" to describe any sort of communication between rider and horse, we will continue to use it.

Physical Aids

The physical aids are:

- **The hands, in combination with the reins and bit.** Since the bit is fastened to the horse's head, and since the horse uses his head for balance, using the hands to increase or decrease pressure on the bit will affect the horse's balance, causing him to react in some way to regain it. Under educated hands, the horse also learns that he can use the bit to help him balance and ground himself more securely. If, instead of the bit, we use a hackamore or other device that presses on the horse's nose, it creates the effect of a barrier as well.

- **The lower leg (below the knee), with or without the spur.** The leg acts in a way very similar to tickling. That is, the tendency is for the horse's body to curl up around it, which prepares him for the extending, forward driving action. In the case of the leg, and especially the spur aid, **the release or taking away of the aid is what allows the horse to go forward.** There is often a learning aspect in the beginning of teaching the leg aid, where the horse gathers himself in response to the tickling effect but has to discover that the release means he can then step forward.

- **The seat.** The active movement of the seat bones within *relaxed* buttocks acts like a massage to release tension in the horse's back, thus enabling the hind legs to extend forward more easily.

- **The center.** The horse will move away from the center if it is applied by someone whom he perceives as threatening, or stronger, and follow it if he perceives the user as leader (see Chapter 3). It is related to, but not the same as, the weight and seat aids.

- **The weight.** This aid has three effects. First, when directed longitudinally through the seat or saddle into the back of the horse's shoulder blade, it sends the horse forward—similar to picking up a person from behind. Second, a small lateral weight shift unweights one side of the horse's body, freeing the legs on that side for easier movement. Third, larger lateral weight shifts require the horse to rebalance.

- **The eyes.** The movement of the eyes and the head movement that accompanies it have an effect on the rider's weight. There is also a more subtle effect of intent, which the horse appears to perceive and respond to.

Learned Aids

The learned aids are:

• **The voice.** The learned effect is the horse discovering the meaning of words such as "whoa." Many horses have learned to respond to a very extensive vocabulary. The physical effect, which really is a psychological effect, results from the tone of voice used; an angry voice produces tension, a calm voice produces relaxation.

• **The whip.** The learned effect is the horse finding that the tap of the whip asks for movement. The physical effect is the tensing of muscles in response to the tap, especially as it becomes stronger. Like the leg aid, the whip tends to bring the horse together, generating power that can then send him forward. When the forward motion is prevented, the power often shows itself as a buck.

Other Aids

Martingales, side reins, gags, and like devices are often considered artificial aids. In reality they are primarily training devices. Whether they are beneficial or harmful to the horse depends almost entirely on the skill and attitude of the trainer. Although I fail to see how some of the more abusive ones could ever be justified!

Throughout the chapters on aids I will be referring to passive and active aids. The concept of passive aids, in particular, is very important to understand. When an aid—leg, hand, or seat—is passive, it means that, while there may be a connection with the horse's body, in no way does this connection disturb the horse by creating tension or imbalance. It is simply there, like white noise in the background, not asking anything and able to be accepted and ignored. It says to the horse, "What you're doing is okay. I'm here, but I'm not going to bother you." The horse, in response, is completely relaxed and unresisting.

Passivity is hardest to achieve with the reins, and hardest for the horse to accept, but a surprising number of horses have also never learned to accept either the leg or the rider's weight without tension.

An active aid is one that asks the horse to do something different from what he is currently doing.

USING YOUR MIND

Much more communication than we realize depends on how the rider is thinking about the result she wants. For example, school horses very often will not pick up the canter for a timid novice who really *doesn't* want to canter quite yet. An inexperienced or clumsy horse will pick up the canter with far less effort for the rider who has a very clear picture in her mind of how a horse picks up the canter.

I also am coming to believe—and you may think this is a little far out— that the horse really gets the message of *what* the rider wants from what the rider is thinking. The aids tell him *how* the rider wants him to do it, and help him to do it that way. I say this because over the years I have seen horses respond to all sorts of different signals that sometimes have very little to do with the horse's mechanics, but the horse still seems to figure them out.

I also had an interesting experience one day with Chris, a horse I was train-ing, who was very reluctant to pick up the trot in the ring. I would always get it eventually, but often only after going twice around. On this day I happened to be riding at the same time as a very inconsiderate teenager who was jump-ing. As we were walking down the rail I suddenly realized that after her next jump she would be coming right at me, and if I didn't move quickly she would jump right on top of me! With this foremost in my mind, I asked Chris to trot. To my surprise, he responded immediately and trotted away before we got jumped upon. Somehow or other he picked up that it was urgent to move.

From then on, when I asked him to trot I also sent a mental signal that it was important that he trot, and I had no more trouble getting the transition after that. Apparently, as a former trail horse, he could see no point in trotting around a ring but was willing to accept that *I* thought it was important.

Whether this "mind reading" is exactly that or the result of the rider's body reacting to what she is thinking is not really important. What is important is that the more clearly you know what you want the horse to do and how you want him to do it, and the more you think and plan ahead to give him a chance to "read" you, the better results you will achieve.

Many riders assume that when the horse doesn't respond immediately, he is being deliberately disobedient. However, if you have taken the trouble to establish a good relationship with your horse, he generally tries to please you and do what you want. If you approach communication with the belief that the horse wants to please, and then give him a chance to work with you, you will often find that you get far better results than if you become aggressive.

I have a T-shirt with the slogan "Attitude Is Everything." This is a motto that could well be adopted by every horse owner. Of course, I don't mean atti-tude in the sense that the word is often used nowadays, to describe someone who is rebellious and aggressive. Rather, I mean an attitude of comfortable con-fidence. It is an attitude that says, "I expect you to cooperate with me, not because you're afraid of me but because I have your needs as well as my own in mind." It is an attitude that sees clearly what is wanted, but is also aware that there might possibly be reasons why this can't happen.

Riding a horse is somewhat like parenting—you can't always be sure you're right, and at least part of the time you will be wrong. But because you are a parent, part of what you need to show is confidence. Sometimes it's better to be positive and wrong, as long as you aren't hurting the horse, than wishy-washy and indecisive. You may have to correct your mistakes later, but your horse will recognize that you want to be strong for him and that your goal is to help him succeed.

7

The Quiet Aids
Making Yourself Heard Without Shouting

I went through phases in my riding career when I felt the need to use all sorts of forceful devices to get the results I thought I wanted. At least I will say that I was never deliberately cruel, and mostly I was following the example of others. Horses got upset and horses resisted, but that was what horses did and you expected it. And usually if you got a little more forceful they gave in. Except, of course, when they didn't.

The ones who didn't gradually taught me, especially as my own knowledge and skills improved, that force accomplishes very little. About the only time you use it is when a horse is being deliberately aggressive—and even then it doesn't work a good deal of the time!

REWARD AND PUNISHMENT

It has been shown that learning nearly always occurs most easily when it is accompanied by positive reinforcement. That is, rather than punishing what you *don't* want, you ignore it as much as possible and instead look for opportunities to reward any effort toward what you *do* want.

This means you must develop the skill of noticing when the horse *starts* to give you the right answer. And you must develop the habit of immediately responding with some sort of encouragement. If necessary, you must also break the habit of marking the incorrect behavior with discipline, or in most cases any sort of notice whatsoever.

Reward is mostly in your attitude. Wanting to please is hard-wired into all social animals, so when you feel and show genuine pleasure in your horse's efforts and successes, he will know it and do his best to repeat the experience. It's something that is common to all of us. *As long as it is sincere*, you can hardly overdo praise. Obviously, praising beyond the worth of the performance is insincere, and the horse will know it and value it accordingly.

To learn more about this topic, read Chapters 8 and 16 of the companion volume to this book, *How Your Horse Wants You to Ride: Starting Out—Starting Over.*

The simplest form of praise is verbal, since you can use it without stopping whatever you are doing. Pats and scratching that special spot are next, and finally, treats. Treats usually mark the end of a training phase, simply because everything has to stop while you give them. Some horses respond very well to treats; others get so focused on the food that they forget about the work!

I find it very important to smile when I am giving whatever kind of reward is appropriate. When I smile, it makes me feel happy and the horse senses that and feels happy too—or so I believe—which adds to his feeling of success. It can be difficult to remember to smile when you are concentrating on teaching something that is difficult for you as well, but it is well worth the effort.

Not exactly praise, but sort of in the same category, is the apology. Every once in awhile you do something stupid that confuses the horse and gets him in trouble. I remember once dropping a rein in midair over a fence. The poor horse put his leg through it, which was more than a little awkward when he landed. Fortunately, the fence was quite small and nothing serious happened except he got his mouth yanked. I felt terrible about it and apologized to him, just as I would to another human. When we approached the fence again, rather than acting frightened by his previous experience, he behaved as though nothing had happened and jumped quite normally.

Ever since then, when I make a mistake that bothers the horse, I immediately apologize and I never experience repercussions.

We talked in the previous chapter about what causes resistance. Now let's talk about the different aids and how we can use them so they are not forcing the horse, and thus cause the minimum of difficulty.

The aids we are concerned with in this chapter are the voice, the eyes, the stick, the seat, the center, the weight, and the legs. All of these are quite easy to learn to use in such a way that your position, and thus your horse's relaxation and balance, are not affected. Hands and reins, being the most complex, will be covered in Chapters 8 and 10.

YOUR VOICE

Your voice is useful in many ways. Since it is one of the major ways you communicate with the horse on the ground, it helps him make the learning transition from ground to mounted work. For example, if you have taught him "whoa" when you are leading and free-longeing, it is fairly easy for him to apply it when mounted, as long as your body is not interfering. Your voice is also very easy to use at a distance, calling or whistling to the horse to come in from the field, for example, so you don't have to walk all the way out to get him.

Horses learn a number of voice commands that they will perform at a distance. Most experienced show horses know all the standard commands, and again, if the rider doesn't interfere, will perform them automatically.

A confident rider also uses her voice to instill confidence in the horse, to reward and, when necessary, to chastise or at least discourage unwanted behavior. But, like all the aids, if it is applied incorrectly the voice will give incorrect results. For example, a frightened rider who babbles nervously at her horse will only make him nervous. Praising a horse who is spooking, in hopes of soothing him, only teaches him that spooking is desirable. Still, unless you are a screamer you can't do a great deal of harm with your voice.

You should remember that talking is associated with the left brain, which means it tends to be a bit controlling, so you should try to offset that by breathing and using soft eyes when you are trying to use your voice to build your horse's confidence. And of course, when talking to your horse it's nice to know that he won't gossip to your friends!

YOUR EYES

Your eyes affect both your body and the way you and the horse think. They affect your body because each time you turn your eyes and head, your whole body subtly adjusts to compensate. You may not be aware of it, but the horse feels the weight shifts and has to adjust as well.

As for thinking, just as we found in free-longeing, the horse will tend to look where you are looking, thus preparing himself to move in that direction. For transitions you look at the spot where the horse would look to plan where to place his feet. For a jump line you look down to a point beyond the last fence on the line, indicating that that is your goal. For a turn you look only as far ahead as the horse needs to figure out how to use his body. Of course, you might glance farther ahead to plan the turn, but you shouldn't ride the turn with your eyes fixed too far ahead.

The horse is also very strongly influenced by whether your eyes are hard or soft. Hard eyes tend to make both rider and horse tense and controlling, so they should be used only momentarily to find a point or direction. In the jumping example above, you would focus briefly on the end point, then allow your eyes to become soft and include the whole line and its surroundings.

Tidbits & Supplements

It was learned comparatively recently that the horse's range of vision is totally different from ours. We see the inside of a sphere, as it were. The horse sees the inside of a wide cartwheel rim, which lifts and drops as he raises and lowers his head and flexes at the poll. Although the horse's range of vision at any given moment is extensive horizontally, it is limited up and down. Thus, a horse who has his head low and overflexed can really only see the ground under his feet, while a horse with his head raised and in normal flexion sees into the distance, but not at his feet. This is yet another reason why horses are uncomfortable having their head movement restricted, unless they have great trust in the rider.

Finally, your eyes make your intent very clear, both to your own body and to the horse. I discovered years ago that if there was a hole in the road that I didn't want to go into with my bicycle, if I stared at the hole I always ended up in it, or at least making a last-minute wobble to avoid it. I found that only if I focused on the line I wanted to ride would my bicycle go that way.

You'll find that developing the habit of using your eyes correctly, in terms of direction, distance, and softness, will change the way you have to use the rest of your aids. Assuming you don't interfere with your horse in other ways, he will require far less in the way of active aids and his responses will be quicker.

YOUR SEAT

The seat aid is frequently misunderstood. Trainers talk about "squeezing your cheeks" and "driving with your seat," but the reality is that you don't use the *muscles* in your seat at all, excepting insofar as they help to keep you upright. If you use your seat muscles they become hard, which causes you to bounce at the faster gaits and also makes the horse tense and prevents him from engaging his hind legs.

Place one hand on your stomach with your little finger just above your navel. Then ask the horse to walk freely forward and feel how your hand is pushed back and forth by the movement of his gait. Now drop your mental eye to your seat and feel how it rolls forward and back on the saddle, like a little paint roller. If you increase that movement by *using the muscles under your hand* (*not* your seat muscles), you will feel that paint roller movement increase.

When you combine this movement with the following seat, especially on a stiff-backed horse, you will feel the horse's gait start to free up and become more forward. Why did that happen? Not because you *drove* the horse forward, but because the soft movement acted like a back rub, releasing tensions along the top of the horse's back, which, in turn, allowed him to step forward more freely behind. If you tense your back and try to push, you will feel the horse shorten and either slow down or perhaps become choppy and rapid because of the loss of balance.

Besides using the active seat bilaterally to get freer movement and a lengthening of stride, as you just did, you can also use it unilater-

> ### *Tidbits & Supplements*
>
> This is a generality and should be considered accordingly, but I often tell my students, "If you get resistance to the rein, add some soft active leg on the same side. If you get resistance to the leg, add some soft active seat on the same side. If you get resistance to the seat, you need to give the horse some more warm-up time or stretching before you try to go on."

ally. That is, you can exaggerate the movement on just one side. Place your hand on the front of one hip bone, just below your waist and a couple of inches in from your side. Get your horse walking and push against that hand just as you did before, when it was in the center. Now you will feel that the seat bone on that side is moving more actively than the one on the other side. If you can shift your center to the opposite seat bone without losing the motion, you should find that the horse begins to bend and turn toward your active seat. What you have done is loosen his back a little extra on that side, so he begins to engage that hind leg more. And that, combined with the centering aid (see the next section), gives you a nice, soft turn.

YOUR CENTER AND WEIGHT

Your center and weight are closely related, but they are not the same thing. For example, it is possible to bend way over to the left, so that most of your weight will be over your left foot but your center will still be to the right—which explains why leaning into a turn doesn't keep you on! Also, you can use your center as an effective aid in ground work, where your weight has no effect on the horse at all.

As we saw in Chapter 3, the horse tends to move *away* from your active center but *follow* your passive center. Since most of the time your centering aid is active, let's talk about that first.

While the center and the weight do not work the same way, they do tend to work together. Your weight primarily influences the horse's balance and his ability to lift one or more of his feet. And if you move your center, it will affect the way the horse feels your weight. Therefore, centering aids, for the most part, must be very subtle.

You move your center by first growing from the top of your head. Then I like to think of it as having a rope under your arm at the shoulder, on the side you want to move your center toward. As the imaginary rope lifts your shoulder up, your side opens up at the waist, allowing your center to move in that direction. Don't tense your shoulder muscles—it's more like your armpit is lifting. This is very easily practiced in a chair, where you can clearly feel your weight shift from one seat bone to the other as you move your center from side to side. Be careful not to twist, but move your center straight across. Also try it standing up to get the feeling of moving your center laterally in half-seat.

Turning

Since the horse moves *away* from your active center, to indicate to your horse which way you want to turn, you move your center slightly *away* from the direction you want him to turn toward. So if you are looking for a left turn you move your center very slightly to the right. Besides encouraging your horse to move the other way, the center shift to the right also moves your weight to the right. This takes the weight off the horse's left legs, making it easier for him to lift them and carry them to the left, thus supporting his body during the turn.

Once the horse has begun to turn, you must immediately move your center so that it stays over him during the turn. If you don't, you will be continuing to tell him to turn and he will tend to spiral inward. If the turn gets too tight, move your center a little more to the inside until he returns to the track you want.

The center does not have any physical effect on the horse. It is more of a psychological, hard-wired, turn-away-from-the-predator effect. So if he doesn't respond, *moving your center off more to the side doesn't help*. In fact it hinders, because it then becomes a different kind of weight aid.

Especially with a young or unbalanced horse, if you move your weight very far laterally it forces him to take a clumsy step in that direction to keep his balance. This is the way many, if not most, people use their center/weight to turn a horse: They move their weight in the direction of the turn and when the weight gets too far over, the horse steps in that direction. This will result in the beginning of a turn, but because the horse is now unbalanced, it won't be a very good turn.

Try this yourself on the ground so you feel the difference. Standing straight with your feet shoulder width apart, move your hips to the left until you are forced to take a sideways step to the left to keep from falling. Return to the original position and move your hips to the right just enough to unweight your left foot, then pick it up and move it to the left. A lot easier that way, isn't it?

Starting and Stopping

Many otherwise excellent riders use their center and weight incorrectly to start the horse. That is, they lean forward, or throw their center and weight forward, or rock forward and back. All of these have the effect of both blocking the horse psychologically and unbalancing him physically. The correct way (which is to say, the way that works for the horse) is to grow and then, without becoming rigid, firm up your lower back so that you can't tip forward, either by collapsing in the upper back or by closing your hip joint. Then you simply *hold that position* as you use the other aids to ask the horse for the transition.

One subtle action on the horse's part is his necessity to collect himself to make the upward transition. This causes him to briefly back off, which tends to make the rider rock forward, which then blocks the transition itself. That's why you have to stay firm throughout the transition.

Your weight is also active here, most especially when you want to prevent him from slowing down, perhaps when you are passing the gate. By keeping your back firm, the force of his slowing down, which would normally throw you forward, is redirected through your seat, via the saddle, back into his body behind his shoulder blades. This sends him forward again in much the same way that you can pick up a small person from behind by placing your hands under her shoulder blades and lifting upward.

My horse is trying to slow down and cut in. The stick and rein are forming
a barrier on the side and my weight and center are sending him forward again.

You might think that since you keep your center back when you want the horse to transition upward, you would want to place your center forward to get the downward transition. But because of the weight factor and your position relative to the horse's front legs, if your center goes ahead of the horse's center you unbalance him forward, making it more difficult for him to stop correctly, rather than less so. The only time the center is used forward to stop is during an emergency dismount, and to a small extent during a pulley rein emergency stop. Otherwise the center is used passively for downward transitions, which will be covered in the next section.

Backing

This is one of the few times your center is deliberately moved ahead of the horse's, and it only works because you begin with the horse standing still so he is not subject to much loss of balance. Now you close your hip angle so that your center is slightly ahead, which tells the horse that you want to move backward, thus preparing him mentally for the application of the other aids.

The Passive Center

Your passive center is used almost exactly the same way you used it in free-longeing to allow the horse to slow down. It's more a matter of intent than anything else. Your thought is simply to allow him to stop on his own, so you become totally passive and let him figure out for himself how to stop. This is a

My center in front of his tells Wills that I want to back up.

great confidence builder for the young horse, who often feels, in his efforts to adjust to the rider's weight, that he *can't* stop. The strong use of reins, which interferes with balance, contributes to his lack of confidence, while the passive center does nothing but say, "It's okay to stop. Take your time, figure it out."

This is also a very effective thing to do with horses who lose their balance when landing from a jump and run off out of control, perhaps crow-hopping as well. If you just sit there with your weight well back and leave the reins loose, or balancing and supporting if you have those skills, as long as you are confident—and realize that the horse is not being aggressive, he's just out of balance—he will gradually get organized and stop on his own. If you force the stop with your hands each time, he just gets more tense. With a horse who has consistently been jumped in a way that makes him lose his balance, it may take a while to regain his confidence. But it will happen, and the horse will become a much calmer, safer jumper.

THE STICK

I can hear you saying, "How can you include the stick in the group of aids that are *not* forcing the horse?" Of course the stick can be used to force a behavior, but if you've ever dealt with someone who has a very irritating and aggressive voice pattern, that's about as aggravating as anything even though it's not physically abusive. It's all in your intent. The intent of the stick should be to use it as an extension of your arm and leg, in that it enables you to apply signals in places that you could not otherwise reach.

Since many horses have been abused with the stick, you should never try a stick on a horse until you have first checked, on the ground, that he is not "whip shy." Standing more or less in front of the horse, move the stick in the air around his head and body, first at a distance, then closer. Then touch him and stroke him with it. Be sure to touch both sides. If he shows any signs of fear with this exercise, spend some time building more trust before you try to ride using the stick.

The first thing to know about the stick is that it should not be used in such a way that it causes real pain. Even if you don't care about the horse's emotions, just as a practical training matter, pain creates fear and fear blocks learning, so the training takes longer. The worst the stick needs to cause is a bit of discomfort; the sort of feeling you would get if someone kept poking you with their finger. It's annoying, so you want to make it stop, so you do something to make it stop. In the case of the horse, watch to see if he is showing discomfort by tensing, or putting his ears back, swishing his tail, or the like. If he is showing awareness or discomfort but is still not giving you anything approaching the sort of result you're looking for, it means he just doesn't know what you want and you'll have to think of a way to show him.

The secret of using the stick in a way that is not abusive—and the same applies to using the leg—is to use it in gradually increasing increments of discomfort and to allow enough time between each increment for the horse to respond. Parelli usually uses four "levels of pressure," which works very well. The first is the lightest touch the horse can feel, which, since he can feel a fly landing on him, is pretty light. The fourth is the one at which he shows discomfort by flinching or tail swishing but does not show by his expression or other behavior that he is feeling pain. The second and third are equal steps in between. The interval between steps should be about three seconds, which gives the horse time to react *and you time to notice his reaction.*

It takes a little practice to apply the levels of pressure evenly and fairly. I find the hardest thing is to remember to return to the first level each time I make a new request. It seems so much more efficient to go right to the level that you know works. Unfortunately, if you do it that way the horse never learns to respond to the lower level of discomfort, so you are effectively desensitizing him.

Ideally, to ask for forward movement the stick should be used either horizontally behind the horse or vertically on his croup. But since neither of those is feasible when you are riding, the stick is usually used on the side of the haunches, fairly high up. Because of the natural crookedness (see Chapter 6), 99 percent of the time the stick should be carried and used in the right hand, so that when you use it on the right side of the horse's haunches you are helping him to straighten at the same time, thus making it easier for him to go straight forward. I know that many instructors advocate carrying the stick in the inside hand to deal with cutting in, but since that is nearly always a crookedness problem anyway, or a centering problem on the part of the rider, it doesn't help that much.

It is very important to learn to apply the stick without any change in your weight. The tendency when you reach back with the stick is to lean forward at the same time, which, as we saw in the previous section on your center and weight, acts as a block, which the horse finds confusing. This is probably one

---

Tidbits & Supplements

I have met several horses who don't understand that you're trying to communicate when you use the stick. Their thinking is that people just sometimes hit horses with sticks. Who knows why? They just do it and so you want to get away, but there's no point trying to figure out what they want. Once these horses realize that you just want them to move their feet, they are very relieved. "Oh, is that all? When you touch me with that thing you want me to move a little? Wow! That's *easy!*"

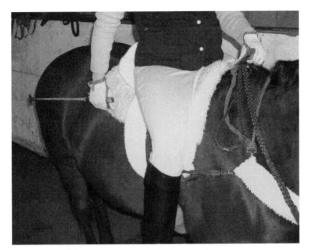

Where to apply the stick. It's important not to
tip forward when you reach back!

of the main reasons horses buck, or even rear, when the stick is applied. They want to move to escape the discomfort but feel there is no place to go, so they move in the only way they perceive as open to them; that is, upward. If you use your lower back to keep your center and weight back without tension, you will not interfere, and if the horse is resisting going forward, those aids will help block him from backing and encourage forward movement. This is especially true if he is already in motion.

One caveat: If you are using the stick to (gently!) encourage a horse who is facing a frightening obstacle, such as water, keep one hand on a neck strap or the saddle. When the horse finally makes up his mind to try such obstacles, it is usually with a sudden big leap. If you come crashing back on his mouth and his back he is not going to be very encouraged to try it again! For that reason, I would never ride a green horse in a challenging situation without a neck strap of some sort ready for use.

THE SOFT LEG

Among the lessons I have taken that I consider the most significant, one I took from the late Nuno Oliveira, the Portuguese Olympic dressage trainer, stands out in my mind. It was the one in which he introduced me to the soft leg. It changed my whole way of thinking about the leg aid. The only thing that surprises me is that everyone doesn't learn to use their legs in this way, because it is so easy and effective.

The standard and instinctive way we use our legs is to turn the toes out and tap or kick somewhat back and inward with the heels. The trouble with this is that the muscles you use to do this are all the ones you *don't* want to contract because they *prevent* the horse from softening and releasing in his back so that he can go forward. In addition, this action tends to tip you forward, which, as we have seen, confuses and unbalances the horse.

Oliveira's soft leg is very easy and effortless to use. There is a learning curve, of course, both for the rider (it took me about two weeks of daily riding to get it programmed in pretty well) and for the horse. In the case of the horse, most of them are so accustomed to being thumped on that it takes them a little while to realize the soft little tap or rub calls for a response.

What makes it a "soft" leg is that you use a whole different set of leg muscles. Rather than reaching back and in with your heel, you reach inward with your toe as though you were going to tap the girth with the stirrup— without actually expecting to do so. Your toe describes a little vertical circle—in and down, then up and out, then down, then in again. At the same time it describes a little horizontal circle as well—in, forward, out, and back. So putting them together it goes in, then forward and up, then out, then down and back. This movement of the toe brings the calf in to the horse, forward along his side, then out and back into its original position.

You can practice on a stool, using one foot at a time, to get the feeling, which you will find is quite easy and natural. In Chapter 1, I talked about a Feldenkrais foot exercise that is very similar, and that tells us this way of using the leg also would improve your grounding, while the other way interferes with it!

Like the stick, the leg aid is applied in gradually increasing increments, with a three-second wait between each increment. It is essential that you do not try to use your leg hard, which would merely make you tense. Instead, for the highest level of pressure you go to the stick, which you should have taught the horse to respond to first.

For increases in speed or gait, the leg should be used at the girth—that is, when the stirrup is at the girth—and should be applied as a tap. To get a tap your calf comes slightly off the horse, then comes in briskly before releasing. If you want the horse to lengthen his stride, the aid is more of a rub; that is, rather than coming entirely away from the horse's side, the inward pressure increases as you bring your leg forward and decreases as it comes back.

For lateral responses you apply your leg in the same way, but place it more or less at the place where you want the horse to yield. As a practical matter you can't use your leg very far back without changing your position in such a way

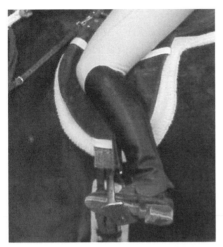

The soft leg, applied in and forward . . .

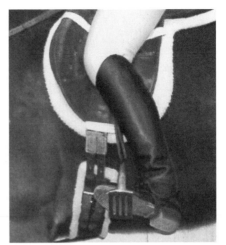

. . . and out and back.

A tall rider on a small horse. She has to bring her foot quite far in to reach his barrel with her calf.

But when her toe is straight, her calf is off the horse.

that you interfere with his movement. "Back" is relative, and is usually only an inch or two. "Forward" follows the same rules. I know there are people who use the leg on the horse's shoulder or neck, but I have seen far too many horses made nervous by this treatment, and there is no reason to do this if your other aids are correct and you give the horse time to learn.

If you let yourself get into the habit of constantly using the leg aid actively, it is very easy for it to become white noise, which the horse learns to ignore. Instead, you should use it actively, as described above, only until you get the desired response. At first you will lose impulsion as soon as your leg becomes passive again, and will have to start over. But after a few tries, the horse will figure out from your center and your intent that you want him to keep going. If you are having a lot of trouble keeping the horse going, look for mistakes in your position or lack of muscle and balance in the horse, or even unsoundness.

If you put enough time and thought into learning and understanding the aids described in this chapter, you will find that almost any horse can be ridden with the quiet aids at whatever level he has attained competence. This, in turn, will result in a far calmer and more responsive horse, and thus a more enjoyable ride.

8

Reins Without Borders
Giving Up Control and Developing Soft Hands

I once had a beginning riding program for local college students. As part of the program, when the students were ready I turned them loose on their horses in small groups, without reins (a practice I later changed for safety reasons). When I set my eight college students loose in the outdoor ring, they were all quite fearless and milled around bumping into each other amid much laughter. The horses were somewhat confused for a few minutes about what they were supposed to be doing. Then suddenly, almost miraculously, the horses, all on their own, formed themselves into a line and started around the ring on the rail, just as if their riders were controlling them! If anything, it was a little better because the riders weren't interfering, except perhaps with their weight. The horses apparently said to themselves, "Nobody is telling us what to do, so let's do what we always do."

∽

The big problem most people have with control is giving it up. As soon as you start saying—to a horse or anybody else—"I'm going to be in charge and I don't want to hear anything from you," they feel threatened. When some one feels threatened, the first thing they try to do is to regain control. And that's how fights start.

Most of that controlling behavior when riding occurs with the rein aids. The horse gets a little quick or he doesn't stop as expected, and right away the rider starts hauling on the reins. From the rider's standpoint, she is afraid of being run off with or bucked off. But since the horse needs to have his head fairly free, as well as freedom to move his front legs, so he can balance himself, overusing the reins is *very* threatening, and frequently *causes* him to run off or buck in his efforts to gain control of his body and balance.

Another reason we humans are so concerned with control on the horse is that other vehicles we deal with, primarily cars, require our constant control to avoid accidents. How often have you heard an auto accident described as "The driver lost control and . . ."?

To learn more about this topic, read Chapters 10, 17, and 18 of the companion volume to this book, *How Your Horse Wants You to Ride: Starting Out—Starting Over.*

LEARNING TO GIVE UP CONTROL

To overcome what is really a control reflex, I found many years ago that if I put a rider *in a safe space with no reins*, she made a number of useful discoveries. First, she discovered that nothing terrible happened. (She was also told that if she felt in the least threatened all she had to do was dismount!)

The most upsetting thing the horse usually does is go and stand by the gate and refuse to move away. If made to move, he walks in a little circle and returns to the gate again. The gate represents safety and security to the horse, and he is very connected to how the rider is feeling. Riders who feel threatened by being without reins will usually spend a fair amount of time near the gate, but they eventually realize that nothing dire is going to happen. Then, if they stay reasonably centered as they keep asking the horse to move, he gets tired of going in little circles and starts to move out more normally.

However, there are always some people who are very threatened by their perceived failure to control the horse. The more the horse goes in little circles, the angrier they get, both at themselves and at the horse. Naturally, the anger makes the horse feel more threatened, so he hugs the gate in an even more determined fashion. Only when the rider is able to say—and mean it—that she doesn't blame the horse or herself for the behavior, will the horse begin to relax.

Needless to say, this is not an exercise to be done by a novice on a skittish horse! However, it is an exercise everyone should practice under safe conditions, and at every gait at which both horse and rider are comfortable.

WHY WE FEEL OUT OF CONTROL

When we feel we have lost control of the horse, what we are *really* feeling nearly all the time is that the horse has lost control of himself. When a horse is running away, he isn't running any faster than he runs at full gallop on good footing. The problem is that you can't stop him, and that's because he can't stop himself. Most of the time this is the result of rider error, that is, riding in such a way that the horse can't get his body organized to slow down. Sometimes it is the result of something frightening in the horse's surroundings. He goes into a panic and takes off so the "lion" won't get him. This kind of bolting, however, only lasts for about fifty yards or so, at which point, left to his own devices, the horse will start to slow down and look around to see what's hap-pening. If he keeps running instead, nearly all the time the rider is causing it by her own fear.

As long as the horse is tense and/or fearful, he can't stop. A skillful rider can help him regain both his confidence and his balance. Once he has done so, *and not before*, the rider can ask him to slow down and will be successful.

So before you try to do much work with the reins, you first have to break the reflex our bodies all have: holding on with a death grip whenever anything goes wrong. This is, oddly enough, one of the big reasons I like to teach my students to ride with a neck strap.

Most instructors have the mistaken idea that using a neck strap teaches you to hang on with your hands. This is like saying that if you let a baby hold your hand when he's learning to walk, he'll never learn to walk by himself. The truth is that if you don't hold on to something with your hands during the learning phase, you force your body to hang on in some other way. This creates all sorts of unnatural tensions that are very hard to eliminate. Conversely, if you learn to ride with a neck strap, which is the natural way, you simply become less and less dependent upon it, until finally you only need it in very unusual situations.

When you ride with a neck strap, your body learns some important things about the use of the hands when riding. First of all, it learns that pulling hard doesn't control the horse (it doesn't know the difference between the reins and the neck strap). Second, it learns that pulling hard only makes your body more tense and less balanced. It learns how a soft connection, along with correct body position, helps the body ground, and that it grounds diagonally. It learns to ground with one hand while the other is doing something else. And, over time, it learns to ground without the assistance of the neck strap in ordinary conditions. Just as a toddler reaches a point where he no longer needs to hold on to something to walk.

That reflex that makes you grab the reins in a death grip arises, of course, out of fear. So let's talk about what we're afraid of and what *really* works to over-come this fear.

I can tell you what *doesn't* work for most people. It doesn't work to tell yourself, or someone else, not to be afraid, whether you say it in a supportive or a derisive manner—although the latter makes things a good deal worse! Fear responses arise in your reflex brain, which is not connected with your reason-ing brain at all. It doesn't hear reason. It only understands successful experience and unsuccessful experience. If the first time you try something it hurts a lot, the next time you try it you will be afraid, no matter what logic tells you. However, if you do something a number of times and it feels good, and then you have one bad experience, you can usually get by it pretty easily because you have a background of successful experience to build on.

It also doesn't work to keep doing the thing you're afraid of if you aren't really ready to deal with it. You only learn that you can't deal with it, for sure.

What we are afraid of, of course, is getting hurt. How do we get hurt? By getting into situations where the horse does something that either our bodies or our minds can't cope with. You don't have to actually get physically hurt; it's enough if you get into a serious situation where you feel like you almost surely *will* get hurt. Not infrequently, we pick up on the horse's mental state as well. If the horse is really angry or really frightened, unless you are very confident you will feel very threatened by that alone.

Except in the comparatively rare situation where a horse falls or runs out into traffic or under a low overhang, you have to fall off to actually get hurt. Running away, in and of itself, should not cause you to fall unless you are a very novice rider. A gallop is a comparatively smooth gait, so unless the horse swerves very violently or stops suddenly, you should be able to stay on. But people do fall in such situations, and they fall mostly because they are afraid. So let's start with that.

You and the horse need to be as secure as possible, both psychologically and physically. Psychologically, the more quality time you can spend together, especially if you incorporate some ground training work on a regular schedule (see appendix C), the more you will trust each other and the less likely you are to scare each other.

Physically, the horse should be kept healthy and sound. Thereafter, the *way* you ride is going to have the greatest effect on his physical security. That's what the Seven Steps and most of the chapters in this book and its companion title (*Starting Out—Starting Over*) are about. It's why both books are called *How Your Horse Wants You to Ride*!

USING THE REINS

As I said earlier, we all have a reflex to grab the reins in a death grip when something goes wrong. That is partly because we're looking for something to hang on to, but also because we have the mistaken idea that somehow, using the reins, we can *make* the horse stop. Every student of riding and every instructor should write out the following in large letters and post it in a prominent place:

It is not possible for a human to *make* a horse stop.

"Oh come on," I hear you saying. "People make horses stop all the time." No, they don't. The horse chooses to stop for one reason or another, but if he doesn't choose to stop, the human cannot *make* him do so. Been there, tried that!

Now, if you happen to be in a position where you can run the horse into an inescapable corner he will stop, but *you* didn't make him stop, *the corner* did. And he might just crash into the wall if he is really terrified. If you can make him fall down he will stop, but again, you didn't stop him, the fall did.

So when we think of stopping, what we want to focus on is not *making* the horse stop, but *making stopping easy and desirable*, so the horse willingly chooses it if the option is offered to him. And that isn't as difficult, psychologically, as it sounds. A horse who has been running for a while wants to stop because he gets tired. A horse who is running out of fear is not enjoying being afraid. If you can remove

> ### *Tidbits & Supplements*
>
> **If you have lost your balance, don't try to do anything with your reins until you have regained your balance again.** This rule will apply for as long as you ride. If you are out of balance, your arms, and thus your rein aids, will be tense, and will only create resistance in the horse and probably get you into deeper trouble.

the fear/danger element, then use your aids so that they *help* the horse stop, the horse will be more than happy to do so.

In the previous chapters, we learned about using the other aids in ways that cause the minimum of interference with the horse and thus the minimum of tension. Now we need to learn how to use the reins in the same way.

You should work on your rein aids only in situations where you don't need your hands for balance. That means you should begin working on the rein aids when:

- You are emotionally and physically secure at least at the walk.

- Your Seven Steps responses are fairly automatic.

- Your other aids are getting a response from the horse without a lot of effort.

- You have done enough work without a leader and without reins that you are comfortable giving up control.

OVERCOMING RESISTANCE AND DEVELOPING SOFT HANDS

I put those two together in the heading because when we see someone who appears to have soft hands, what we are seeing is that even as the horse is apparently responding to all requests, he never seems to resist. As I said earlier, the horse resists because he is unable to respond at that moment. That nearly always happens because the horse has to bring the next foot forward to put it down so he can keep his balance, and the rein is being pulled in such a way that

---

Tidbits & Supplements

Many writers and instructors don't like to use the word "pull" when talking about the reins, because they feel it implies using strength or otherwise causing discomfort to the horse. But there aren't really any better words to describe that aspect of what you do with the reins. You must just take the word to mean "pull in a way that does not cause resistance."

---

if the horse yields to it he won't be able to take that step. So he "resists" to keep his balance. Therefore you, as rider, have to learn how to pull the reins in such a way that you don't interfere with the movements the horse *must* make.

There are two basic hand effects—ways in which you apply the reins—and some variations. This is another topic that is covered in far greater detail in *Starting Out—Starting Over*, and unless your hands are already very good, I strongly recommend that you read it. I also recommend that you try these hand effects on the ground first, perhaps with another person as well as with the horse, to learn how they should feel.

All hand effects consist of either pulling, following the motion of the horse, releasing, or some combination of these.

Because of the way the muscles in the horse's shoulder and neck work, the direction of a pull that asks the horse to yield should always be on or above a line drawn from the bit to your elbow. (There are times you *don't*

Maintaining a straight line from elbow to bit enables the
horse to ground and step forward freely.

want the horse to yield, which will be addressed later in this chapter.) This position makes it easiest for the horse to give to the reins and still remain grounded.

The pull on the reins should also ground the rider. For this to happen, you must hold your hand and wrist so that the pull is transmitted into your body in a way that grounds you, rather than pulling you up onto your toes. By holding your hand so that both the back and the top of it form a straight line with the wrist, the whole muscular system of your body is engaged so that the pull on the reins pulls you down either onto your heels or your seat bones, depending on whether you are standing or sitting (see the photos on page 168).

Releasing is an essential part of using the reins. You *must* release the reins any time the horse starts to take a heavier or more rigid feel on the reins than *you* want. Since you can always let the reins out—assuming they are long enough—the horse can never pull by himself; you have to help him do so. A release is always a quick move, and always directly toward the bit. It must continue until the *horse* releases. That is, if the horse extends his head and neck when you release the reins, they will not become looser so you must continue to release until there is no longer any tension on them.

The Active Hand

The hand effect that allows the horse to most easily yield is the active hand. It consists of pulling the rein very smoothly as long as the horse is not resisting, until you feel the horse starting to respond. If he yields, you maintain whatever pressure you have reached, but if you start to sense resistance you *very quickly release as soon as you feel the slightest tension*. This is followed by a repeat, again engaging the rein very slowly and smoothly.

Because the horse can only stop one leg at a time, and because he needs to stay grounded, when you are using an active hand you virtually always use it with only one hand, while the other maintains steady passive contact (see the section below). Your active hand is used on the side that feels the stiffest and most resistant, while your passive hand is used on the softer side. During a difficult transition the horse may change sides in his effort to work out his balance problems.

The Passive or Following Hand

The passive hand, also called the following hand, is the other hand effect that is used most frequently. For your hand to be passive, the contact on the horse's mouth must be absolutely even. That is, it must follow the slightest movement of the horse's head so that the pressure never changes.

The pull under your little finger pulls your hand out of position.

By using the muscle under your forearm to pull, you can keep your hands and wrists soft and straight.

Pulling with a straight wrist keeps you grounded.

Pulling with your hand cocked upward lifts you on to your toes. Pretty scary if your horse's head is down on the ground!

Tidbits & Supplements

Like all four-limbed animals, humans have different gaits. That is, we have different body patterns depending on whether we are walking or running. Running is not simply walking faster, as you can easily envision if you think of how the body of a human race walker looks, as opposed to that of a runner.

This is considered a very advanced technique, but it need not be if your body follows normal gait patterns. That is, when you take a step with your legs and feet, your upper body reflexively responds so that your arms swing in the appropriate way, depending on the gait you are in.

When you are on the horse and following with your seat, his movements under your seat bones are the same as would be created by the same gait in your own legs. This, in turn, creates the same pattern in your upper body. Therefore, if you are on a horse who is walking and your body is working correctly (in other words, normally), your arms will naturally move in conjunction with the horse's front legs, which move in conjunction with his head movements. For that reason, the following hand is a normal and natural movement.

Therefore, the following hand is not too difficult to learn, *provided that you are very comfortable and secure, particularly with your following seat*. You especially need to be very free of tension in your neck and shoulders. Naturally, it takes some practice before you can follow the horse's movements well without too much effort.

If at all possible, you should practice at first on a horse with a nice free-swinging walk who doesn't make you nervous and is not overly sensitive about his head. Start in a large but safe space, although if you are relaxed about it, walking home from a trail ride is another good way to practice to passive hand. The horse will be more comfortable during your learning process if you attach the reins to the side rings of an ordinary halter (see pages 21–22 for fitting the halter).

If you can find someone to work with, you can practice on the ground together. You need something to use for reins. One of you is the "horse" and walks in front, holding one rein in each hand with the long end trailing out the back by the little finger. The "rider" holds the reins normally and follows behind, *staying in step*. At first the "horse" may have trouble allowing her arms to swing naturally, but eventually you can walk around together keeping a steady, soft, grounding feel on the reins. Take turns being horse and rider. The rider should try things like pulling the rein as the "horse's" arm is swinging forward, and keeping her arms rigid, so the "horse" understands how these things feel to a real horse.

On the real horse, begin with the reins dropped (but knotted or draped over the pommel so they can't be stepped on) and allow the horse to walk around freely. With your arms dangling freely by your sides, go through the Seven Steps until you feel very soft and relaxed. Your arms should begin to swing in step with the horse's front legs, although the movement will be much smaller. You may need someone to watch you and tell you what's happening.

When you pick up the reins, remember to keep your wrists soft and straight and your elbows bent. Your elbows should hang just in front of your rib cage. You should have the sense that your arms are hanging from your shoulders and your hands are hanging from your wrists. You may find it easier at first to hold the reins western style, with the rein coming from the bit in between your forefinger and thumb and exiting by your little finger. In the beginning you will probably need to take a moderately firm hold to feel and follow the motion. If so, you will need to keep your hips a little open and perhaps use your voice or leg to keep the horse going.

Look for the horse to take big, firm, regular steps, not short, choppy ones, and try very hard to resist the temptation to steer now that you have reins. If the horse starts cutting in, hanging around the gate, or walking in little circles, check that your lateral center is not falling to the outside and that your outside rein is not tighter than the inside one. Closing your eyes helps you feel these things—*if* it doesn't make you nervous. Ask the horse to walk briskly, perhaps allowing him to follow another horse or having a ground person keep him going with her center or a longe whip—whatever works and is safe.

Working at the walk helps teach you to follow movement, while working at the trot—providing your trot skills are good—teaches you to keep your hands quiet while your body is moving, since the horse's head movement at the trot is minimal.

The Holding Hand

If you take a firmer but still elastic hold and ask the horse to maintain or increase his pace, you get what I call the holding hand. You follow the horse's movement in the same way, but with an increased feel that requires the horse to push into it to remain grounded. If the horse stretches his neck out against the pull, you release enough to allow him to do so, without removing his support. Think of picking up something heavy in each hand, as opposed to carrying nothing. You have to make an extra effort with your whole body to carry the things comfortably without collapsing. This increased hold is used where the horse needs more help with his balance, such as moving downhill at speed or in extensions. It helps the horse to ground more deeply without interfering with the engagement of his hindquarters.

If you use the holding hand with one hand only, it's like carrying something heavy in just one hand. At first you may lean toward the weight, but you find this very awkward and unbalancing, so you soon learn to lean *away* from the pull, making it easier to balance and to ground more firmly on the opposite foot, which engages more, as well. It is this hand effect that gives you the turn starting from the outside hand. It allows the horse to lengthen and engage his body correctly at the beginning of the turn, rather than shortening and cramping himself, which is so often the result of beginning the turn with the inside rein.

Just as we raised the hand a little when we wanted the horse to yield to the active hand, so we lower the hand a little (being careful not to lose the soft, straight wrist) to help the horse take the holding rein. The horse should have no feeling of hanging or hauling on the rein, simply an increased feel. The horse takes the rein as needed and turns away from it, and, assisted by the other aids, begins a turn.

The Fixed Hand

The fixed hand is probably the most difficult to use. The rider takes a soft hold that doesn't quite follow the horse's movement. Thus you get a little release and take with each step, like a very minimal active hand. If it can be done so that it is really nonthreatening, the result is softening of the horse's jaw and poll.

Parelli has a ground exercise to give you the feel. With your hand on the horse's crest, hold one rein up, then slide the other hand down the rein several times, as if you were playing the trombone, gradually establishing contact using just your thumb and forefinger. Then you place your other fingers on the rein, one at a time. If it's done smoothly, after a few seconds the horse will release the tension in his jaw so that you have a very soft but still grounded communication with each other.

Combing the Reins

Combing the reins is another way to help the horse to relax his jaw and poll. Many horses have been hung on so much that as soon as they feel any sort of steady contact, they immediately tense up. When you comb the reins the contact is constantly alive and soft. To comb the reins, take them in one hand with the palm down and a finger between the reins. Starting with your arm extended but not stiff and the reins in the lightest possible contact, draw your hand

Combing the reins.

smoothly up the reins toward your chest. As you run out of space, reach out with the other hand, place it on the reins, and draw it toward you in the same way. Continue to comb them until you feel the horse beginning to relax and soften, probably reaching out with his head and neck in the process.

You can also comb just one rein, crossing your hand over as necessary, if the horse is very stiff on one side.

If the horse is very stiff on one side you can also comb just one rein, crossing your hand over as necessary.

The Taking Hand

The taking hand is the hand effect most often taught and used, and the easiest to abuse. Here the rider takes an increased hold, as with the holding hand, but with a raised rather than a lowered hand position. The pressure is not eased when the horse tries to take, but only if he gives. This is the same effect as picking up something heavy with one hand and, instead of leaning away from it and grounding yourself, you give to it and lean toward it. Since you are *not* grounding, this position is somewhat awkward and insecure. It is my feeling that it should be used primarily in connection with the Parelli one-rein stop, where the horse is deliberately disengaged behind, thus making it difficult for him to grab the bit and run.

The hand effects are combined with rein effects and the other aids to *help* the horse find the best and easiest way to perform the desired task. Once you understand clearly that resistance is *never* "just an attitude problem" (even a so-called attitude problem has its origin in fear of some sort) you will find that there is always a way to get the results you want without a fight. You may have to be patient, to go back and look for original causes, or to improve your own skills, but in the end your results will be correct and permanent. And you and the horse will both feel happy and successful.

Part III

Setting Out into the Real World

9

Stirrup Stuff
Sitting or Standing, Be Solid and Secure

When I was young and most horse shows were a good deal less formal, many of them ended with a groom's class. It was a jumper class, and the grooms came out mounted on their charges, many of them pretty valuable and highly rated show jumpers. The catch was that the grooms all had to ride bareback! Watching this group—mostly men in those days, but a few women as well—ride those big, athletic horses over some very sizable fences with nothing on the horse's back except themselves was one of the highlights of the show. Somehow they managed to stay on when they rode against time, cutting corners as sharply as they could, with no stirrups to stabilize them—not something most of the audience would ever dream of trying!

∽

Riding with your feet in the stirrups is pretty much a given for most people. Certainly nearly all fast work, especially if it involves turns or substantial fences, is made considerably easier with the lateral support of the stirrups and the additional shock absorption provided by your leg joints.

So riding with your feet in the stirrups should be much easier to do correctly than riding without them. But when you look around, most riders, unless they're quite advanced, constantly complain about the difficulties of riding with stirrups. "I keep losing my stirrups"; "I can't keep my heels down, no matter what I do"; "I can't keep my feet still"; "My feet are always stuck out in front of me;" and, less commonly, "I can't seem to keep from tipping forward."

Every rider seems to have one or more of these complaints—plus some I probably haven't thought about. But, although they seem different, what they all come down to is that the rider is not able to figure out how to ground in her stirrups, whether she's sitting or standing.

Why is grounding in the stirrups so difficult? Well, we've already worked on the biggest problem, which is simply becoming relaxed and comfortable about sitting five or more feet in the air on top of a live and therefore

To learn more about this topic, read Chapters 11, 12, 13, and 14 of the companion volume to this book, *How Your Horse Wants You to Ride: Starting Out—Starting Over.*

unpredictable animal. Everybody has to learn to balance while sitting before they can stand—just think how much easier it is to ride the bus or train sitting down than standing—so we started out by learning to ground in full seat and just didn't worry about the stirrups.

What is it about stirrups? After all, most of us can deal with standing and walking pretty well. But put us up on the stirrups and suddenly it's as if we'd never learned to stand up at all! Well, to begin with, they're narrow. Most stirrups are less than two inches front to back, so you can't use either your toes or your heels to help you. And they're so *wiggly*! There they are, hanging from the ends of those straps, swinging all over the place; you can hardly *find* them long enough to get your feet into them, much less keep them there. And no matter how you try, it never seems to get very easy.

In fact, there's a very good reason for that, and it's hard-wired into our brains. If you're walking along and you suddenly feel the ground underneath you becoming unstable—maybe it's a pebble or a loose board or a patch of ice—your first reaction is not to commit your full weight to that foot. That is, you don't want to try to ground on something that might be going to give way underneath you. So it's going to take a while, and some study, to overcome this reflex and replace it with successful experience, before you're going to be comfortable on the stirrups. You have to give your body time to learn. That means sticking to pretty easy stuff—a lot of walking and jogging—during the learning period. (Figure skaters don't start doing double axels the first week!) You may be able to be a bit creative; for example, if you have the right horse, quiet trail rides in congenial company are a great way to put in the necessary "miles" before you feel comfortable in the stirrups. So, where do we start?

THE FIXED LEG

When you ride without stirrups to learn grounding and relaxation, you allow your whole leg to hang freely and it is the weight of your legs that holds you down on the horse. Your toe hangs lower than your heel and your lower leg hangs a bit in front of your knee. That's fine as long as you are sitting, but when you stand up you will need to have your feet back underneath your center, so to prepare for that we will use the fixed leg. In other words, you will place your leg in stirrup position but without the stirrups. You can work on the fixed leg either in the saddle without stirrups or on a bareback pad.

Tidbits & Supplements

I, personally, prefer wider stirrups and managed to find some that are about three inches front to back. I also have a pair of even wider, padded endurance stirrups that I use for long rides and for students who are having a lot of trouble relaxing their feet. Some people might think the wider stirrups are dangerous because of the possibility of your foot getting caught, but your foot is much less likely to slide around on the stirrup if you are properly grounded, so the risk is actually not as great.

Begin by going through the Seven Steps, with special attention to shaking out your legs. Do the wringing out exercise (page 118), and then, using your hands on the pommel or neck strap, lift your entire leg away from the horse and shake it out again. If you have a ground person available, ask her to swing your lower leg back and forth. It should feel almost detached. You need to think about not letting your thigh start to take hold, which it is going to want to do when you start to fix your leg.

First you're going to find the correct foot position with your knee straight. Straighten your leg and hold it out in front of you a bit so you can see your foot and ankle. Keep your toe straight ahead and lift it up. Now, *without turning your knee*, lift your toe up and turn it out as far as it will go comfortably. This position gives your ankle far greater flexibility, which is essential for half seat work. It also brings your knee in closer, while having your toe straight ahead brings your calf in closer. You will need both positions for different things. Play with this for a few minutes until you have a good feeling for both positions. Then let your foot and leg fall back down, shaking out if necessary to return to your relaxed leg position.

Now you're ready for the fixed leg. Fix your legs one at a time at first. Begin by swinging one lower leg forward and back a couple of times, finishing with it back so your heel is under your pants side seam on your hip. Look for tensions in your upper leg. *Your knee should not rise up at all.* Let your leg hang loose and shake it out again, then reposition your foot under your hip. Do this a couple of times to get the feeling of bringing your leg back without tensing and drawing it up or turning the knee out.

Once you can swing your leg back under you without unnecessary tension, then the final move is to fix your foot. Begin by simply lifting your toe without any ankle rotation. Allow your knee to fall slightly away from the saddle if it wants to. This is the leg position we call the ∩ position, and it is used for all

> ### *Tidbits & Supplements*
>
> There are a number of muscles that flex the leg at the knee. Some of them also rotate the knee outward, some inward. You have to experiment to learn how to bend your knee without creating any outward rotation of either the knee or the shin.

sitting work with stirrups and also used when you apply the lower leg aid. It allows your thighs and buttocks to stay open and soft and your calf to come in against the horse for the application of the leg aid.

Now, *without allowing your shin to rotate* (which it may do when your knee is bent), rotate your toe out from the ankle, lifting at the same time, just as you did with a straight leg before. You can allow your foot and calf to come away from the horse a bit, as long as there is no shin rotation. This is the leg position we call the Λ position. It is used in all work where you are standing in the stirrups. It gives maximum flexibility of the leg joints, as well as keeping the knee tucked in behind the knee roll for emergency longitudinal support.

Practice going from relaxed leg to fixed leg ∩ position or Λ position and back to relaxed leg. Try both positions at the walk, and the fixed leg ∩ position at the sitting trot as well. (Posting with fixed leg will be covered in the posting section.)

USING THE STIRRUPS

Making the Stirrups Even

Many people ride with uneven stirrups, at least partly because they don't get them even in the first place. This needs to be done from the ground where you can see exactly what you are doing. You really can't tell accurately by just looking at them from the front, though, because the horse may be standing crooked or the saddle may not be sitting level on him.

If you don't already know your approximate stirrup length, begin by making a guesstimate for the length of one stirrup by putting your fingertips on the stirrup bar, then holding the stirrup up against your fully extended arm. The bottom of the stirrup should come about to your armpit. This makes a longish stirrup, but for the beginning work we want it that way.

Now let that stirrup hang straight down. You are going to measure its length against the saddle flap, then measure the other stirrup against the flap to make them even. If the stirrup hangs less than the width of your hand below the flap, used your closed fingers to measure the distance from the bottom of the flap to the top of the stirrup, then adjust the other stirrup to the same length. If necessary, punch extra holes between the regular ones.

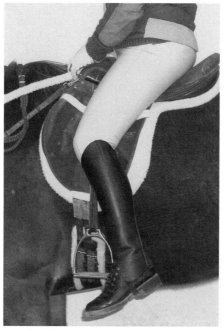

Preparing for the fixed leg. My leg
is long and relaxed and my heel
is under my side seam.

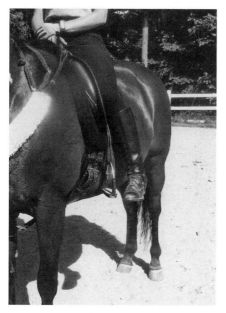

Fixed leg ∩ position.

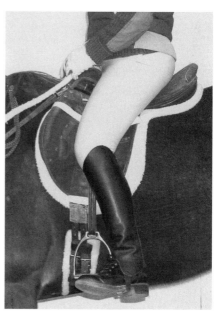

Fixed leg Λ position.

Measuring for even stirrup length.

If the stirrup hangs down further, so your hand is no longer accurate, take the stirrup and fold it back up against the leather so it is upside down. Then measure with your closed fingers again, now from the bottom of the stirrup to the bottom of the flap. (The bottom of the stirrup may be above the bottom of the flap, but it doesn't make any difference as long as you make both stirrups the same.)

Adjusting the Stirrups from the Saddle

Every rider should be able to adjust her stirrups from the saddle using only one hand, unless the leathers are very stiff. It just takes a little practice and is an important safety consideration.

Without removing your foot from the stirrup, open your knee so that you can reach the stirrup leather with the hand on the same side. Hold both reins in the other hand throughout. Going in from the front, slide your fingers under the loose excess strap, close to the buckle. Put your index finger lightly against the buckle tongue so that you can keep track of which hole it was in if it should pop out suddenly.

Pull up on the strap, using some pressure with your foot and some wiggling of the strap to hold the buckle more or less still, and break the tongue out of the hole as the strap moves. The buckle should, ideally, remain against the bar, though this isn't always possible with stiff leathers. Be sure not to move your index finger away from the hole as you pull.

If you are trying to shorten the stirrup, after you feel the tongue break free pull up as much as seems necessary. Then cautiously slide your index finger down to the hole you want, if necessary either pulling more leather out with your hand (don't lose count!) or pulling it back down by pushing on the stirrup with your foot until the hole and the tongue are together. Use your index finger to point the tongue into the hole, then push down a final time with your foot to set it, and set the buckle against the bar.

If you are trying to lengthen the stirrup, after the tongue breaks free use your index finger to open it further if necessary, so it doesn't go into a hole before you are ready. Find the new hole with your index finger, then lower the strap below the buckle, wiggle it a little, and let the buckle slide down it to the new hole. Use your finger to place the buckle tongue in the hole.

The buckle will now be several inches below the stirrup bar. To bring the buckle back up to the bar, put your hand around both the buckle and the strap, so you are holding them firmly together. Lift your foot and lift the strap and buckle up above the bar at the same time. Hold them there and push down on your foot, pulling the under strap through the bar until you hear the buckle hit the bar. You may have to do this last move several times to get the stirrup all the way into place.

Adjusting your stirrup while mounted, step 1.

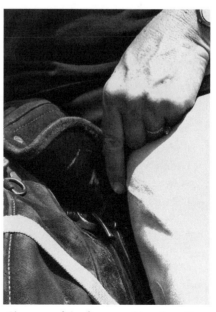

Close-up of the finger and hand position while adjusting the stirrup.

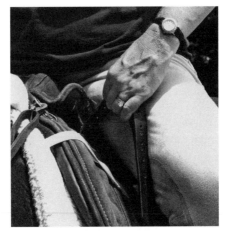

Bringing the buckle back
up against the stirrup bar.

Grounding on the Stirrups

For your foot to be able to ground in the stirrup, it must be placed so that it rests on the natural grounding point of the foot. This is called the *bubbling spring* in martial arts, and is located as shown in the figure on page 20. When you do a teeter-totter, you can feel that as long as the bubbling spring is on the ground you are secure, but the second it starts to come up your balance is gone. This grounding point should be placed on the back bar of the stirrup. For most of you, your foot will feel rather far through at first, but as we said earlier, because your foot is grounded it is actually safer than having your foot placed farther out.

Tidbits & Supplements

If I find myself in a dangerous situation with a horse—which I try very hard not to do—where bailing out may become necessary, at that point I draw my foot somewhat out of the stirrup, being careful to stay as grounded as possible but still able to quickly kick free if the horse goes down.

The stirrup should be placed relative to the saddle seat so that when you sit with fixed leg—the back of your heel under your pants seam—the stirrup, hanging vertical, is in the correct place relative to your bubbling spring. If there is much variation from this, or if you have a great deal of difficulty finding your balance in half seat, you may need to make special adaptations to your saddle, as described in Chapter 4.

Checking to see if the stirrup hangs in the
correct position longitudinally.

THE SEVEN SEATS

Most of us were taught that there are two seats, or positions, we use with stirrups. One is *full seat*, also called *three-point* or just *sitting*. The other is called *half
seat*, or *two-point* or *jump seat*. I am going to use the terms *full seat* and *half seat*,
but in actual riding there is more than one version of each position. We will
begin with the three full seat positions.

Full Seat, Legs in ∩ Position

The first position is full seat, legs in ∩ position. Your stirrups should be adjusted
quite long, so they hang only an inch or so above your foot when your legs are
fixed. If possible, find a ground person to help you at first.

1. After doing your Seven Steps, fix your legs in ∩ position.

2. Ask your ground person to take your calf and lift your knee up and drop it
a couple of times. **Don't help!**—which is hard not to do. You want your leg to be
dead weight as much as possible. If you have no ground help, do your best to lift
your thigh up while allowing your calf to hang down and your foot to stay fixed.

Full seat ∩ position. Gravity is doing all the work.
My leg is completely relaxed and my heel is down.

3. Now have the ground person turn the stirrup so that the outside of it faces back, and then pick your foot up for you and drop the bubbling spring onto the stirrup. She (or you) should lift and drop it several times until the whole weight of your leg from mid-thigh down rests on the stirrup. You should feel that your foot could not slip out, because there is too much weight on the stirrup.

This position is exactly like the first fixed leg position you tried, and exactly like your bareback position except for the fixed leg. It is the position used most often, since it is used for nearly all sitting work.

Full Seat, Legs in ∧ Position

The second full seat position is full seat, legs in ∧ position. Everything should be as above, except your stirrups can be one hole shorter if you like.

1. From the ∩ position described above, rotate your toe outward so that your ankle flexes. Be sure you don't push your foot forward as well.

2. At the same time, allow your lower leg to drift away from your horse a little, so that your knee comes in a little more snugly and your weight falls a bit more on the inside edge of your foot. The inner edge of your foot should be resting against the inside post of the stirrup.

Full seat, legs in Λ position. My foot is quite far out
to the side, giving me a wider base.

This position is particularly useful for giving you a little firmer grounding and a wider base of support. If you are walking on the trail and suspect the horse might spook, placing your feet this way adds a large measure of security in case of a sudden sideways movement. Try it on some turns, comparing it with the ∩ position, and see how solid it feels.

The other place it is commonly used is in sitting work in equitation classes, since many judges like to see a deep heel. Your foot and ankle in the ∩ position are relaxed, but your leg is so constructed that the heel doesn't drop very much. In the Λ position you get greater ankle flexion, and thus a lower heel. It makes it more difficult to present a soft sitting trot, which equitation riders may find frustrating, but that's the way the game is often played.

Full Seat Forward

The last position is full seat forward, and for this we first have to study how one leans forward and still keeps the back in a correct position. Since all the half seat positions involve some degree of leaning forward, this is preparation for the steps to come, as well.

The secret to leaning forward correctly is to move only in your hip joints, which is harder than it sounds until you find the trick. Our tendency is to round our back as we lean forward and arch it as we lean back, both of which interfere with its flexibility and thus our ability to follow the horse's movement.

To lean forward and back correctly:

1. Sit in a straight chair with both feet on the ground and go through your first five steps.

2. Place both hands on your back: one at your waist and one between your shoulder blades, or as high as you can get from below, or place one hand on your upper chest and one between your shoulder blades.

3. Grow again, then sway forward from your hips, letting your hands tell you if there is any movement at all in your back (see the photo on page 189).

4. Sway back to your original position, again checking for any movement.

Practice this until it comes very easily, taking your hands off when you think you have it right. Watching yourself in a mirror as you do this exercise is a plus.

On the horse, sit first with your legs in ∩ position. Sway forward only as far as you can and still feel balanced. Since your stirrup hangs in front of your seat bones, your center is still over your base, but now your base is also in your feet instead of just your seat bones. As you lean forward, allow your chin to rise so your face remains vertical but no more than that.

Practice swaying forward and back until you can do so smoothly, maintaining your balance and keeping your back still. Your hips should move as if they were coated with oil.

Full seat forward. My face should be vertical
but I am still relaxed and grounded.

Now try the same exercise with your legs in Λ position.

With your legs in ∩ position, full seat forward is used when asking the horse to back. With your legs in Λ position, it is the "down" position of the posting trot. You also might use it on the trail if you were walking across an awkward, low obstacle that the horse might scramble or hop over.

Three-Quarter Seat

For half seat work you will need a somewhat shorter stirrup—less so for the three-quarter seat, more for closed position. You will also need some sort of neck strap (see appendix A) if you are to really learn the half seats correctly. After all, you held on to the handlebars of your bicycle when you were learning to ride it; it was only later that you could let go.

The first half seat position is one I call three-quarter seat, because you don't rise fully out of the saddle. As a ground exercise, practice getting out of a straight chair very slowly with your arms folded, observing how you have to lean forward and at what point you can shift your weight from your seat to your feet. Lift just your seat *bones* off the chair a little. That's the three-quarter seat.

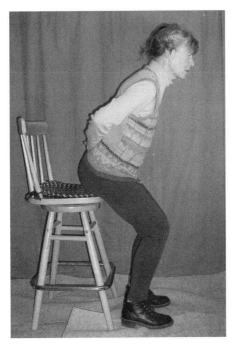

Trying out the three-quarter seat.
My hands are making sure my spine
doesn't flex or collapse.

You don't actually get up; you just shift your weight from your seat bones to your feet. Your buttocks should still be touching the chair lightly. Let your weight back down onto your seat bones but don't lean back. Practice shifting your weight from seat to feet and back, keeping everything else as it is.

Then, on the horse:

1. Begin in full seat, Λ position. Either fold your arms or hold them both out in front of you. You might also want to close your eyes, if it is safe to do so.

2. Slowly lean forward as if you were going to do full seat forward. Continue until you reach an angle from which you think you could stand up. Remember, all you want to do is to shift your weight off your seat bones and onto your stirrups. Your seat should not leave the saddle.

3. Try to stand and see what happens. If you have to lean forward more or make a big effort, you did it wrong. Try again. When you get it right you will just float upward with very little effort, almost imperceptible to the observer.

And your stirrups will not move! Except perhaps away from the horse a little as your weight comes down more on the inside of the stirrup than the outside. That is perfectly okay. What causes the stirrups, and your feet, to swing back and forth is having your center shifting forward and back instead of staying in the same place, directly over your bubbling spring on the back bar of the stirrup.

Three-quarter seat.

When you sit, stay in the same closed hip angle until you are fully seated. Then, if you want to rest, sit up straight as a separate movement. Never sit down and lean back simultaneously until your posting is perfected! (You'll see why later on.)

When you have figured out the hip angle and your balance at the standstill, take up your neck strap. It should be adjusted so that when you are holding it in your three-quarter-seat angle, your elbows hang slightly in front of your shoulders.

In three-quarter seat, with your hands on the neck strap, lean back (open your hip angle) very slightly, just so there is a little pull on the neck strap and you feel that if you let go you would sit down, but not hard. *Be careful not to pull your hips forward* so that you lose your centering. You should also feel that you are in no danger of tipping forward. *The pull should go from your hands through your body and all the way down to the stirrups.* Look for tensions, and try to pull on the neck strap the same way you pulled the reins (see page 168).

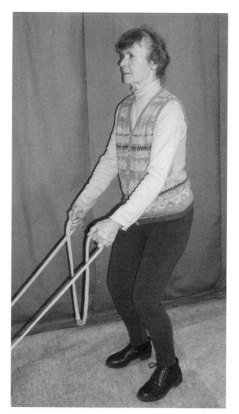

Using the neck strap in a standing
position. Even though the pull is forward,
my weight is firmly on my heels.

Tidbits & Supplements

Because of the natural crookedness of our bodies, the tendency is for the right side of the pelvis to be tipped back a little. During sitting work this places the rider's weight toward the back of the seat bone, creating a little tension in that buttock muscle. Both sitting and in half seat, the right foot tends to be pushed forward more than the left because of the changed angle at the hip. It also creates a little vertical twist in the upper body, which causes the rider's right hand to tend to pull inward toward her midline, instead of straight back on a line with the bit and her elbow.

To correct this crookedness, while sitting, push the top of your right pelvis forward to bring it even with the left side so that you feel yourself sitting in the same spot on both seat bones. Experiment both sitting and standing to improve your awareness of being square.

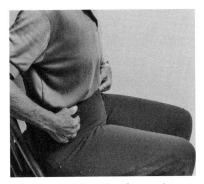

The top right side of my pelvis is tipped back and I am sitting on my right buttock.

Bringing the right hip bone forward has leveled me up.

Now do some walking around in three-quarter seat. The pressure on the neck strap and on your stirrups should remain constant, indicating that you are free of tensions, that your body is moving with the horse, and that your center is not moving around relative to your base. Your buttocks should be resting very lightly on the saddle but all your weight should be in your stirrups.

Keep a little soft bend in your knees, as though you were going to kneel. This will help prevent you from jamming your heels down and pushing your feet out in front of you. Glance down at your feet now and then and make sure your toe has not crept out in front of your knee. Also look at where your knees rest against the saddle flaps. Both knees should be at the same level and at the same distance from the fronts of the flaps.

The three-quarter seat is a good place to start trying to feel your feet following the horse's movement. Since your seat is resting lightly on the saddle, you should be able to feel your following seat. If not, let yourself sit for a moment in full seat, forward, until you feel your seat following, then lift up into three-quarter seat again so you can feel it with the lighter pressure. Then try to feel how your feet are following as well; that is, when your left seat drops, your left foot drops down and a little inward as the horse's barrel swings to the opposite side to allow his left hind foot to step forward. This is much more subtle than the following seat, but with a little practice you'll start to feel it.

Three-quarter seat is a preparatory training position for half seat, but it has two other uses. The first and most important is to get you grounded in your stirrups when you first mount, or any time you have lost your grounding while doing sitting work.

When they first mount, most riders immediately shove their feet down onto the stirrups in an effort to ground. It doesn't work! First of all, when you are sitting your center is behind your feet, so pushing on them sends them forward. And second, you are using muscles to push your feet down, rather than relaxing and using gravity. Instead, develop the habit of mounting and immediately finding your three-quarter seat, using it to help you relax and ground. This also makes it easier for a horse with a cold back—one who has trouble supporting your weight before he is warmed up—and that is the other use for the three-quarter seat.

Half Seat, Open Position

The next seat is half seat, open position. It starts from the three-quarter seat but lifts you high enough off the saddle that you won't bump it at the faster gaits. As a preliminary ground exercise, go back to your straight chair and find your three-quarter seat position—lean forward by closing your hip angle until you can fairly effortlessly lift your seat bones, but not your seat, off the chair. Now let your arms dangle by your sides and very slowly stand up, the rest of the way, being careful to stay right on your bubbling spring points. Notice what happens to your hip angle. Although you leaned forward—that is, you closed your hip angle—to *prepare* to stand, when you actually go to stand up, your hip angle opens again so that, in effect, as you go up you lean back again, until you are straight up.

For half seat you will probably want your stirrups another hole shorter than you had them for three-quarter seat and the neck strap perhaps a little longer.

1. On the horse, after doing your Seven Steps, begin in three-quarter seat with your slightly shorter stirrups. Hold the neck strap but don't pull on it at all at first.

2. Now, keeping your center carefully over your bubbling springs (go slowly and adjust your upper body if your weight changes in your feet), stand up just enough so you are clear of the saddle by an inch or so.

3. Open your hip angle just enough so you have that same light pull on the neck strap that you had in three-quarter seat. This puts you comfortably behind the horse's center so that you don't get ahead of him every time one of his feet hits the ground.

4. At the standstill, grow both down and up from the saddle to avoid the tendency to curl up.

Practice going from three-quarter seat to half seat until you can stay very balanced and centered throughout the change. Also work on using the neck strap to ground yourself without tension.

When you begin working in half seat at the trot, you may tend to tip forward or back too much at first as you search for longitudinal balance. To correct yourself if you are falling back, close your hip angle (bring your shoulders forward) as much as necessary to bring your center forward over your feet. If you are getting ahead, begin by pushing your hips back (again closing your hip angle, but with a different objective) to move your center back. Once you are recentered, open your hip angle again until you have the right amount of pressure on the neck strap or the horse's neck, depending on which seat you are working on. Try this on the ground, feeling how it changes the pressure on your feet.

Keeping your torso straight laterally (your spine at 12 o'clock), use your legs to push your center first to one side, then the other. This is how you handle lateral centering in half seat. Try to avoid any tensions. This is something else that can be practiced on the ground first.

When you are comfortable, it's time to try the trot. If possible, practice on a horse with a smooth gait and little hesitation. If he will follow quietly behind another horse, either in the ring or on the trail, that will make things easier.

Because of the nature of the gait, half seat doesn't work very well at the walk, so start in three-quarter seat. Ask the horse to gently trot, and as he does so lift your buttocks off the saddle so you aren't being bumped. Adjust your longitudinal center by closing your hip angle or pushing your hips back as necessary, until you find the place where you can just stand there while the horse trots along underneath you.

Remember that this is an *open* position, meaning you keep your center from getting ahead by keeping your hip angle a little more *open* than necessary, compensating with a light pull on the neck strap to keep yourself from falling back. Think of a jackknife that is opened just a little beyond the vertical, so that its tendency is to open the rest of the way, rather than close.

Half seat, open position.

Don't curl up like a snail
hiding in its shell.

Keep your body long,
then folded, not crouched.

Half seat, open position, is a training exercise in the beginning. It enables your body to find its balance naturally, using your hands to help until your reflexes figure out what to do. Your hold on the neck strap will gradually diminish and become more even and you will find yourself grounding comfortably in the stirrups. Eventually you will find your balance so that the neck strap is no longer necessary for normal situations (see "Half Seat, Balanced," page 200). As you become more advanced, you will be able to use the reins to ground both you and the horse, without interference. Useful when you are galloping down a steep hill!

Half seat open is also used any time you face a situation where you need to be in half seat but you're expecting that the horse may not want to go forward. The most common situation is when you are confronted with an obstacle that the horse is very unsure of and that he may try to jump, even if it is not necessary. Going into water is the best example. The open position enables you to keep your center behind your horse's, as he perhaps backs and sidles, and the neck strap will prevent you from landing hard on him if he takes an awkward leap.

Half Seat, Closed Position

The next position is half seat, closed position. This is the one you will be using for jumping, and you will, I think, find it a blessing.

We have already established that:

The horse needs to feel balanced all the time in order to be free of tension and able to ground.

The rider is frequently the cause of the horse losing his balance, as her weight moves around.

Except in extraordinary circumstances, the rider cannot cause the horse to lose his balance backward, because the horse's hind legs support him.

So it follows that any position must have at least the one goal of preventing the rider from getting ahead—that is, in front of the center of the horse. There are a couple of exceptions, but this is nearly always the rule.

In the full seats, where the rider's center is over her seat bones, her seat bones rest in the lowest part of the saddle. This sits over the lowest part of the horse's back, which is, in horses of normal conformation, several inches behind the horse's center. Because the rider's seat is more or less fixed, if she has control of her back and hip joints it is comparatively easy to stay behind the horse's center. This is one of the main reasons why so much training is done at the sitting gaits. It is simply easier for the horse to balance the rider and himself.

In the half seats, the rider's center is over her stirrups. More specifically, over her bubbling spring point, which should be resting on the back bar of the stirrup. Ideally, when the stirrup leather is vertical and the horse is on level ground, this will be about even with the back of the girth and thus slightly behind the horse's center. However, because the rider's seat is not fixed and the stirrups are all too moveable, staying behind the horse's center in half seat is far more difficult. Hence the neck strap and open position work just described.

When it comes to jumping and cross country work, in most instances the open position is not appropriate. (Although for centuries people jumped in the "backward seat," which is simply an open position, and, when done correctly, not at all harmful to the horse. It is still used in steeplechase and many people use it for drop fences.)

In open position you stay back by simply leaning back from the hip very slightly, using the neck strap for support. So, how do you stay back while leaning forward?

The secret lies in that technique I mentioned in the open half seat section of pushing your hips back when you feel yourself getting ahead. Pushing your hips back *closes* your hip angle, so while your center moves back, your shoulders move forward. Because of the closed hip angle, as your center moves back your seat does *not* contact the saddle. This allows you to be pushed back by the thrust of the horse during a jump, without being "left behind"—in the worst sense. But you'll find out more in the jumping chapters.

First let's do a ground exercise to clarify this pushing-back feeling a little more. You'll need something to push against, such as a windowsill or a dining room table. A mirror beside you would also be helpful.

1. Stand about a foot away from the table, find your grounding, and bend your knees as though your feet were in the stirrups.

2. Close your hip angle to about forty-five degrees and place the heels of your hands against the table. You should be far enough away so that your elbows can hang in front of your shoulders a little. Try to keep your face more or less vertical throughout the exercise.

3. Now increase the pressure on the table, and at the same time allow your hips to go back and your hip angle to close. Notice that your hips must go *down* as well, because they are attached to your knees by the thigh bone. That's why you must have shorter stirrups for jumping—to allow room for you to move downward.

Using your arms to keep your
center back in closed position.

Think about the pressure on your feet. As you pushed your hips back, the pressure probably went onto your heels. If you did this in stirrups, the stirrups would shoot out in front of you and you would lose their support. To overcome this, as you push your hips back and down, push your knees forward as well. Play with this for awhile until you can feel it clearly. Check your grounding frequently. If someone is around to help that you don't mind doing this with, have them try to push you forward by pushing on your butt while you brace against the thrust using your hands and feet, all the while holding your position. You will find that it is a surprisingly strong and stable position.

On the horse, shorten your stirrups two holes. You may have to experiment with the adjustment, since both your own and the horse's conformation are factors. For learning purposes you should probably keep a finger on the neck strap just in case, but you won't be using it for support.

Take up your open position, but then, instead of opening your hip angle and pulling on the neck strap, close your hip angle and place your hands, knuckles down, on the horse's neck. They should be side by side, on either side of the neck and parallel to it, but close to the top of it. How far up the neck you place them will depend on the length of the horse's neck and your arms, but probably somewhere in front of the withers. As before, your elbows should hang just in front of your shoulders.

Closed position. My closed hip angle enables me to follow an active forward movement, while my hands on the
neck prevent me from getting ahead of the horse's center.

Your hand and wrist position are especially important if you are to maintain your grounding. While you had to use the heel of your hand to brace
against in the ground exercise, on the horse you *must* use the straight wrist position when you brace against your knuckles, to transmit the push all the way
back down to the stirrups (see the photos on page 168).

Also glance down and make sure your feet have not pushed forward. Your
toe should not get much past your knee and your stirrup leather should remain
vertical, not swing forward.

As on the ground, if you can, find some one to try to push you forward to
test the strength of your position. It has to be strong enough so that if the horse
stops suddenly, or you are taking off or landing from a large fence, you will not
go ahead of the horse's center and unbalance him.

When you feel secure at the standstill, practice the closed position at the
trot just as you did the open position. Start from three-quarter seat at the walk.
As you move into the trot, close your hip angle and place your hands on the
horse's neck. It's a good idea to grow quite vigorously before you start, because
the closed position tends to make your body want to curl up in a ball even more.

As you begin to get comfortable with the closed position, try working from
closed to open and back again, finding each position securely before changing
to the other.

Besides being the position for jumping, the closed position is also used for
riding up hills. In addition, we will be using it in a modified form to work on
the posting trot.

Half Seat, Balanced

The final seat of the seven is half seat, balanced. This is what you will arrive at after your body has had plenty of practice in the open and closed positions. It simply means your reflexes develop to the point that, *provided the horse is going forward*, you will no longer need your hands to help you and you can deal with the normal fluctuations of gait and terrain without conscious thought.

You are neither behind nor ahead of the horse, you are *with* him. It's rather like those people who have ridden the subway for years and stand calmly in the aisle, not holding onto anything, reading their newspapers while the train sways and rocks and changes speed. Their bodies have solved the problem and made the performance effortless. And so will you.

TROUBLESHOOTING EXERCISES

There are two exercises that many people find helpful to consolidate their balance in the stirrups. They both force you to get it right, in the sense that either you do them correctly or you can't do them at all.

The first is called *short stirrups* or *jockey stirrups*. By taking away any possibility of leg grip, it forces you to ground. You must have some sort of neck strap for this exercise and it needs to be quite long, so a martingale yoke or the horse's mane won't work. Adjust the neck strap so it reaches at least a foot above the horse's withers.

Your stirrups need to be very short. When they are the right length, the top of your thigh will be horizontal and about level with the horse's withers. You might want to just try this position once without stirrups to see how short your stirrups will need to be.

If you don't want to put extra holes in your leathers, you can wrap them as follows: Undo the buckle completely but don't remove the stirrup from the stirrup bar. There should be holes in the leather where it goes through the bar. Slide the stirrup up the leather toward the bar until the bottom of the stirrup is level with or a little below the bottom of the saddle skirt. Take the buckle end and start wrapping it around the shaft of the stirrup iron, on the side nearest the horse's hindquarters and as close to the top as possible. Keep your wraps snug, as your weight will pull them tight anyway. Wrap until the remaining leather will just allow you to buckle it up under the protective flap over the bar. You will probably have to adjust the wrap a bit to get it to come out right. Wrap the other stirrup, making sure they are even and the wraps are snug.

You will either need to get a leg on or use a bareback mount from a tall mounting block. If absolutely necessary, you can wrap the left stirrup after you mount.

A correctly wrapped stirrup. Wrapping only
around the back shaft keeps the stirrup
at the proper angle for your foot.

Once mounted, and with the horse standing still, take the neck strap and try standing up. Be sure your eyes are soft and stand up gradually the first time, so your horse gets used to the idea of having you so high up above him.

1. Stand up all the way until your legs are almost straight and grow a little to be sure you are not curling up, which will be your tendency at first. Adjust the neck strap again if you need to.

2. Allow your knees to drop down and forward so you are in an open half seat position. The bone on the inside of your knee should be right at the top of the skirt, about level with the stirrup bar. That will give you a little support in front of your knee to help stabilize you longitudinally.

3. Work with your balance standing still until you feel reasonably secure. Make sure you're well grounded on the stirrups and experiment with pushing your hips back and opening your hip angle to move you back, then with closing your hip angle to move you forward. Also practice sitting and standing up again in case you need to sit down while the horse is moving.

4. Now start moving around, first at the walk, then the trot. Keep your eyes soft and be careful not to pull on the neck strap so hard that you make yourself tense. Your hip and shoulder joints, especially, need to be very loose.

Once you get the knack of this, it is a lot of fun. You can even canter and hop over little fences quite successfully. And it is a real confidence builder.

Jockey stirrups.

The second exercise is called *Mexican* because I learned it from General Humberto Mariles, the Mexican Olympic rider, who used to hold wonderful clinics in Mexico City. This exercise forces you to find longitudinal balance in closed position without using your hands.

Again, you will need to have your stirrups shorter than usual, but only by a couple of holes. You can experiment with the length after you have tried the exercise. Very often, simply shortening your stirrups another hole or two will make the seemingly impossible possible. One caveat: This exercise cannot be done in a saddle with a very deep seat or a high cantle.

The rules are very simple: All you do is bend forward and allow your hands—holding the reins—to drop down level with the horse's shoulder points. But you may not touch the horse with your hands at all! Keep your hands and wrists straight, which in this case will also be vertical. You will have to round your back a little to reach down that far.

Your hips will have to push back quite a bit to keep your center over your base. Allow your knees to drop forward a little, as though you were going to kneel. This allows you to use your stirrups to help hold your position without having your feet just shoot out in front, although they will be more forward than normal.

The Mexican.

Once you sort of have the idea, start walking and trotting. You will find it easier with the horse's movement holding you up, as it were. Again, you can also canter and jump—jumping is surprisingly easy from this position, and we will be talking about it more in the jumping chapters.

The Mexican can also be done with the fixed leg, which really forces your awareness of centering, although it is something of a torture if done for long periods.

Like many such exercises, the effects may not be apparent while you are doing the exercises themselves, but you will later find that your regular positions are more secure and correct than before. Plus, the exercises are kind of fun and a nice change of pace from the same old thing.

POSTING

Posting is one of the earliest skills most riders learn, so we would expect most people to post correctly without effort. But this is not usually the case. In fact, good posting except at advanced levels is quite rare. Keeping your center over your base is a difficult task when you are only trying to maintain *one* position. When you are changing positions at every step, it may seem impossible.

Let's begin with a ground exercise that will help you feel what posting should be and also understand what your body is really doing. You will need something like a tack trunk, although if you're not too tall a straight chair can be used as well. If you have one, place a fairly high stool just behind you so that you can sit on it lightly.

1. Stand facing the tack trunk with your toes touching the bottom of it. Keeping your torso upright, bend your knees until they are also touching the trunk. Allow your arms to dangle freely from your shoulders.

2. Bend forward from the hip, allowing your buttocks to go back at the same time. If you have a stool, allow your weight to rest on it but don't straighten up.

3. Keeping your knees in place, bring your hips forward. To do so they must open, so your shoulders come up and back.

4. Depending on your saddle, the horse's gait and thrust, and the conditions, your overall angle may be more closed (A) or more open (B).

5. Move your hips forward and back, forward and up, back and down. Keep your arms relaxed and dangling, and think about keeping your weight constant on your bubbling spring points throughout the movement.

Tidbits & Supplements

When you are sitting the trot or riding it in half seat, you resist the movement that is throwing you back—that is, the forward movement of the horse—at each step, either by leaning into it, as in half seat, or by keeping your hip muscles a little firm in full seat. When you post, by contrast, you resist the thrust of one step by going forward and yield to the thrust of the next by allowing yourself to slide back and sit. Which pair of legs you resist and which pair you yield to determines which diagonal you are on. The yielding gives you a little rest, while the resistance puts you up on your stirrups and gives you the greater shock absorption. Therefore, posting is much less effort for your whole body, especially if the trot is prolonged, and it enables you to trot without tiring pretty much as long as the horse can keep going.

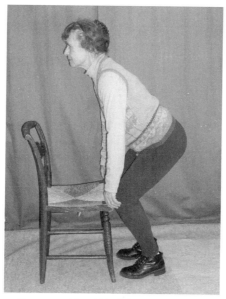

Down position (A) of the posting trot.

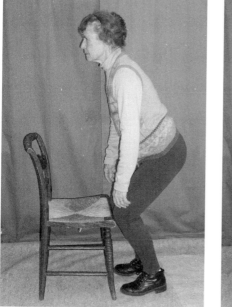

Up position (B) or down position (A).

Up position (B) of the posting trot.

The principal difference between this posting on the ground and posting on a trotting horse is that on the horse there is no need to pick yourself up. The motion of the horse does the lifting. That's why we bounce at the trot unless we have learned to absorb the shock of the gait. So, from the point of view of the rider, *posting is a forward-and-back movement rather than an up-and-down movement.*

I have found that novice students can pick up the feel of the posting rhythm most easily without stirrups, using a fixed leg. This avoids the problem of keeping your center over your feet, which can be difficult until your hips are working smoothly. I know many riders have nightmares about the pain of working on the posting trot with a fixed leg, but that only happens if you try to lift yourself by gripping with your thighs. Gripping tires you and locks your hip joints as well. If the horse has a reasonably active gait so he lifts you up, posting correctly without stirrups for a moderate length of time should not be torture. Chaps or full seat breeches will give you a little better surface, so that your legs don't slide up and down too much. You can either be on a bareback pad or in the saddle without stirrups.

1. At the walk, fix your leg, then close your hip angle slightly and place your hands on the horse's withers as you did for closed position. Think about your following seat, then imagine that as your *outside* seat drops, your hips are going to close and go back and down, and as your *inside* seat drops they are going to open and go forward and up. Don't worry about what your upper body is doing, or going up and down, or anything except what your hip joints and pelvis are doing. Don't forget to keep your leg fixed and lean slightly forward. This will create just enough tension to bounce you up when the time comes. Keep your face vertical.

The down of the posting trot, fixed leg.

The up of the posting trot, fixed leg.
This horse's trot is slow and smooth so
there is very little bounce to lift me up.

2. Continuing to think about your following seat, put your horse into the trot. Use your hands to help you get started, if necessary. Try to follow the rhythm you practiced above, but don't worry if you miss.

3. If the horse starts to get bouncy, as you get bounced up, open your hips and let yourself be bounced up, then close them and let yourself be pushed back down. Let your hands keep you from getting too far forward. *Don't get grippy with your thighs* if you can help it. There should be no need to grip, because if the horse is bouncy you're going to let him make you post, and if he is smooth you can just sit and perhaps ask him to move along a little bit.

If the horse has a good rhythm and his trot is bouncy but not too rough, you should get the feel of moving your hips in his rhythm without too much trouble. Think about having very slippery hip joints, perhaps coated with oil.

When you are beginning to feel comfortable with posting on a fixed leg, you can try with stirrups. However, I do not recommend that you try posting with stirrups if you are still having trouble keeping centered over your feet in half seat. One thing at a time!

In the saddle, first try posting at the standstill. With your knuckles resting on the horse's neck, try to keep a steady pressure on your knuckles and stirrups as your hips move forward and back. If your center is moving in the same vertical plane (as it should be), your stirrups will not move at all.

If you are having trouble with the balance concept, try posting with your arms dangling and your eyes closed, which more or less forces your body to figure out the problem. Keep in mind that every time you get up out of a chair or sit down, you are performing part of a post, so your body does know what to do. It just has to apply that knowledge. If you feel your knees starting to grip or lean against the knee roll, your center is still moving around.

When you're doing well at the standstill, try posting at the walk, again thinking about soft, loose hip joints, light, steady pressure on your knuckles, and even pressure on your feet. You should *not* press harder on your knuckles as your hip joints close, which would mean that you were going forward rather than staying centered and simply rotating *around* your center.

Finally, try the trot. The big difference will be that at the standstill and walk you had to push yourself up, but at the trot the horse should do *all* the heavy lifting. That is, you should go no higher than the horse lifts you (see the photo on page 209). Do not try to push off your feet; simply stay grounded. Your forward angle, plus the gait itself, will start you bouncing up.

Begin in three-quarter seat at the walk, pressing with your hands lightly on the horse's withers and finding your following seat and feet. As your outside seat drops, say to yourself "down," and as your inside seat drops, say to yourself "up." (Actually, as we now know, it should really be "close, open" or "back, forward," and you can certainly use those words instead if they create a better picture.) Put your horse into the trot and look for the posting rhythm first, then you can refine your balance. Your thought should be to stay very steady and grounded on your hands and feet, just as you did in half seat, This will give you the balance and relaxation you need. Then the movement of your hips gives

The down position of the posting trot with stirrups.

The up position of the posting trot with stirrups.
Compare these photos with those of the fixed leg
posting (pages 206 and 207). The upper body angles
are different, but I am always centered.

you the posting. Moving back and forth between half seat for balance and posting for rhythm is often helpful.

One problem many people have is they get a little double bounce as they sit. This is because when you're standing up and leaning forward, your buttock muscles are working to keep you from tipping over. When muscles are working they get tense and hard, and this causes a bounce. At the standstill, start to post, and, as you start to come down onto the saddle, release your lower back muscles and allow your seat to sink softly into the saddle just for a second before going back up again. Practice it a few times, then try it at the trot. Besides preventing the double bounce, this move also helps make posting less tiring by giving you a tiny moment of complete rest in each stride.

All these different positions and techniques are going to take a while to perfect, but they are well worth the time. Only if you can stay soft and grounded will your aids be correct, and your horse soft and grounded as well.

10

Rein Effects

Looking at Rein Aids from a Different Angle

Some forty-five years ago, when I started working with my trainer Bill Hillebrand, one of the first things he did was make me aware of rein effects. Although I knew about them, before Bill I had never really thought about how the angle of the rein relative to the horse's body and track might affect the horse's entire body. Far less had I thought about its relationship to the horse's comfort, and thus his attitude and his overall soundness. Bill was particularly critical of riders who constantly used indirect reins. "Hock breakers" he called them, because of the way they interfered with full engagement of the horse's hind legs. I learned many important things from Bill, but perhaps in terms of my horses' health, that was one of the most useful.

∽

The term "rein effects" refers to the several positions and directions in which the rein can be pulled, each of which has a different effect on the horse's body and thus produces a different result. This is a much neglected field of study, except for advanced dressage students, and even then is usually just a "once over lightly." The result is often a frustrated student and an annoyed horse.

The rein effects and hand effects are closely related. Using different hand effects will change the way your horse responds to a particular rein effect, and vice versa. Just to make things even more confusing!

GROUND WORK

When you ask the horse to perform an action, the part of his body that actually gets you where you want to go is his feet. So you need to know in what directions his feet will move. The things the horse can do comfortably with his two sets of feet (front and hind) are:

211

To learn more about this topic, read Chapters 11, 12, 13, and 19 of the companion volume to this book, *How Your Horse Wants You to Ride: Starting Out—Starting Over.*

- Move so that the hind feet follow in the track of the front feet as they walk a straight or curved path (normal tracking). If the horse is backing, the front feet follow the track of the hind feet.

- Move so that the front feet step out of the track of the hind feet. The hind feet walk a straight track, the front feet cross over (shoulder in).

- Move so that the hind feet step out of the track of the front feet. The front feet walk a straight track and the hind feet cross over (haunches in/travers, haunches out/renvers).

- Move so that both sets of feet cross over (leg yield, half pass/traversale, full pass).

- Move so that both sets of feet cross over in opposite directions (turning on center).

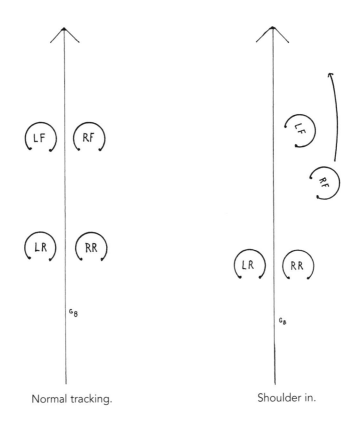

Normal tracking.   Shoulder in.

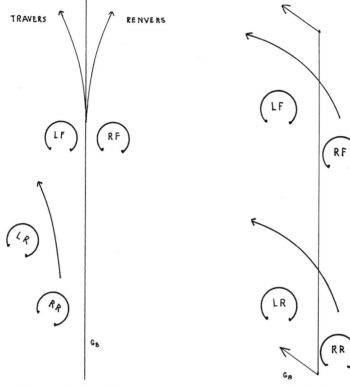

TRAVERS   RENVERS

LF   RF

LR

RR

G_B

Haunches in/haunches out.

LF

RF

LR

RR

G_B

Leg yield or half pass.

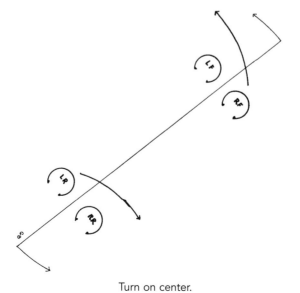

LF

RF

LR

RR

G_B

Turn on center.

We also need to consider *how* the feet cross over; that is, whether the crossing foot passes in front or behind the other.

It is through the use of the various rein effects that we can cause the horse to move his feet in different patterns. To help you understand this more clearly, let's look at the diagrams and then work with the horse on the ground to see how the movements of the horse's head affect the rest of his body in normal riding situations. You will need a quiet horse who leads well and a quiet work area free from distractions. If possible, work with another person so you can take turns leading and watching the horse's movement.

The best thing for the horse to be wearing is a snug halter or a longe cavesson that won't twist around, with the reins or ropes fastened to the side rings on his nose. Thus when you pull sideways you won't be twisting his head. If you and the horse are both experienced, use a snaffle bridle with reasonably large rings so it won't pull through his mouth.

Rein Effects Without Opposition

Opposition refers to the direction of the pull on the rein, and simply means that the pull is in the opposite direction to the horse's movement. In other words, a pull back more or less parallel to the horse's track. This is another reason for staying in front of the horse's head when leading.

1. Lead the horse in a straight line, staying in front of his head so the direction of pull is forward and thus there is no opposition (known as the *leading rein*). Allowing for the natural crookedness, his hind foot track will be on a line with his front track and probably somewhat in front of it (normal tracking). (See the photo on page 216.)

2. Now lead the horse to the left by bringing the left rein to the left, but making sure the pull is still somewhat forward (known as the *opening leading rein*). As long as there is no opposition, the tracking will remain normal throughout any turns you may execute.

3. You can also use a western-style *neck rein* to turn (which you can do from the ground if the horse will carry his head low). If the horse is wearing a bit with a shank, you can use just the rein on the far side, led across his neck a few inches behind the ears. As you use it to get the turns, you will get the same result as when you used the opening leading rein. If you are using a snaffle, you will have to use some opening leading rein on the near side as well to keep the bit from pressing against the inside of the horse's face and blocking him.

Tidbits & Supplements

Western riders use the neck rein and English riders use the leading rein because of the types of bits used by the different disciplines. Western riders traditionally use a bit with the rein attached at the end of the shank. When you lead the rein to the side even a little, away from the horse's head, the bottom of the shank also moves. This causes the top of the shank to press into the side of the horse's face, which he will tend to move away from. Therefore, the western rider presses the rein against the side of the horse's neck so he turns his head *away* both from the rein pressure on his neck and the bit pressure against his face.

English riders usually use a bit with the rein attached directly at the horse's mouth. When you lead the rein to the side, the bit presses against the *opposite* side of the horse's face, causing him to turn *toward* the rein.

Now let's experiment to find out how to use the reins to move either just the forefeet or just the hind feet laterally, without creating any discomfort or resistance in the horse. These are the same exercises we learned in Chapter 1, but now we are using the bridle.

Begin with the horse standing still and square. (When the horse is moving forward, other aids are needed to teach him to move his feet laterally, rather than tracking normally. These exercises help him understand the possibilities.)

To move the forehand, use an opening leading rein with just the rein nearest you to bring his head to one side, but not more than about thirty degrees, until he takes a step *toward* you with his front foot. Be sure to pull the rein straight out to the side, perpendicular to the horse's head, or a little forward, *not* back (which would create opposition). Use your hand actively or holding, as necessary, and follow his head around with your hand. With a little encouragement, the horse will respond by stepping with a front foot in the direction of the pull. If you don't get a step, move around his head and tap or press on his other shoulder to give him the idea. (Just don't lean, which would cause him to lean back.) As with the walking turn, you could also use a neck rein, either alone or in conjunction with the opening leading rein.

To get the horse to step over with his hind foot, you usually need to bring his head further around to the side, which traps his front foot and forces him to move the hind foot instead, but to the opposite side. If necessary, add a leg

The neck rein in my right hand turns the horse left
without changing his tracking.

aid by pressing or tapping on his barrel or haunch with your hand, as you learned in Chapter 1. He should step with his hind foot *away* from the direction of the pull on the rein.

Experiment with both sides and both ends of the horse, rewarding and praising as you get the result you are looking for. This can be quite difficult for some horses, so be prepared to be patient and accept the smallest effort.

You will often find the horse will move more easily or differently in one direction than the other. Generally speaking, a horse who is heavy on his forehand will find it easier to move his hind feet (turn on the forehand), while a horse who is balanced more toward the rear will move his front feet (turn on the hindquarters). A horse who is quite stiff laterally will be more likely to move both sets of feet at once (turn on the center).

Part of what you should be noticing throughout all these exercises is **that the horse will always try to do whatever is necessary to rebalance himself** as you change his balance by turning his head. When you get resistance it's because the horse needs, or thinks he needs, to do something differently so he can get or keep his balance. When there is nothing to unbalance him—no lateral pull on the rein—his legs just follow along. When you pull his head a little off to the

Moving the front feet laterally. Brandy is crossing her right fore foot well in front of her left fore foot. Many horses find this crossover difficult at first.

Moving the hind feet laterally. Brandy's head is turned much further, so she moves her hind feet rather than her fore feet.

side, that throws the weight of his head to that side, so he steps over with his front foot underneath it. When you bring his head around so far that he can't step over with his front foot because it is "nailed" to the ground, he moves his hindquarters over so he is straight again. That is, if he can't get his head over in front of his body, he'll move his body over behind his head.

Turning on the center. Brandy is quite flexible to the left,
so while her right fore foot is crossing over well,
her left hind foot will not cross over her right hind
very much, as it would in a stiffer horse.

Also notice whether the horse steps in front of the other foot with his crossing foot, or behind. Nearly all the time you want him to cross the foot in front, since this enables him to keep going forward. About the only time you would want him to cross behind is if you were asking for a very fast 180-degree turn, such as a cutting horse might do.

The Three Sections of a Horse

Besides understanding the directions in which the horse can move his feet, you need to understand the different directions in which the horse can move his body and how these moves affect his feet. The horse's body is divided into three movable parts, all of which can move in different directions relative to one another, and which are joined by more or less flexible sections. The three parts are:

1. The head

2. The shoulders and front legs

3. The haunches and hind legs

The head and shoulders are joined to each other by the neck section, and the shoulders and haunches are joined by the body section. Think of a little wooden toy train. Each of the three parts is a car in the train, and the hooks that join them are the flexible sections. Each part can work separately, or two adjacent parts or all three can work together.

Tidbits & Supplements

As I said in Chapter 1, I find that, to accommodate the natural crooked-ness, I can make it easier for the horse if I ask him to first step to the right with his front feet, then to the left with his hind feet, then to the left with his front feet, and finally to the right with his hind feet. Thus he starts with the smallest, easiest bend to the right and finishes with the greatest, most difficult bend to the left.

Rein Effects in Opposition

As we saw on page 214, as long as the horse is going forward without restriction, the three sections of his body perform as one. Now we will see that when we add opposition the sections interact in different ways. Opposition simply means pulling back on the reins in the opposite direction to the horse's forward movement. It is one of the major factors in how the reins affect the horse. The best way to learn this is by backing the horse in hand.

You need a horse who backs easily, or else you may frighten or confuse him. The horse should be wearing the same equipment as before. Once you learn the techniques, you can use this method to build the horse's confidence.

1. Stand directly in front of the horse, holding one rein in each hand six to twelve inches from the bit or halter.

2. Keeping the horse's head and neck straight, ask him to step back one step (one diagonal pair of feet) at a time. He should back in a straight line.

3. Now bring his head a little to one side. If he is still backing willingly, his hindquarters will step to the opposite side and as he backs, his shoulders will follow. In this situation he is actually "going forward" (see page 136) while backing up, so he tracks as he did when you were leading him forward.

4. Next, place him so that his tail is about five feet from a wall or fence and back him toward the fence. As he approaches it he will want to stop backing. That is, he will no longer "go forward" and if, at the same time, you turn his head quite far to one side you will find that his shoulder section pops out to the opposite side while his hindquarters swing toward the same side to which his head is turned.

This is not always easy to demonstrate when you want to, but unfortunately can be all *too* easy when you don't want to!

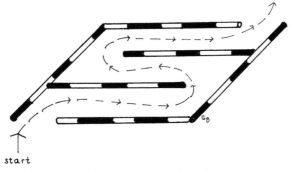

This maze, which I took from Linda Tellington-Jones'
TTeam text, is used for working the horse in hand. He
can go through either forward or backward.

You can try backing the horse into a narrow space, such as between two hay bales, or for an even greater challenge, through a maze. I have found these to be excellent exercises to help students understand how the sections of the horse work with and against each other.

When you are riding the horse rather than working from the ground, you have one serious handicap in rein effects: You are never in front of the horse's head, but always behind it. This means there is a certain amount of opposition in any rein effect, as opposed to when you are controlling the horse's head from the ground while leading him from in front. As soon as the direction of pull gets behind an imaginary line drawn through the horse's mouth, you are creating some opposition. This helps the horse to ground, and also gives the horse an advantage if he wants to take it.

In addition, you will remember from Chapter 2 on leading that in order to control the horse you needed to be in front of his head at all times. This is true both physically and psychologically, and of course is not possible when you are sitting on him. However, to balance that disadvantage, you have the advantage of being above him. This gives you the same psychological benefit as being in front, and also means you can raise the rein relative to his head. *Because of the structure of the horse's neck, if the direction of pull on the rein is more than forty-five degrees upward from the bit there is a minimum of opposition created.* As we will see later in this chapter, we can vary the amount of opposition to create different rein effects.

Opposition can be either *direct* (along the line of elbow to bit), *opening* (outside that line), or *indirect* (inside that line). Direct and opening reins act very similarly, while indirect reins tend to be more restricting.

Direct opposition can be used in two desirable ways, depending on the associated hand effect. If you use it with an active hand(s) the horse will either slow down, turn, shift his weight back, or some combination of these. If you use it with a passive or holding hand the horse will take the bit and ground with the hind leg opposite to the working hand(s). However, if you use opposition with a *taking* hand any way except very carefully, the horse will *compress* and become rigid, which is not desirable. The horse is unable to respond, and everyone gets angry and frustrated.

Compression is at the root of most of the control problems people have with the reins. Here are a couple of little exercises you can try on your own to gain an understanding of the effect of compression on the horse's body.

Go through the Seven Steps on the ground, making sure you finish with a long neck. Reach up with your arms and move them as though you were swimming the crawl with big, long, free strokes. Continuing to "swim," draw your head in like a turtle. You can hardly bring your arms above your shoulders.

Now walk around, keeping yourself tall, swinging your arms, and walking freely. Pull your neck in as before. Notice that your arm swing is immediately restricted *and that your stride is considerably shortened.*

The pattycake exercise will also help you understand the concepts of opposition and compression. You will need a partner, preferably someone about the same size. Work in a fairly large space (the barn aisle is good). Face each other and place your palms together with your hands at about shoulder height. The "horse" will be walking forward and the "rider" will walk backward. The "horse" must be careful not to push so hard that she pushes the "rider" off balance. (The "rider" is theoretically sitting on the "horse's" back.) You should play the part of the horse first.

The pressure on your hands represents the pressure on the horse's mouth through the bit. Walk around experimenting with different degrees of pressure, trying to discover how much opposition—that is, pressure from the other person—you can handle without tension. At first she should try to give you comfortable support. Keep your arms straight but not stiff and *don't* allow tension to build up in the rest of your body. All the pressure should go from your hands *through* your body into your feet, and if the other person lets go you should be able to easily rock back and rebalance. You will find that you can take longer stronger steps against stronger pressure.

In addition, try having the "rider" use too much pressure, that is, more than you can handle without tension, so you can feel how it restricts and tenses your whole body. You can also feel how it forces you to "hang" on her hands, just as a horse hangs on too heavy a feel on the bit.

Knowing what we do about the importance of the horse having free movement in front, both for balance and to allow free movement behind, you can easily understand that opposition has to be handled very carefully. When you feel resistance in the horse, it is nearly always because opposition has been used in a way that restricts him.

The rule about opposition when riding is never to use more than the horse can comfortably accept.

Now let's use the horse again and see how opposition affects the movement of his feet. Keep in mind that for optimum balance the horse should step forward with his hind feet to a point under his center.

1. First, *lead* the horse in a smallish circle around you. To the right is probably the easiest for him. Make sure the circle is not so small that he can't bend around it. He should be in normal tracking. Notice how his inside hind leg steps forward under him.

2. Without pulling back on the rein, gradually diminish the size of the circle so that the horse can no longer bend and has to cross his feet over to keep turning. This will be a moving variation of the exercises on page 212. You will see that the crossover foot steps *in front of* the other foot.

3. Continue with the same size circle, but now pull firmly *back* on the rein (the *direct rein of opposition*). Without seat and leg aids to encourage the horse to keep moving forward, the crossover foot will now step *behind* the other foot.

As I pointed out earlier, for nearly all purposes you want the horse always to be stepping *forward* when he crosses over, so that he keeps his impulsion and balance. Another reason why we need to use the rein in opposition very carefully.

Opposition is a real trick to deal with. The right amount of opposition helps the horse to ground and gives him something to push against, as when we use the passive or holding rein correctly.

Here's a ground exercise to show how this works. I did it against a windowsill, but you could use a heavy table. Whatever you use just shouldn't move and should be about waist height. Stand with your feet a couple of feet away from the table and place the heels of your hands against it as though you were going to try to push it, but don't try to push yet. Feel the pressure of your feet on the floor. Now push hard against the table with your hands, keeping your back a bit rounded so the pressure goes through your body into the ground. Feel how much harder your feet are pressing into the ground. That's how the reins help the horse to ground and push forward harder.

Next, let's find out how the hind legs and the reins pair up. Still pressing against the table, first lift your right hand and foot up and push with just your left hand and foot. Then put your right foot down and lift your left foot up and push again (right foot against left hand). You will find it much easier to keep your balance when the push goes diagonally through your body, left to right or right to left. You can also push much more firmly.

While opposition can help the horse, too much opposition blocks the movement of his legs and he loses his balance. If you think about movement, you can see how, to be effective, each foot must ground (get a good grip on the riding surface) and then immediately lift again. Think of walking briskly and catching one foot on something so that you can't bring it forward. Unless the foot comes loose, you will fall. So the reins can be pulling and the horse can be grounding against it, but then the reins must allow the foot to come off the ground again. When the rider's hand is following the horse's movement this occurs naturally, but when the rider is asking, say, for a downward transition, there must be some release to allow the foot to step forward as freely as necessary. In other words, even when you are using your hands actively in some way, you must allow them to follow as well.

How much of a release must occur depends on a number of variables, none of which need really concern you. What concerns you is how the horse is reacting (how he feels on the other end of the rein)s. For example, if he loses his balance forward, he will need to use his front legs to save himself. You can recognize this because he will attempt to free up his front legs and thus regain his balance either by leaning on the bit to try to push it out of the way, or by bending his neck to loosen the reins so that his neck muscles can relax. This is where your understanding of hand effects will allow the rein effects to work the way you intend.

Indirect Reins of Opposition

So far, except in one case we have used the reins either *leading* out in front of the horse, *opening* out to the side away from the horse's body, or *direct*—straight back. What happens when we use them toward the horse's body, *indirect*? Aha! That's a whole different kettle of fish. As long as you keep the reins direct or opening or leading, the horse's head and shoulders can move in more or less the same direction. This is also true when you use them indirectly with no opposition, as you did with the neck rein. But when you use indirect reins *of opposition,* you interfere with the relative direction of the sections of the horse.

This is a little harder to demonstrate on the ground, so if it upsets your horse, don't do it; just look at the picture.

1. With the horse standing square, stand by his girth and bring the near rein back and toward his withers, working actively with the rein until his head comes around toward his side and your hand is up more or less over his withers. You will also need to maintain passive contact with the other rein.

2. Keep gently and carefully forcing this position until he takes a step *away* from you with his front leg.

If you look at him now, you will see that he is bent away from you like a bow, with his head and quarters toward you and his shoulder away from you.

This shows the effect of the *indirect reins of opposition*, in this case used right about at the withers—the most common position and the rein effect that is most often used incorrectly. By pushing the shoulder out and misaligning the hindquarters relative to the front end, the horse is trapped and cannot use his driving hind legs effectively. If he is trying to do something really aggressive and dangerous this is a good way to prevent it, but unless you know how to use it safely you can also cause the horse to fall. In fact, it is this rein effect that is used to get trick horses to fall for action shots in films.

Classically, there are two indirect reins of opposition: in front of the withers and behind the withers. The first shifts the horse's weight to the opposite shoulder, and the second to the opposite hip. However, I find this a bit limiting because I think that in practice the horse doesn't get as precisely off balance as that, so the knowledgeable rider can use the indirect reins of opposition at an infinite number of angles, depending on the horse's needs. As a general rule, one can say that wherever the rein points, the horse's weight will be shifted to that place.

Tidbits & Supplements

One good use for this position is mounting. If you bend the horse's head somewhat to the left or mounting side using an indirect rein, his weight will shift over his opposite shoulder but his left hind leg will be pretty much underneath the stirrup, making it fairly easy for him to balance the rider's weight during mounting. However, it takes a very skillful eye to make sure he is in a good position, so it's better to teach him to stand without so much restriction. But it's a useful thing to know about.

Brandy has shifted her weight over her left fore in response to the indirect rein of opposition. Notice that her front legs are not quite vertical. My right hand, holding the rein, is just in front of her withers.

The two techniques that use indirect reins in an emergency situation are the pulley rein and the one-rein stop, which disengages the hindquarters. The pulley rein is most effective with a horse who is already running, and is executed as follows.

1. Place your left hand, knuckles down and with the left rein held normally, on the horse's neck just in front of the withers. Your thumb will be on the right side of the horse's neck.

2. Without pulling on it, bring the right rein up between your left thumb and forefinger.

3. As the horse's head is coming up during the gallop stride, use your left hand to brace against as you pull sharply up on the right rein with your right hand, carrying it toward your left shoulder.

This indirect rein technique takes a little work. It should be practiced just for the moves, without applying force, because it is very hard on the horse. If you get it right, he will stop dead in his tracks.

The one-rein stop is more effective with a horse who hasn't gotten started yet.

1. With your right hand, use a taking hand combined with an indirect rein in front of the withers, at a fairly sharp upward angle. If necessary, begin with a little active hand to get the horse to begin yielding.

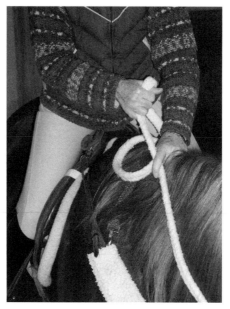

Preparing to use a pulley rein.

2. When the horse yields and brings his head around, change to an opening rein and add some right leg behind the girth to get the horse to step his quarters to the left (disengagement).

3. When the horse begins to submit, ease the aids and allow him to step forward normally. Repeat as necessary until he settles.

ON THE HORSE

Now let's name and describe the rein effects as they are used while riding. The opening and leading reins are treated in most texts as the same thing. This is true on the ground, when your hand is actually in front of the horse's head. However, the opening rein usually taught for riding is actually an opening rein of opposition, and I have so named it.

The riding leading rein, when carried away from the horse's neck, becomes an opening leading rein. When asking for a turn you usually use the leading and opening leading reins more or less together, depending on the horse's response, so they are treated as one rein effect.

> ### *Tidbits & Supplements*
>
> You will sometimes see a rider who uses the indirect reins of opposition most of the time. Because it is very restrictive to the horse's hind legs, it makes them hit the ground too straight and is very hard on the horse's hocks. The trainer I mentioned at the beginning of this chapter was extremely fussy about this, and would never allow me to use this rein effect for more than a step at a time. The next step he would always have me open or release the reins to allow the horse to step forward. That's a good rule.

Rein Placement

The first two rein effects listed here involve almost no opposition.

1. *The leading rein.* The rider's hand is brought forward and upward so that the rein pulls up at least a forty-five degree angle when viewed from the side. Viewed from the top, the line of pull is directly parallel to the track of the horse's feet or *away* from his neck (*opening/leading*). *Effect:* The horse's head, neck and front legs move toward the rein. His hind legs may track or, in the case of the opening/leading rein, may move in the opposite direction.

2. *The neck rein.* The rider's hand is brought forward, upward and close to the horse's midline so that the rein pulls up more than forty-five degrees when viewed from the side and *against* the horse's neck when viewed from the top. *Effect:* The horse's head, neck, and forehand move away from pressure on the neck and from pressure on the muzzle from a bit with a shank. His hind legs move as described in the leading rein.

3. *The direct rein of opposition.* The rider's hand is brought straight back, parallel to the track of the horse's feet when viewed from the top. Viewed from the side, the position varies but is *less than forty-five degrees. Effect:* This depends on the hand effect the rider is applying. When used with both reins and one active hand, the horse yields and shifts his weight back. If used with two reins and the passive or holding hand, he pushes forward into the bridle from behind. Used with one rein and an active or taking hand, the horse yields and steps to the opposite side with his hind legs. If the hand is holding, he pushes forward with the opposite hind leg and bends his head and neck away from the rein. *This is the rein effect that most people use, and have so much trouble with because of the two entirely different results.*

4. *The opening rein (of opposition).* The rider's hand is brought away from the horse's neck so that the rein pulls out to the side relative to the horse's track when viewed from the top. Viewed from the side, the line of the rein varies but is less than forty-five degrees. *Effect:* The horse steps toward the rein with his front legs and/or away with his hind legs. He may or may not turn his head toward the rein. If his head is turned away the opening rein will not bring it back. But, used with the active hand, if his head is already yielding it will yield more. (This occurs because of the relative position of the hind leg on the same side—if it is already forward and under him, he will yield more. If not, he will resist.) Two opening reins have the same effect as two direct reins of opposition but are more restrictive laterally and less longitudinally. That is, the horse can go forward more easily but finds it more difficult to bulge to the side.

5. *The indirect rein of opposition.* The rider's hand moves inward relative to the horse's track when viewed from above. The angle inward varies, depending on what part of the horse you want him to shift his weight toward. *Effect:* The horse's head and neck yield in the direction of the rein at the bit, the horse's shoulders yield to the pressure of the rein at the shoulder, and the horse's hind legs move laterally in the same direction as the horse's head. The horse's weight is shifted to opposite shoulder if the pull is in that direction, and to his opposite hip if the pull is in that direction.

When riding, a rein effect used actively with one rein is usually balanced with a passive or supporting rein on the other side.

HIGH AND LOW REIN EFFECTS

In addition to the various effects that result from the lateral movement of the reins, the upward or downward direction of the pull also has a major effect on the horse. We have already seen something of the effect of an upward pull in the description of the leading and neck reins.

The base position from which we work is a straight line from elbow to bit. We do this because, as I said in chapter 8 on using the reins, it is the easiest for the horse to accept. With the reins in this position the horse can find a connection through his body into the ground using the pressure on the reins, and in almost exactly the same way, you can connect your pull to the stirrups or the seat of the saddle. I don't know who the first genius was who made that discovery, but it is a very easy guide to follow. The angle of that line is upward, and you must move your hand along that line as you release and pull. So you move your hand *toward the bit*, that is, downward and forward, to *release* pressure on the rein, and you move your hand *toward your shoulder*, that is, upward and back, to *increase* pressure. Try it on the ground in front of a mirror a few times. Using a piece of shock cord as a rein will give you a feeling for pulling without creating resistance. Combing the rein as you pull will do the same thing.

Because of the shape and structure of the horse's neck, when you raise your hand relative to the bit so that the direction of the pull is more upward, the horse finds it more difficult to push against the bit. Therefore, **raising your hand gets the horse to *give* to the bit.** When you lower your hand it makes it easier for the horse to push against the bit. Therefore, **lowering your hand gets the horse to *take* the bit.**

Pulling *up* to get the horse to raise his head if it is curled down by his knees doesn't really work very well, because the horse needs to stretch out first and raising your hand makes that hard for him. A very forward single hand, lifting lightly, will sometimes work, but a low holding hand that gets the horse to take the bit and stretch is usually more effective.

Pulling *down* to get him to lower his head if his nose is stuck way up and out doesn't work either, because in that position his neck vertebrae can lock very easily. Instead, you must adjust the height of your hands to get an approximation of the straight line, then use your hands passively or lightly holding. From that position the horse is able to take the reins, drop his head, and round his back.

Making It All Work

The ways in which the horse can resist the reins are almost too confusing to explain. The way you learn to deal with them is to put yourself and the horse in the least threatening situation you can, *put away all your desires and expectations*, and just experiment.

Every time the horse resists he is simply saying, "Stop what you're doing and do something different." Maybe you only have to stop for a step, but you must realize that it is up to *you* to change if you want to get the horse to change. You have to find out what will work for you and your horse together. That may not be the same as what works for someone else. The way you sit on the horse, the way your hands move in relation to his head, your confidence or lack of it, will all have an effect on the way the horse responds.

While the rein effects are very logical, they are somewhat complex and you aren't going to figure the whole thing out in one reading. This is one of those chapters that you should read, or perhaps only read part of, then go off and think about and experiment with. After a few weeks or months, come back and look at it again. It requires a lot of thought and study to fully understand how all the rein effects work. But, like all aspects of the aids, they are applicable to all horses, and so are always useful and important.

11

Hills and Cavaletti
Preparing for the Great Outdoors

Many years ago I used to take my students foxhunting regularly with the Fairfield County Hounds in Connecticut. We tried to go out on weekdays when it wasn't too crowded. That great teacher and horseman, the late Emerson Burr, manager of the Fairfield Hunt Club, would often bring his group of novice ladies as well. Many of them were quite timid, and their especial bugaboo was jumping downhill—as it is for many more-experienced riders as well. I can still hear Emerson's voice in the distance as he watched one of his charges approaching a downhill fence, crouched over her horse's neck in terror. *"Lean back!* **Lean baaaaccck!"** Since they all arrived safely at the end, I can only assume his directions were taken to heart.

∾

Up to now we have tried to make everything as easy as possible for the horse to do, so we have pretty much stuck to level ground and nonthreatening situations. Often when the physical situation becomes threatening to the horse, he gets tense and difficult to control—not because he wants to, but because his body has become difficult for *him* to control.

One of the ways we can avoid having a physical situation become threatening is by training ourselves and the horse ahead of time, under controlled conditions, in the best way of handling the problem. And of course, that's what we've been doing throughout the book. But now you're ready to go out into the real world and there are some new situations you're going to encounter.

HILLS

Hills are one of those threatening situations that make many otherwise happy horsemen miserable. It's not so much going uphill, but what goes up must come down and downhill is a real bear for many riders. As usual, let's start with some ground work and analysis of the problem.

> To learn more about this topic, read Chapters 7, 11, 12, and 13 of the companion volume to this book, *How Your Horse Wants You to Ride: Starting Out—Starting Over.*

Ground Work

First of all, you need a hill. It doesn't have to be very long, but it should be long enough so you can walk three or four steps up or down and still be on the hill. It helps if you work with another person, so you can look at each other.

1. Stand on the hill, facing uphill. Do the first five of the Seven Steps. Make sure your feet are firmly grounded, then start thinking about how you are standing relative to the hill. You should become aware that your body has the same stance it would have on level ground. That is, your center is directly over your base. Or, to put it another way, if you drew a straight line from your center to your bubbling spring point, that line would be perpendicular to an imaginary horizontal, the level ground. But, relative to the line of the hill, you are "leaning forward."

2. Now turn around and face downhill. Direct your soft eyes *straight ahead, not down* (this is *especially* important if you are afraid of heights). You will find that the same conditions apply. Your center is vertically over your base, but now, relative to the hill, you are "leaning back."

3. Go to level ground and feel how you are standing, then go back to the hill and stand both uphill and downhill. Play around with this until you really begin to feel how your body relates to hills.

4. Stand on the hill again, facing uphill. Bend your knees and take up a balanced half seat position. Adjust your hip angle so you feel comfortably centered and think about what that angle is. Now go to the level, take up the same position, and compare your upper body angle on the level with that on the hill. Depending on the steepness of the hill, there should be a noticeable difference in the two, with your angle on the hill being much more closed. This is because on the hill you have to resist gravity pulling you backward down the hill. Also, because of the angle from the horizontal you have to close your hip angle to keep your center over your feet.

5. Now take up a position facing uphill, standing as close to the bottom of the hill as you can and still be on the slope. Then walk slowly but firmly up the hill to the top and a few steps on level ground, adjusting your hip angle as you go. You will find that you feel *most* balanced and grounded when your hip angle closes more as you start to walk up the hill and opens up as you reach the top. This is because of the combination of gravity and thrust. On the hill, gravity is pulling you backward and the thrust of pushing up the hill is also pushing you

I am standing on an uphill slope. Tilt this book so
the ground in the picture is level and you'll see how
I am "leaning forward." This little hill was so steep that
I felt the need to close my hip angles, as well.

Now I'm standing on a downhill slope. Compare this
with my uphill stance.

back. On the level, gravity is only pulling you down and it takes less thrust to
move you on the level.

6. Next, stand on the slope near the top, facing downhill. Assume your
half seat position. You will notice that your back is quite vertical or even perhaps leaning a little backward from your hip, because gravity is now pulling you
forward. If you like, step back to level ground and compare the positions.

Standing in half seat on an uphill slope.

Standing in half seat on the level.

Standing in half seat on a downhill slope.

Standing incorrectly on the downhill. My feet are pushed out in front of my center, so I have to lean forward to compensate. Compare this with the previous downhill pose.

7. Now walk down the hill onto the level. Keep your eyes up and be careful of a tendency to lean too far back. Feel how your feet hit the ground. You should find that your hip angle is slightly more closed when you are moving than when you are standing still on the downhill. This is because while gravity is pulling you forward, the movement is pushing you back, so you have to lean a little forward to compensate.

8. Finally, walk a big oval. Go straight up the hill onto the level, then make a smooth turn, walk straight back down the hill onto the level, and back up again. When you're on the level, try to get a smooth, centered flow to your steps and then keep that flow on the hill, especially on the downhill. If your steps get very short and choppy you haven't found your balance yet. If you're really centered, your downhill steps will actually be longer and freer than the uphill ones, because there is more space in front of you to take the steps. You will also feel a lot more movement in your joints, which you will notice again when you ride.

To summarize all this, your center must stay over your base for you to be grounded. For your center to stay over your base, you must adjust your upper body angle to allow for thrust. The two thrusts are those of gravity and forward motion. When you ride uphill the two are added together, so you have to lean forward more to keep your center in place. When you ride downhill the two offset each other, so you lean forward less.

The first sentence of the preceding paragraph applies all the time, not just when you're on a hill. However, working on the hills really brings it home to you and helps make your half seat position more secure at all times.

Tidbits and Supplements

When you are riding uphill, the angles of your legs require more stretching in the backs of the calves. This need for stretching may make your ankles tense and you may find it difficult to keep your heels from coming up at first. Standing in half seat position on the uphill is a good exercise to help the muscles and tendons stretch out a bit.

On the Horse

One might think, from reading that summary paragraph above, that going downhill should be easier than uphill—and in terms of effort it certainly is. Imagine a retaining wall that's about two feet high. Standing on top of it and jumping off is easy. Jumping up onto it isn't easy at all, unless you're pretty young and athletic. But downhill is much harder psychologically. In the first place, if you have any fear of heights at all, looking down is very disturbing. Looking downhill from on top of a horse can be terrifying.

You should have a quiet horse for the mounted exercises because you will want to stand still on the hill for several minutes at a time. Most hills have grass on them, so if he is a voracious grass snatcher you may need someone to hold him. He should be wearing a neck strap of some sort, which should be a little longer than usual. You may want to adjust your stirrups a hole shorter than normal, especially for the uphill work.

Because the horse has to make a greater effort going both uphill and downhill, if the hill is at all steep or long you should always ride it in half seat to distribute your weight more evenly over his back.

Start the exercises only after you and the horse are both thoroughly loosened up. During your warm-up do some work in half seat, being conscious of your body angles and their relationships to each other and to the saddle. Again, it is very helpful if you can do this with another person so you can look at each other.

Going Uphill

1. Place the horse on the slope at the bottom, facing uphill. Take up your half seat. You will find a moderately closed position, with your hands pressing lightly on his neck, the most comfortable.

2. Become aware of how your lower body relates to the saddle. Your center will still need to be vertically above your base—in this case the stirrup—and the stirrup leather will need to be perpendicular to an imaginary

Uphill position on the horse.

Standing on the level.

Downhill position on the horse. Compare the upper body
angles in all three positions.

horizontal, just as it was on the flat. However, the horse and saddle are now tipped uphill, so that relative to the seat of the saddle your center will be ahead of it and your feet will be behind the girth. A line drawn from your center to your base should pass through or slightly behind the horse's center. Compare your position in your mind to the one you took when you were on the ground. The positions should be identical, except now there is a horse under you.

3. Go through the first five of the Seven Steps, then ask the horse to walk up the hill. If the hill is at all steep, even at the walk you will feel your hips tending to slide backward. This is normal. Just try to keep your feet back so they stay below your center and allow your hip angle to close as much as necessary. You may find yourself with your tummy resting on the pommel. Climbing long, very steep hills requires some help from the horse's mane or the neck strap to keep you from sliding back too far. As you come onto the level, allow yourself to straighten up so you stay balanced.

4. Walk back down the hill in full seat at an angle to the hill rather than straight down, using the least steep side, and practice walking uphill and onto the level a few more times.

To summarize, **going uphill the horse is pushing forward all the time, both to move and to counteract gravity, so your upper body position has to be very far forward to compensate.**

Going Downhill

1. Place the horse on the slope facing downhill. This should not be a very steep nor a very long slope, so at first you may want to place him quite near the bottom. If you are really nervous, place him so that his first step will put him on the level.

2. Begin by checking your leg position. One of the main things that makes downhill difficult is the tendency to try to brace with your feet. This pushes them out in front of you, forcing you to lean farther forward to keep your center over your base. Turn your head so you can look over your hip to your heel and look for that vertical line. Also, your toes should *not* be in front of the vertical dropped from your knee (see the photo on the bottom of page 234).

3. Holding the neck strap, take up an *open* half seat position. Keep your eyes up and your knees soft so your feet don't slide forward ahead of the knees. Now your center will be behind the seat of the saddle and your feet will be a little in front of the girth, but a vertical line drawn from your center to your base should still pass through or a little behind the horse's center.

4. Go through the first five of the Seven Steps. Again, if you're really nervous, don't go on until you are comfortable standing in half seat at the bottom of the hill. When you are finished, sit down into full seat before walking down even a short way.

5. Once you feel confident, take the horse up the hill so that he is about three steps from the bottom, facing downhill. Take up your half seat, get comfortable, and ask the horse to walk down onto the level, thinking about staying centered and grounded all the way. Make sure you are looking straight out with soft eyes, not down with hard ones. One of the things you'll notice is that your following seat and stirrups have to be a lot more active on the hill than on the level. This extra movement also contributes to the difficulty of riding downhill.

To summarize, **going downhill the horse is pretty much allowing gravity to move him forward and keeping the brakes on to keep from going too fast. So your upper body must be fairly upright to offset this braking effect.**
Gradually increase both the length and the steepness of the slope until you can walk down a moderately steep slope without difficulty. Then combine your uphill and downhill techniques by riding the same sort of long oval that you walked in the ground exercise (page 232). Notice particularly how your upper body angle changes and how your leg appears to swing back and forth relative to the saddle as you go from up to level to down. Compare the leg positions in the three photos on page 237. The leg is the same in all three; it's the angle of the horse that is different. *What is **really** happening is that your leg is staying still and the saddle and horse are tipping up and down.* Therefore, your leg must *not* grip or you won't be able to keep your center and base aligned. Later on, you'll see how this also applies to jumping.

Here's another way to think about dealing with hills. When you're riding hills you have to take into account two things: the force of gravity and the force of the horse's movement. The gravity is constant, the movement isn't. Making it fairly simple, your leg position handles the gravity part and your upper body handles the horse-movement part. This is the same thing you do on the flat. That is, you always keep your feet under your center, but your upper body angle changes depending on whether the horse speeds up or slows down.

Crossing the Hillside

Riding across the side of a hill presents problems of its own, mostly problems of centering. Gravity tends to throw your center down the hill, so you must press strongly with your downhill leg to hold your center in place, in the same way you used it for lateral centering on pages 187 and 194. However, if you bring your center too far uphill, it begins to act as an aid to move the horse laterally *down* the hill, which is disturbing for him. This can be especially difficult at the canter, with its lateral thrusts. There are no new techniques to learn here, just practice.

One little tip about riding the hillside is that the horse will nearly always tend to slip downhill. Therefore, if you are trying to ride a particular line, to go through a gap or over a fence, always aim for the uphill side of your goal. When you get close to it, turn and ride through or over the center.

If you and your horse are going to get the maximum enjoyment out of your trail rides, learning to deal with hills is important. As you can see, it isn't all that difficult. Logic and a little time well spent will soon solve the hill problem for you both.

Tidbits & Supplements

Ground poles are very useful for teaching the horse balance and management of his feet, so it is worth the effort to buy or make yourself a set. The poles should be at least four inches in diameter, and ideally should be made or placed so that they don't move easily. They should also be fairly heavy and solid. If you use PVC pipe or something similar, you may want to cap it and partially fill it with sand to give it the necessary weight. You should not use the very thin-skinned variety of PVC because it cracks easily, creating dangerous sharp edges.

You can buy plastic blocks that are slotted to hold poles at several low heights (there are photos of them in Chapter 13). Or you can place them in an X-frame that can be rolled over to change the heights.

You will also need at least a temporary "jump lane." Use the arena wall or rail on one side. On the other side, lay poles that are parallel to the wall and the length of your jump poles away from it, resting on supports that are about four feet (1.3 meters) high. By using a jump lane you avoid the problem of steering and perhaps interfering with the horse's head at the wrong time. It's helpful to place "wings" (poles with the outer ends resting on the ground at either end) leading into the lane.

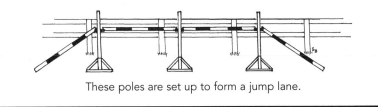

These poles are set up to form a jump lane.

GROUND POLES (CAVALETTI)

Ground poles, also called cavaletti, have numerous purposes, but in this case, we will use them to introduce you to dealing with obstacles (which is the other thing, besides hills, that starts riders shaking in their boots.). In this chapter, we will only concern ourselves with obstacles the horse can step over without jumping. With practice a horse can step over an object up to about twelve inches high, from the walk, with no more effort than just lifting his feet a bit higher. But it does take practice, so if you want to be able to walk over logs and similar things, you will need to raise the height of the obstacles a little bit at a time.

If you know nothing about the horse's attitude toward walking over poles, start by leading him over them on the ground. Begin with a single pole. Give him lots of time and just let him follow you back and forth until he walks over it comfortably. You can tell right away by his attitude whether he is accustomed to them.

Once the horse is leading well over a pole on the ground, you can start riding him over it. As usual, before starting any new work have him well warmed up and review your position with the Seven Steps. Even though he was quiet with the poles on the ground, many horses have quite a different attitude toward obstacles when they have a rider on their back. So many horses are ridden over obstacles badly that they are often very tense about it—which is why *you* are going to learn to do it right!

Your intent is important with obstacles. If you are thinking, "I'm going to ride *up to* that pole," the horse is quite likely to walk up to it and stop, or at least hesitate strongly since he isn't sure where to go next. Instead you should be thinking, "I'm going to ride from here to there on that line. On my way is a pole, but that only concerns me in that I have to be ready to tell the horse to keep going." Your eyes are a very important part of this intent. Soft eyes, looking toward the far end of your line and including the obstacle, give the horse a very clear idea of your goal.

Using a single pole in a jump lane (see the box on page 240), ride in full seat with your center firmly behind the horse's center. You should have a neck strap adjusted so that you can hold it while seated. Put your horse into a nice forward walk with one hand on the neck strap and just keep thinking about your Seven Steps as you ride toward the jump lane. When you reach the end of the wings, let your reins slide through your fingers a bit so there is some slack and firm up your back a little bit. Many horses will hesitate, especially the first time, as they go to step over the pole. If you are not prepared for it, this hesitation will cause your shoulders to swing forward, which will unbalance the horse just as he is about to step up over the rail. That's the kind of thing that makes horses nervous about obstacles.

If you do everything right, chances are that the horse will just walk calmly down the jump lane, step over the pole, and keep going. However, if he has had previous bad experiences, he may react in one of three ways.

1. Weaving. The horse walks a crooked path as he approaches the obstacle. This occurs as the result of tension, combined with natural crookedness. Use your center laterally to correct him and also keep it firmly behind his center to encourage him to go forward. Emphasize your following seat and use voice, stick, or leg, or a combination, to encourage him to keep going forward. It is important that whatever driving aid you use does not make him *more* tense, so be careful about getting too aggressive or tense yourself. Usually, once the horse discovers that you aren't going to haul on his mouth or bang on his back, he starts relaxing and going more forward.

2. Refusing. The horse comes up to the pole, stops, and refuses to step over the pole. Do *not* punish him for stopping. Stopping is harder for the horse than going on, so he only stops if he either thinks he can't make it over the obstacle or he will get hurt if he tries. Urge him quietly to step over the pole, keeping your soft eyes and your breathing, and thinking about being very relaxed in your shoulders. Be very careful not to rock your body or tense your thighs. Usually clucking and tapping lightly with the stick work better than the leg. Have a good hold of the neck strap so if he does by any chance leap over it suddenly, you won't hurt him. If it is apparent he isn't going to go over right away, turn him around and approach the pole again with a little more impulsion, thinking about the end of your line and your following seat, and keeping your center behind him. As long as he is walking toward the obstacle, keep your aids light and praise him. If he begins to slow down, ask him to move on but become passive as soon as you get a response. If he continues to stop after several attempts, try leading him yourself or getting someone to lead you both. Be effusive with praise and treats when you get the result you want. Very often people will "solve" this problem with a hard whack with the stick just as the horse gets to the obstacle, but in many cases this results in the horse associating the obstacle with whacks from the stick.

3. Rushing. The horse gets up to about the wings, then grabs the reins and races over the obstacle. This is the result of having had his mouth hauled on when he went *over* the obstacle. Use light, active hands as the horse approaches the lane, slowing gradually and stopping about twenty feet away, that is, *before* you reach the point where he would grab the reins. Let him stand for a minute, then turn away and repeat. Gradually bring the stop closer to the lane, turning away after the halt each time. Then, with the pole placed just within the wings, stop the horse at the edge of the wings, hold your neck strap, and *release the reins* until you are holding just the buckle. Ask the horse to walk

The three-pole pyramid, a slightly higher obstacle.

forward. Be prepared for him to race over the pole the first time and perhaps even crowhop a little on the other side, so keep your weight well back. If you do nothing drastic he will quickly stop. Once he finds out that you aren't going to haul on him when he is trying to get over the obstacle, he will settle down. One caveat: If you are *very* timid, you're better off getting some one else to teach this to your horse—if you can trust them to do it right.

As I said earlier, the chances are the horse will simply walk quietly over the pole. After a little practice you can start making the obstacle higher. The simplest way to do this is to take three poles and build a little pyramid of two poles side by side with the third pole resting on top. Then repeat the whole process.

Before you go any higher, you should practice riding over the pole in something more like a jumping position. You don't want the horse to jump, but as the obstacle gets higher it will be easier for him if you aren't sitting right on his back. And if he has to hop a little to get over, you are less likely either to be unseated or to hurt him.

When your upper body is already inclined a bit forward it becomes harder to keep it from tipping over even further if the horse hesitates. If the horse is just about to step or jump over something, which requires him to lift his front, it is essential that you do nothing to disturb his forward balance. Therefore, you will take up an open three-quarter seat with a moderately firm pull on the neck strap. Take up the position on the far side of the ring from the jump lane and make sure the horse is walking comfortably forward before you try the poles again. Then proceed exactly as before, starting with a single pole. If the horse had difficulty in the beginning he may revert briefly to his bad habit, so be prepared to do a little reschooling.

A walking crossbar.

Once he is comfortable with you in three-quarter seat over the three-pole stack, you can look around for some slightly higher obstacles. Old telephone poles are good because they taper, so you can get quite a variation in height. Solid obstacles are easier than open ones for the horse to judge and step over. You can also build a little crossbar, which looks more solid than a straight bar and is therefore easier for the horse to judge. Place the standards quite far apart so the angle of the rails is not steep.

Be sure you take up your three-quarter seat well ahead of time. If you wait until you get to the obstacle the horse won't have time to adjust his balance, so he may stumble or stop.

You should know that if you approach even a low obstacle at any gait faster than a walk, the horse is liable to jump it, so although you probably aren't aiming for the Olympics, you may want to read chapter 13 on jumping as well. Jumping is a lot easier than you think!

12

The Real Fun Begins
Cantering and Galloping

Lewis, a friend of my son, had just one riding experience. He was visiting in the Midwest, in corn-growing country. His host invited him to ride and put him on his horse in the middle of a cornfield. No sooner was Lewis seated then the horse took off at a gallop straight down through the tall rows of corn. After what seemed forever, according to Lewis, the horse finally slowed down and stopped. Lewis managed to turn the horse around, and he immediately took off at the gallop and returned to the starting point, where his owner was waiting. Lewis dismounted gratefully and never rode again. But in describing the experience to me, he said that he never felt as if he would fall off, except at the very end when the horse stopped rather abruptly.

∾

Flying along effortlessly on a good horse, with his body completely under both his control and yours, is an unbelievable high. It's been my experience in both hunter pacing and eventing that, although it is nice to come home with a ribbon, the experience itself is such fun that you don't really care one way or the other. And the horse is so obviously having a ball as well!

Most of the riding that people consider really fun involves some degree of cantering or galloping. As the horse stretches out into the gallop, which is a four-beat gait, the gait tends to flatten and become smoother and easier to ride as long as he keeps going in a straight line.

Because it is a three-beat rather than a two-beat gait, closer to the walk than the trot, many people find cantering on a horse with a good gait easier than trotting, especially sitting. However, while it may be easy to canter, it is difficult to canter well. This may explain, in part, why so many horses have problems with it.

If you look at video of a high-level rider at the sitting canter, you can see that her seat does not leave the saddle *at all*, any more than at the walk. The vertical line from the shoulder through the hip to the ankle is maintained

To learn more about this topic, read Chapters 7, 8, 12, 13, 15, and all of Part IV of the companion volume to this book, *How Your Horse Wants You to Ride: Starting Out—Starting Over.* (Canter work requires *all* of your basic skills, once you get past just staying on.)

throughout the stride, and her inside leg stays long and soft. If she is in half seat the stirrup leather remains vertical, showing that her center is not moving longitudinally and her shoulders are quiet.

Most riders find the canter difficult to follow smoothly at first because it is not a human gait and the weight shifts are quite complex. As the horse moves and his weight shifts back and forth and side to side, the rider's body has to move to compensate and keep her center over the horse's. The weight shifts during the horse's walk are also quite complex, but since the gait is slow and there is very little bounce to it, and since we walk ourselves, we don't have a hard time following it. The trot is a very balanced gait, with the diagonal pairs of legs moving together, so it is fairly easy for the rider to stay centered. It is also easy for the horse, which is why the horse will nearly always choose to trot rather than canter if he feels at all unbalanced.

In the canter, however, the horse's weight moves from back outside to front inside to back outside in the course of each stride. In a well-balanced horse who keeps his legs pretty well under his center, the change of vertical movement forward and back will not be great—in fact, one of the signs of a good canter is that the horse's withers move on a consistent horizontal rather than up and down. The lateral movement is more difficult to cope with, particularly when riding on a turn. As the horse rocks to the inside the rider tends to slip to the outside, then the centrifugal force of the turn tends to hold her there. The usual result of this is the rider gripping with her inside thigh, which makes her less able to center and more likely to bounce off the saddle, which in turn makes her more likely to bounce to the outside.

PREPARATORY WORK

The canter, as I said, is not a human gait—unlike the walk and the trot, which are two different gaits in humans just as they are in horses. However, since our front "legs" no longer reach the ground and the canter requires that at one point all the weight will be on one front leg, it is not a gait we can use. But the canter is still hardwired into our brains, since we are four-limbed and once ran on all fours. Whatever you can do to revive that memory will help you to be comfortable in the canter.

Since the movement of the horse is directed into your body through your seat or the stirrups, the more your body knows about what it's supposed to be doing, the better it will be able to follow. It's rather like finding it easier to follow your dancing partner if you already know the steps.

You should, first of all, watch as much good cantering as you can, with horses both free and being ridden. It has been demonstrated that you can learn a skill more effectively by spending time watching it being performed well than if you just go ahead and start working on it on your own. Watching a video, then imagining yourself cantering on the horse, will begin to wake up your brain and your reflexes.

If you have access to a swimming pool, and instruction if necessary, the sidestroke is actually a canter pattern and even includes the two "leads." And you can imagine yourself on a cantering horse as you swim.

There are also skills you should be perfecting at the other gaits that will help your canter. Because of the difficulty with the lateral motion of the canter, it is very important for you to be *completely secure in your lateral balance* at a fairly brisk sitting trot, both on the straight and around corners, before starting canter work. If you can work at the trot without stirrups and with a loose leg, your inside leg position will tell you clearly whether you have good lateral balance. If it is at all weak, your inside leg will draw up and back rather than hanging and swinging freely.

For longitudinal centering, you should be able to do transitions from trot to walk without losing your center forward, both in full seat and half seat. Trotting over cavaletti with the same requirements would be a bonus.

Your following seat should be good enough for you to be able to sit an ordinary trot without your seat leaving the saddle *at all*. Riders often think that because the trot is a bouncy gait, it is acceptable for your seat to leave the saddle a little and come down again as long as it isn't apparent to the observer— especially if the observer happens to be a judge! However, even a little bouncing becomes very uncomfortable for the horse after a while. More important in terms of cantering, the little bounce means that your thighs, hip joints, buttocks, and lower back are not as soft and flexible as they need to be. When you start cantering, the little bounce becomes a little bigger, which makes centering harder for you and makes it hard *on* your horse. Cantering in most horses is a smoother, less bouncy gait than the trot—but not always.

The fit of your saddle is an even bigger factor in the canter than at the walk and trot. If it isn't comfortable, or tips your pelvis the wrong way, or is too big so that you slide around in it, sitting the canter will be more difficult to learn. It is also important that the saddle sit level in the middle of the horse's back. Some not-too-well-made western saddles that seat you far back on the horse's back make the gait much more difficult to sit correctly.

Once you feel you're ready to try cantering on the horse, you have a choice of learning in half seat or full seat. I recommend that if you have a horse with a slow, smooth gait, learn the canter first as a sitting gait because there is a rather tricky hip movement that occurs just before the moment of suspension that is harder to learn in half seat. If you start out in half seat you may find it harder to learn to sit than if you learn full seat first.

The best horse to learn on is one with a good, active walk to get your pelvis moving freely, who will pick up the canter directly from the walk and can canter slowly and smoothly. An ideal area for the first cantering trials is a largish ring or smooth field, either level or with a slight uphill. It should be at least eighty feet (twenty-five meters) wide, and one hundred feet (thirty meters) is even better. If you have a smooth trail that goes slightly uphill for a longish stretch, that is another easy place to learn. You only canter for a short distance in the beginning anyway, but downhills should be avoided for quite a while, as should anything more than a very moderate uphill.

If you are fortunate enough to have a horse with a slow, shuffly little canter, learning on a bareback pad is the way to go. As you have already discovered, it is easier to relax your legs without stirrups and the bareback pad makes it fairly easy to keep your lateral balance.

Before attempting to canter, spend some time working on your following seat at the walk. Place your hand on your front, palm against your body and fingers slightly spread, with your little finger just above your navel. Using *only* the muscles that are under your hand, push the hand forward in rhythm with the horse's movement as he walks, thus exaggerating the effect of the movement on your pelvis. Check to make sure you aren't squeezing with your thighs or buttocks to move your pelvis. Notice how you roll from your seat bones to a gentle pressure on your crotch, and then back. If you loop your reins around the fingers of the hand that is on your front, you can then place your other hand on the small of your back and feel how your spine goes from flat to hollowed, *not* flat to rounded. Practice this until it becomes really easy and automatic. At the canter, you should be just as grounded and connected to the saddle in your seat bones as you are at the walk.

If your horse doesn't have a smooth, slow canter, you will probably want to use the half seat. Still at the walk, take up the half seat but

---

Tidbits & Supplements

We used to have a wonderful horse named Chipper whom you could put on a big circle with a child on him bareback. When you said the word "canter," Chipper would slide into a gait that was not much faster than a walk but had a true canter beat. After experiencing that, none of our students was afraid of cantering!

raise yourself a little more off the saddle than normal. Now place your inside hand over the front of your hip joint, so your little finger is on your thigh and your thumb is on the point of your hip. Have your other hand on the neck strap to help you ground.

As the horse walks, feel the same opening movement in your hip joint that you felt before, but now your back will simply become more upright, then close again. You should notice how your fingers spread and come together as your hip joint opens and closes. Your grounding should remain absolutely even on both feet. Again, practice this until it feels very automatic.

PICKING UP THE CANTER

One thing that makes cantering tricky is getting the horse to pick it up without tension or excessive speed. To take the canter in balance, the horse has to be somewhat collected. This does not necessarily mean that you have to understand collection. A well-trained horse will collect himself when he feels the canter signal. If the horse does not collect himself—if, for example, you get the canter by making the horse trot faster and faster until he "falls" into the canter on a turn—the gait will be sprawly because the horse will be on his forehand. That means his center will be more over his front feet than his hind feet. Try walking on the ground, leaning so far forward that your weight is over or ahead of your toes, and you'll feel how awkward and uncontrolled it is. Some trainers use this method to get a young horse cantering in the ring, "so that he learns to go forward." But what he learns is that, because he is so far out of balance, cantering is scary!

The horse should pick up the canter by rocking back over his outside hind foot, then picking up and stepping forward with the other diagonal pair, and so on. You begin by putting your center slightly to the outside, as if you were asking for a turn to the inside. This frees the horse's inside legs and also indicates to him that he will want the inside lead. Your center and weight should also be a little back and holding, as in any upward transition.

Then the usual signal for the canter is to give a little lifting active hand (page 167) with your outside hand as your outside seat drops, which tells the horse to rock back. This is followed immediately by the use of both legs (page 158) as your inside seat drops. Your outside leg should be applied a little behind your inside leg. A very effective addition to these aids, which will sometimes work just by itself if the horse is anticipating the signal, is to use an active inside seat (page 151) at the same time or a little before the legs are applied. Make sure your center remains on the outside and a little back as you use this aid. The outside rein must also be eased to allow the horse to go forward. (Some people like to use an inside indirect rein instead of an outside rein, but I do not consider this a good rein effect for novices. However, horses can be trained to almost any signal, including one trainer who taught her horses that a normal cluck meant trot, but a kissy noise meant canter.)

There are several techniques you can use to help the horse collect himself for the canter. One is to trot, then bring the horse *lightly* to the walk and imme-diately ask for canter. Another is the diminishing circle exercise. You have the horse walking well forward on a circle in the opposite direction from the way you want to be cantering. For learning purposes your circle would be to the

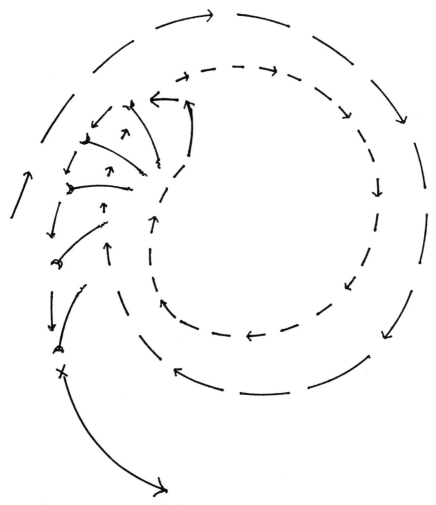

This pattern is one way of helping your horse collect himself for the canter.

right. Then you make the circle about ten feet (three meters) smaller in diameter. Next, reverse your horse toward the *outside* of the circle, using your aids as for a turn on the haunches, but lightly, and as soon as he has reversed ask for canter. The beauty of this method is that after you have done it a few times the horse knows what's coming, so he is ready for it.

Especially if you are working in half seat, you can also ask for the canter from the trot just as the horse starts around a corner. The turning changes the horse's balance just enough so that the canter comes more easily than the trot. Usually the corner he turns to start toward home works the best. If he tends to be tense at the far end of the ring, riding across the midline of the ring and then asking for the canter as you turn the corner toward home may get you a quieter start. You can combine this with the trot-walk-canter technique quite effectively. It is also the most likely method to produce the correct lead (see page 254).

A method that works well with horses who are quiet on the trail is to be trotting up a slight hill in a line. The first rider asks for canter, and all the others have to do is to *allow* their horses to move freely and they will pick up the canter automatically. However, this must be done out of the trot, so is best if the riders are going to canter in half seat. Also, some horses find it too exciting.

Many horses tend to drop their heads for the first couple of strides of the canter, even propping and hopping a little bit. This is not necessarily an aggressive action, but merely the horse's attempt to stretch out his back and round it for the canter, and then rebalance. Therefore, it is important to keep your center well back when you are asking for canter and be ready to let your reins slide, then gather them up again. If you do this, the horse will nearly always pick himself up and canter normally after a couple of strides, while if you keep the reins tight and let yourself be pulled forward he will not be able to get his balance and may even pull you off unintentionally. Starting on an uphill also helps avoid this situation.

You will probably need to experiment a bit to find which system works best for you and your horse. If your horse is really reluctant to canter but will trot fast, it nearly always means he feels unsure of his balance, either because of your skills (or his previous rider's) or because of the size of the arena.

If you know how to do it, you should train your horse, either longeing or free-longeing, to pick up the canter on a voice command. The word is usually spoken as "can*ter*" with an upward inflection in your voice on the second syllable. If you can clicker-train him, so much the better. This will make it much easier for you to concentrate on your position rather than having to think about the aids.

Tidbits & Supplements

A technique often used in riding schools is to have the horses walking in line around the arena. The first horse canters and the second horse continues walking until number one has either reached the end of the line or at least gotten well out of the way. Then the second horse is asked. Since he saw the first horse canter away and horses are such copycats, he usually will pick up the canter quite willingly, especially if he has done this exercise before. The problem is that the horse can anticipate too much and start off with a rush or a buck, so it requires an experienced instructor to keep matters under control.

CANTERING ON

As I said earlier, if possible you should pick up the sitting canter directly from the walk, at least while you're learning. Your lower body is already moving at the walk in almost the same pattern as at the canter, whereas the trot is quite different, since it lacks that diagonal roll, and the pattern of the footfalls, and thus the back movement, is totally different. You will probably find it helpful in the beginning to hold your saddle at the canter just as you did when you were learning the sitting trot (page 122).

Since you will need to use the outside rein to start the canter, put the inside hand *with the rein in it* on the saddle just before you give the canter signal with the outside rein. Then, as soon as you get it, let the reins slide through your fingers a bit so you don't bump the horse's mouth while your body is learning. It is not uncommon for a beginner to get the horse cantering and then forget to let go, so the horse canters one stride and then trots again. Frustrating for all!

You should certainly not make any attempt at steering until you are following the canter fairly well, since, as you already know, when your body doesn't feel secure the tension shows up immediately in your hands. In any case, your centering probably won't be very good at first, so the horse will have enough problems steering himself without your interference.

Try to concentrate on your Seven Steps, especially the centering and following seat, and on being as loose as possible—even if you feel floppy at first. If you start to bounce too much and your horse won't break to the trot immediately, stand up in half seat and grab the mane or neck strap until you can bring the horse back to the walk and start again.

If the only horse you have to learn on has a very fast or rough canter, or if you have lower back problems, you should start learning in half seat instead of sitting. In this case you would hold the neck strap instead of the saddle with your inside hand. Begin from a walk, if possible, in half seat, picking up the canter on a corner and on an uphill if you can. Keep your position as open as you can without becoming stiff. As with the sitting canter, pay particular attention to your centering and following the stirrups.

Things to look for:

● At the sitting canter, your seat should stay right down on the saddle or the bareback pad. Your seat *bones* may lift and drop a little, but the flesh of your buttocks doesn't leave the horse. If you're in half seat, your feet stay firmly resting on the irons. Your spine stays directly above the horse's spine.

● You want lots of activity in your hip joints and lower back.

● Your head and shoulders should be fairly still. Don't try to force this, but work on being more flexible from the shoulder blades down.

● In half seat, you should have the sensation that you are simply standing there on flexible legs and the horse is cantering along under you.

● Have fun! If you find cantering really disturbs you, it means your body isn't quite ready. Or it may mean the horse is insecure and you are sensing it.

Tidbits & Supplements

As should have become apparent, a big factor in learning the canter, especially sitting, is having the right horse. If your horse's canter is really uncomfortable it might be worthwhile to take a few lessons on a school horse with a good gait, if one is available.

While training the horse is not within the scope of this book, it is worth saying that a rough canter is usually the result of trying to get the horse to canter too slowly or in too small a space for his balance and muscling. This happens to all too many horses, and I think is the reason that so many riders have trouble with the canter. Allowing the horse to canter more freely until the canter smoothes out, and then using a diminishing circle to slow it down, is something most riders can do if they are ready to canter at all. This work is usually done in half seat until the horse's back relaxes and he can "allow" the rider to sit.

LEADS

Just as correct diagonals are an important part of the posting trot, correct leads are an important part of the canter. When the horse is turning, he can balance best if his inside hind leg comes well up under his center. During the canter stride the leading hind leg comes farther forward under the horse than the other hind leg, so we want the horse to canter on his inside lead.

Knowing which lead the horse is on is mostly a matter of practice and feel. On the wrong lead on a turn, most horses feel as if they had grown an extra leg! When you are first learning to canter in a ring you will probably have some help, and your instructor will tell you if you have the wrong lead. When you are on your own it is a little difficult to tell by looking down at the horse's feet, since both front legs come forward at almost the same time. You also have to lean forward to see them, which should be avoided while you are learning to sit. What you can sometimes do is lean forward only a little, and you will then be able to see just the leading foot as it comes forward, but not the other one. The problem with looking for the lead is that if you're not very good at it you end up riding along with your head down, which doesn't help your balance or your seat.

Luckily, most well-trained horses will take the correct lead most of the time. And if you accidentally get the wrong lead, you can ask for a simple change of lead. If you bring the horse back to the trot then ask again for the canter, if possible just *before* a corner, you will usually get it right the second time. The simple change of lead is also used when you want to change direction while cantering. The best way to do that is to canter across the long diagonal of the ring, break to the trot as you cross the center, then ask for the canter on the new lead as you approach the opposite corner.

Incidentally, there is no such thing as a wrong lead on the straightaway, which is one of the advantages of cantering on the trail. However, if you are on a long trail ride the horse should be asked to use both leads in the course of the ride, so that he uses his muscles evenly.

Tidbits & Supplements

Deliberately cantering on the outside lead (called the *false lead* or *counter canter*) is used to teach the horse more advanced balance. Naturally, it takes a great deal of skill on the part of the rider and strength and experience on the part of the horse.

Lead Changes

There are, as you no doubt know, two ways to change your horse's lead. One is the simple change, where you break gait and start again, and the other is the flying change where the horse maintains the gait while he changes. There are two ways to execute each of these: a basic way if you aren't planning to do any really refined work, and another way that is more precise. The second way, especially for flying changes, requires a good deal of preparatory work for the horse and is not within the scope of this book.

The best way to learn basic lead changes, both simple and flying, is across the diagonal of the ring. You start with them when your position is secure enough at the canter that you can use your aids without tension. You should also be able to ask for and consistently get either lead on the rail, with very little effort and minimal aids.

Simple Lead Changes

Many horses find the change from left lead to right easier, so you should start with that. However, if your horse seems to be having a problem, try it the other way. With your horse well warmed up, and after you have done some canter work:

1. Pick up the left lead canter and with the horse cantering quietly, as you start down the long side of the ring, turn and begin to canter across the diagonal. In the beginning, ride from the far end of the ring toward the gate, which will give the horse the incentive to take the lead in the direction he would like to go—home.

2. As soon as you have turned on to the diagonal, immediately and smoothly ask the horse to break to the trot. You would like the break to occur as you reach the midpoint.

3. Then ask the horse for the same kind of transition to the walk. This is just a test to see if the horse has maintained his balance during the first downward transition. If he is unable to come to the walk easily, he needs to improve his balance at the canter before you attempt any sort of prompt change of lead.

4. If you are successful in step 3, turn around and begin again, so that you are going around to the left, and repeat steps 1 and 2.

5. As you approach the end of the diagonal at the trot, keeping your horse well in front of you, ask him to walk. As he gathers himself for the walk, ask for the right lead and send him strongly forward into the canter. **Don't forget your**

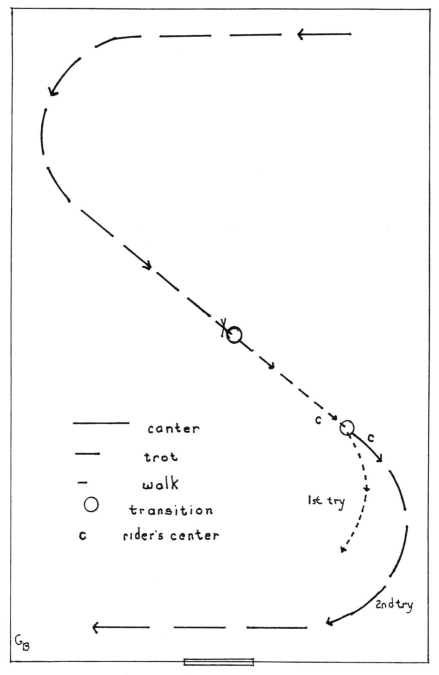

Where to ask for a simple change of lead.

centering aid. **The slight shift of your center to the outside (in this case, the left) is the clearest signal to the horse of the change of direction, and thus the necessity to change his lead.** The other secret to any good lead change is that you must send the horse forward, not hold him back. Later you can modify your aids so that you don't get more speed than you want. Be sure your eyes are up and soft and you are looking forward and around the corner.

6. After you have executed the left to right change successfully a few times, try the right to left.

7. Gradually reduce the number of trot strides, first by moving your downward transition closer to the far end of the diagonal so that you can use the wall and the corner to get the new lead, then later by moving the transition back to the midpoint and asking the horse to pick up the new lead when he is on the straightaway.

Eventually, you and the horse will reach a degree of skill where he will break gait; you will shift your center and send and get the new lead with one trot stride or even none at all. This last is called a *break and change*, and is not the same as a flying change. It is very quick and efficient for anything except showing. (It is not considered correct for dressage, and flying changes are required in hunter classes.)

Flying Lead Changes

For the horse to be able to do a flying lead change, he must first be well balanced and grounded in the canter. He should work in a moderately rounded frame and step well up underneath himself. He should be in a fairly forward canter, so that the moment of suspension is long enough for him to change his leg—that is, hold what was the initial leg of the old lead off the ground long enough for the new leg to get to the ground and start the new lead. A big enclosed field is a better place to work on this than a small ring or arena.

There are a number of ways to practice (or teach) a basic flying change, but I have found the following one to be the most successful. Again, with the horse well warmed up and working freely, begin by doing some simple lead changes as described above, so the horse is thinking about changing leads. When you are ready, start the same pattern as for the simple lead change. Then:

1. As you come through the diagonal on the left lead, move your center a little right, apply your right leg a little back, and ask for the beginning of a leg yield to your right leg. Use your hands to restrain the horse lightly, just so he

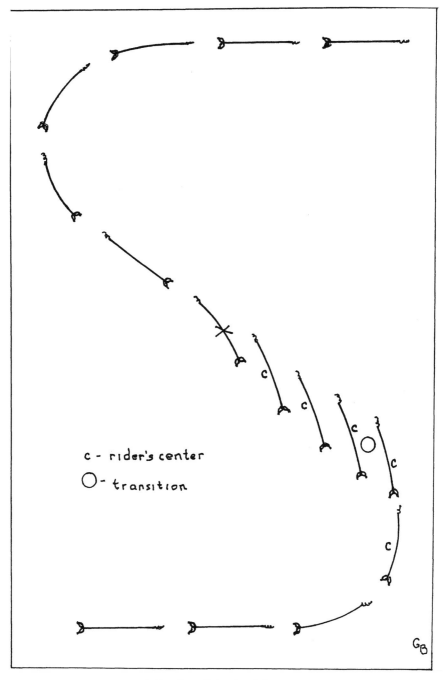

c - rider's center

O - transition

Asking for a flying lead change.

doesn't think you want an increase in speed. The leg yield will start positioning his body and leg for the new lead by bringing his right hind foot in front of his left, and will also force him to collect a little bit.

2. When you feel him begin to yield to your leg and as he approaches the end of the diagonal, as his left front foot hits the ground, move your center quickly *but not too far* to the left, look a little right, and give him the leg aids for the new lead: left leg back, right leg at the girth. Keep your weight and center back and send him strongly forward. Be sure you don't pull hard on the reins, especially the inside (right) rein.

It may take a few tries to get the complete flying change, but if you and the horse are ready you should find it fairly easily.

The right-to-left change is often more difficult to do correctly. Many horses find the right lead more difficult, so staying balanced long enough to completely execute the change can be a problem. Since the natural crookedness tends to place the horse's quarters to the outside, you often end up with a change in front only. You need to have a good feel for the horse's body position, which has to be correct for him to get the left lead. Riding him well forward and keeping his head to the outside (right) while he is learning the change will help.

It is also essential to *complete* the change *before* the horse hits the corner. If not, he will lean to the inside and be unable to change correctly, if at all.

Another place where it is often easy to get flying changes is on the trail. When the horse is well warmed up, choose a place with good footing, a moderately long straightaway, and a turn at the end. The turn should be sharp enough to make the correct lead desirable, but one that you can take without slowing down. Put the horse into the lead that he will *not* want to be on for the turn. Let him canter forward, though not out of control, down the straightaway, then just *before* he starts the turn, send him on with the aids for the new lead.

GALLOPING

The gallop is not exactly the same gait as the canter. Instead of the nonleading diagonal pair of legs hitting the ground together, the hind leg hits first. Thus the gallop is a four-beat gait, and is therefore smoother than the canter and easier to follow with your body.

Difficulties in the gallop arise from the speed. As long as you have plenty of room and no sharp turns, like Lewis in the story at the start of this chapter, the gallop is easy. But if you run into a situation where you are "driving too fast for conditions," the horse, and you, can become tense and get into trouble. Also, the presence of other horses galloping or something happening to spook the horse can both result in the kind of panicky running where the horse is out of control of his body, and thus out of your control.

So the answer to happy galloping lies in choosing carefully the places where you gallop. A racetrack is ideal, of course, and next best is a large enclosed field, so that you can circle. Dirt roads or wide trails that are fairly straight, long, and preferably slightly uphill are also good as long as there is plenty of space. Also choose your company carefully; inconsiderate people and badly trained horses can teach your horse things you would rather he didn't know. And, as always, build your horse's trust so that if something happens to scare him, you can get him to listen again.

Serious problems with the gallop, such as bolting, are covered in Chapter 15.

Cantering and galloping are really joyous things to do for both rider and horse, as long as there is no fear involved. However, you must realize that *a good cantering seat comes out of a good seat at the walk and trot*. If you have been working slowly and carefully all this time, you shouldn't have any trouble now.

13

Jumping Made Easy
The Half Seat Revisited

Did you know that any sound horse can jump four feet (1.3 meters)? And that most of them can jump it from a standstill with a rider on their back? My sister Lee found out about that the hard way many years ago. She was sitting on a little horse we had—actually a pony—who liked to jump just about anything but was a bit nervous. They were standing in front of the paddock fence talking with friends and without thinking my sister struck a match to light a cigarette. Before she knew what happened she was on the ground and the horse was on the other side of the fence. Did I mention his name was Sky Rocket?

∾

Believe it or not, jumping is one of the *easiest* things to do on a horse. Oh, I'm not talking about Olympic-level stuff, just the kind of thing you meet on the trail or even in the hunt field. Single fences of the kind that any horse can jump easily. Perhaps that story about my sister isn't a very good example of how jumping is easy, but it shows that it is easy for the horse. And generally speaking, what is easy for the horse should be easy for the rider. While we're on the subject, what usually gets the rider in trouble is not having the horse unexpectedly jump, but having him unexpectedly *not* jump!

The usual assumption is that the horse has to be *made* to jump and that given a choice, he will stop. But in reality, if the horse is experienced, is being ridden correctly, and the jump is within his easy range—that is, less than four feet (1.3 meters) and not in difficult terrain—it is far easier for him to jump than to stop. Consider the whole picture when a horse is jumping: He canters or gallops calmly toward the fence, organizes himself in the last few strides, and sails over the jump in the rhythm of his canter stride. The whole movement flows together as one. Stopping is a very different matter. During the approach the horse and his gait are tense and uneven, and the stop, far from flowing smoothly, is strained and violent; a massive effort that raises dust and drops rails. Certainly the horse would find it far less difficult to jump.

261

To learn more about this topic, read Chapter 13 of the companion volume to this book, *How Your Horse Wants You to Ride: Starting Out—Starting Over.*

So what causes refusals and run-outs? The answer is very simply that the horse doesn't want to try the jump because he doesn't think he can make it safely over and is afraid of falling. Earlier in the book I described a horse who had been so traumatized that he was afraid to try to step over a pole on the ground. This fear of failure is virtually always created directly by the rider/trainer, both by the way she uses her body—allowing her weight or hands to disturb the horse's balance—and by her judgment in choosing what to jump.

Our primary concern is the first category, that is, learning to use your body correctly. In the next chapter, we'll discuss some of the factors that make an obstacle more or less difficult, to help prevent mistakes in judgment.

When we start thinking about telling the horse *what* to do, we need to know what he *will* do. Basically, the rider can only make him move in two dimensions; forward and backward—or faster and slower if you like—and sideways. When we start thinking about "making" the horse jump—a third dimension—we must first realize that this is impossible! Let's say you are riding around the ring and a friend draws a line in the sand and then says, "Let's see you make the horse jump four feet high when he gets to this line." Could you do it? Not unless the horse is a trick horse trained to capriole on command! No, what makes a horse try to jump at all is the obstacle itself. In addition, if the horse loses his footing badly enough just before the obstacle he won't jump, and there will be nothing you can do about that except hope he doesn't fall on top of you! There is no way you can pick him up and carry him over the fence. **So the existence of an obstacle in the horse's path makes the horse jump, and the way the horse approaches it, combined with his experience, is what makes the jump successful.**

Therefore, your goal with your body is a very simple one: Since there is no way you can *help* the horse lift his body into the air over a jump, your concern is to *stay out of his way* and *allow* him to negotiate the obstacle *without interference*. Besides having your body under control, this means almost entirely giving up *control* (but not necessarily support) with the reins in the immediate area of the jump. I'm sure you're thinking there is no way you will get the horse over the fence if you can't steer him, but you're wrong. At some point you may reach a degree of skill where you can help the horse balance over jumps, and can steer without interfering, but for at least some of you that's a long way away!

For now, if you have followed this book (and the companion volume, *How Your Horse Wants You to Ride: Starting Out—Starting Over*) all the way through, you have all the tools you need to ride passively over fences. So let's explore further. The first thing we need to learn is what factors make going over a jump different from riding on the flat.

THE HORSE'S BODY OVER THE JUMP

The action of the jump is typically divided into five parts: the approach, the liftoff, the flight, the landing, and the departure. Let's talk about them one by one. As usual!

The Approach

The approach can begin as much as eight or ten strides away if the horse is experienced and has a good eye for distance. During the approach the horse needs to determine two things. One is the right degree of speed/impulsion that will carry him over the jump with the least effort by giving him the most momentum.

Obviously, the faster he is going the longer he can stay in the air, but also the harder it becomes to make the transition from straight ahead to up and the harder it is to find the right spot from which to leave the ground. This last point is his second concern during the approach: how he should moderate the length of his stride so that he reaches the front of the fence at the best spot. This is usually a distance from the fence that is about equal to the height of the fence.

In terms of the physics of motion, the ideal approach is at a constant speed, with no thrust except that which results from the gait.

The Liftoff

This is the crucial part of the jump for all concerned. If the horse is unable to get his front legs high enough into the air to clear the fence, he will catch them on it and very likely fall. Not very desirable! The horse gains this lift by planting his front feet firmly on the ground, well out in front of him, then uses the power of his forehand to lift it into the air, folding his legs in the process. Only then do the hind legs hit the ground, actually ahead of where the front feet left, to prepare for the flight.

Since the horse's motion during liftoff is converted from straight ahead to upward, the thrust during liftoff is the same as that of a downward transition; that is, the rider's body will be thrown forward.

The Flight

The flight occurs as a result of the horse's speed approaching the jump, combined with the power of his hindquarters to push his body through the air. The hind feet hit the ground and send the horse forward exactly the way they do at the beginning of any gallop stride. He goes up because at that moment his body is pointing up.

The thrust is that of an upward transition; the rider's body will be thrown back.

The Landing

The horse lands on his front feet, which is to say, on his forehand. His front feet then lift off again in the first gallop stride, after which the hind feet land, as in the liftoff, in front of where the front feet landed and assist in lifting the horse up and forward.

The motion is converted from downward to straight ahead, and the thrust is that of a downward transition; the rider's body is thrown forward.

The Departure

The horse continues in the gallop, usually taking a stride or two to fully rebalance. The thrust during the rebalancing is that of a downward transition. Once balance is recovered, the thrust is that of the gait alone.

The approach. I'm just about to place my hands
on the horse's neck for my closed position.

The liftoff. My upper body angle is about the same as in the preceding photo; the horse has come up to me. It's not perfect, but I'm old, the horse was unfamiliar, and I hadn't jumped in ten years!

The flight. My center is well behind the horse's center, as it should be. He took a big jump, and we just caught the moment when he had unfolded his front legs and hadn't yet folded his hind legs.

The landing. The horse came down a bit heavily, but I was able to stay back. (He was a little out of practice too!)

The departure. The horse brought his head up to free his front legs and rebalance, and is just about there.

THE RIDER'S BODY OVER THE JUMP

I'm sure you noticed in the preceding paragraphs that in each case I described the thrust that would result from the horse's actions. That's because it is the thrust that disturbs the balance of the rider's body, which in turn affects the horse's balance and function. Many years ago I worked in a publishing house and was asked to edit a book on jumping. The author, an Argentinean, described taking an experienced jumper and tying a weighted dummy on him in all different places. The only criterion was that the dummy must be fastened so that it could not move at all. The horse was then sent through a jump lane. No matter where the dummy was placed on his body, the horse negotiated the jumps without difficulty.

Then the dummy was removed and a rider of the same weight mounted the horse. He was instructed to move his body as much as safely possible while the horse jumped. The result was catastrophic! The horse was unable to get over the jumps without taking them down—and almost himself as well. So the very sensible conclusion the author reached was that the most important factor in successful jumping is to ride the horse so that the rider does not move relative to the horse. It took me a great many years to find the solution to this problem, but once I did, my students and horses found jumping a very easy skill to learn.

As we said, the crucial moment in the jump as far as the horse's balance is concerned is during liftoff. If, when the horse is trying to lift his forehand up, the rider does something to interfere with or prevent that lift, the horse is going to have trouble getting over the fence.

There are two things that can happen that will interfere: The rider's body can come forward ahead of the horse's center, thus throwing additional weight onto the horse's forehand as he is lifting; or the pressure on the reins can be reduced suddenly and drastically, affecting the horse's head and thus his balance. The first is called *getting ahead* of the horse; the second is called *dropping the horse*. For the moment we are concerned with the rider's body, so we'll leave the rein problems until later.

Everybody always worries about getting left behind—having their body flung back as the horse takes off in flight. Even though this looks terrible, and can be quite painful for the horse if the rider's hands grab on the horse's mouth and her seat comes down with a crash on his back, it is nowhere near as *dangerous* as getting ahead. Worst case, if the rider is badly left behind, the horse will be pulled down and land with his belly on the top of the fence, an ignominious position but rarely resulting in anything except a few scrapes and a good deal of embarrassment.

Worst case if the rider gets *ahead* is that the horse hangs his knees on the fence, flips completely over, and lands on his back with the rider underneath. Not good!

So now we're faced with the problem of not getting ahead of the horse, but not getting left behind either. If we look at those descriptions of the parts of the jump again, we see that first, during the liftoff your body gets thrown forward. Then during the flight it gets thrown back, and during the landing it gets thrown forward again. Forward, back, forward, and all occurring very close together. How are you *ever* going to learn the timing of that? The answer is amazingly simple: you aren't. **You aren't going to try to learn to move back and forward and back to offset the forward-back-forward thrust.**

One of the things that has been mentioned many times in this book is that the horse cannot lose his balance backward. Being behind the horse's center is never going to get him into trouble. **So what you're going to do is stay back the whole time.** Now, don't give up and go away yet. If you look at the photographs on pages 269 and 270, you'll see that this looks just like what you want it to look like. We're not talking about a "left behind" kind of staying back, but something quite different. We're talking instead about the sliding back that happened to you when you rode your horse uphill.

Let's look at some photographs and use some imagination to understand what it is you're going to do. As the horse approaches the jump, you're going to take up a moderately closed position with your fists pressing lightly into the horse's neck. When he gets to the liftoff point, the thrust is going to try to send your body forward. But you aren't going to let that happen, since that would unbalance him. Instead, you're going to use your hands and feet to hold yourself firmly in place so that you can't go forward. (What's really great about this is that if the horse *does* stop you are already positioned to prevent yourself from falling forward.)

Then the horse is going to take flight, which will thrust you back. And you're just going to let that happen, exactly the way you did when the horse went uphill. Your hips will slide back along the saddle and the hip angle will close so that your upper body comes down close to the horse's neck.

Then the horse will land, throwing you forward, and again you resist firmly with your hands and feet. Your hips will open and your shoulders come up, but your center won't move ahead of the horse's center. Then the horse will gallop away and you will come up into a balanced or open position.

At no time was your center ever allowed to get ahead of the horse's center, and when it slid behind during the flight you didn't lose your balance backward, but just kind of slid back like a car rocking on its springs. All very graceful, effortless, and unbelievably easy.

A more closed approach position, appropriate for learning and
for jumping over a small fence where the thrusts are less.

My stirrup is still vertical and my belt is well behind the girth, as is my center.
Although the horse's nose is tucked in a bit, there is some slack
in the reins, showing that it was his choice.

I am still pressing myself back a little, as the horse hasn't quite
started to go forward again after the landing.

RIDING THE BASCULE

Bascule is a word that has been much misunderstood. Most people take it to
mean the way the horse rounds his back over the jump. It really refers to the way
the horse's body tips up and down as it moves through the air. Literally, *bascule*
is French for a type of see-saw, which describes the motion quite clearly. (The
French got into this somehow, which is why we say *bascule* instead of *see-saw*.)

Now let's look at the jumping from that aspect. The horse goes up, then
over, then down. It's just like that exercise where you rode the horse up the hill,
onto the level, then back down again, except you don't have to turn around at
the top.

In fact, jumping is very much like riding hills. If you go back and take a
look at Chapter 11, you'll find a description (on page 238) of how your legs and
the saddle change their relationship to keep your center over your base as the
horse goes up and down. Take a look at the photos on page 237. Note where
the whip is, relative to the girth, in each photo. Also notice that my leg is in
exactly the same position relative to horizontal in all three photos.

The same thing has to happen as the horse goes through his bascule over
the jump. As the horse goes up, your legs go back relative to the saddle flap. At
the top of the fence your legs are in normal position, and as the horse comes

down your legs come forward. And as we said with reference to hills, what is *really* happening is that your legs are staying still but *allowing* the horse to tip up and down inside them. This is why gripping the saddle with your legs while jumping makes you *less* rather than more secure, and things like calf blocks on the saddle hinder rather than help.

The bascule effect also adds a gravity thrust to the jumping thrust. That is, during flight as the horse is going up over the fence gravity pushes your upper body back, and as he is coming down your upper body is pushed forward. You will be dealing with these thrusts in exactly the same way as you did on the hills. That is, you will be more closed on the way up and more open on the way down. Of course, when you first start jumping, the hill aspect won't be very noticeable because you won't be jumping very high fences. However, as a preparation for jumping, spend some time riding up and down hills, paying attention to what your body is doing and trying to make the movement as effortless as possible.

PREPARATORY WORK

Cavaletti Again

We're going to start over ground poles, so you should build a little jumping lane such as described on page 240. Start with one pole but have several available. A jumping lane, or wings if you are jumping single fences, is very important psychologically. A jump constitutes an obstacle in the horse's path. Horses are pretty logical animals. If it is obviously easier to go around the obstacle than over it, which is certainly the case if the obstacle is narrow, the horse's first thought will be to look for a way around. This means he won't be thinking about how to get over it. Therefore, even if you are quick and capable enough to guide him over it, he probably won't jump it very well, which is disturbing to you both.

This first exercise is especially important for people who have had previous jumping experience. Almost without exception I have found that those people have a very difficult time learning *not* to jump ahead of their horses. It is almost impossible for them to learn from any sort of half seat position, since their bodies are so conditioned to going forward at the jump. By approaching the jump in a full seat upright position, they change the pattern and fool the body into thinking it is doing something different.

The horse should be wearing a neck strap, which should be adjusted for the first exercise so that you can hold it easily in full seat. You can either be in a saddle or on a bareback pad—which might be a little easier, provided you know the horse will jog quietly over a series of ground poles. If you aren't sure about the horse, keep your feet in the stirrups so you can switch to half seat or posting if he goes too fast.

1. In full seat, holding the neck strap, walk through the jump lane as described on page 241.

2. When the horse is walking through quietly, take up a slow jog and let him jog over the pole. You will feel a little more thrust and bounce over the pole. Try to keep your center back the whole time and allow your back to be flexible so that you don't bounce on the horse's back. This can be a bit tricky, because you have to keep your buttocks and hip joints soft so you can follow, but your lower back firm so you don't tip forward.

3. When one pole is easy, add more poles, up to four, and repeat the exercise. (See the box below.)

The purpose of this and the next few exercises is also for you to learn to *feel* the thrusts, while only resisting the thrust that throws you forward. *So, you will be allowing your torso to sway back but never forward.*

The next step is to raise the obstacles so the horse first has to hop, and, for the more advanced rider who is working at the canter, eventually jump over them. We will continue with this "backward" seat for a little while longer, but don't think of it as a total waste of time. Besides the reasons described, it is by far the least threatening way to handle jumping downhill and over drop jumps.

Unless your horse is fairly smooth gaited in his normal trot, you should now begin to ride in open half seat (page 193) rather than full seat, so you don't get bounced around too much. In any case, you will want your stirrups. Allow a little extra length in the neck strap because the horse stretching over the

---

Tidbits & Supplements

When using them in groups, the poles have to be placed at a distance apart that fits the horse's stride. For a fifteen-hand horse, three feet (1 meter) is about right for walking, four feet six inches (1.5 meters) for a brisk trot and nine to ten feet (3 meters) for a quiet canter. But since every horse's stride is different, and because you also have to take the horse's boldness and experience into account, experiment until you find a distance that works well for you. If you work alone, this means a fair amount of dismounting and remounting until you get it worked out.

Trotting a small fence in the "backward" seat. My arms have straightened a bit as the thrust throws me back, but the neck strap keeps me from hitting the horse's back.

jump will tend to pull you forward. Your half seat should be as upright as possible without being stiff.

First set up three poles in a stack (page 243) and work over this at a slightly brisker trot. Then set up a second stack about nine feet (2.75 meters) beyond the first stack. **This is as much as you should attempt unless you are ready to work at the canter.** However, you may work up to the same point using closed position (described later on in this chapter).

At the trot over the slightly higher obstacle, you will feel the thrusts much more clearly. That means you have to keep your back very firm as the horse approaches and starts to step over the fence. Your elbows must also be very springy so you can allow your arms to straighten as you sway back when he pushes off behind.

If you can work with someone and watch each other, you can get a clearer idea of how much you have to hold yourself back at liftoff. It's a good deal more than you think, because the combination of the hesitation, which you often get, with the change of direction from forward to upward, increases the thrust. And the idea is not to allow your center to move forward relative to the horse *at all!* Allowing your upper body to sway back is fairly easy, and there is very little landing thrust because the arc is so flat and the horse usually steps forward pretty well on the far side of the fence.

Tidbits & Supplements

If your horse has a four-beat gait such as a rack or tolt, you should *not* approach a jump in that gait. The horse finds it almost impossible to engage both hind legs simultaneously and jumping off of one hind leg can lead to a fall. You may have to work at the canter to avoid a four-beat approach.

Little Jumps

When you are ready to ask the horse to jump, encourage him to increase his pace as you get close to the first stack, so that if possible he hops it, takes a small canter stride, and hops the second one. Some horses are inclined to jump easily; others prefer to trot until forced to jump by the height of the obstacle.

If the horse isn't jumping, try setting up little crossbars in place of the stacks. Start small, then increase as necessary until the horse will hop over them. If you can fit a canter stride in just before the first obstacle, the horse will then jump rather than step. But whatever he does, *don't go forward!* You should feel a constant light pull on the neck strap throughout the exercise, increasing when he thrusts forward over the jump.

What you are going to find when the horse starts to make a little jump is that you will stay firmly back against the neck strap during the liftoff, with your elbows bent and your back upright. Then, as he takes flight, your upper body will sway back—the neck strap will prevent you from banging on his back or mouth—then come back to vertical as he lands. Be sure to keep your arms relaxed so the horse doesn't pull you forward by the neck strap. You may have to play with the adjustment of the neck strap to find the right length.

What is really surprising is how *late* in the jump the swaying back takes place. Over a small crossbar the horse has almost landed on the other side before you feel yourself getting thrown back. This is why most people get ahead of the horse if they try to go forward when he does. That point comes much later in the sequence than you expect. As with the lower obstacles, if possible you should practice this with someone else so that you can watch them, or get someone to videotape you.

Tidbits & Supplements

You might think that going forward early would keep you from getting thrown back later, but it doesn't. If your body has gone ahead of the horse, when he takes flight there is just that much more distance for you to get thrown back! As a result, you get thrown back harder.

Jumping a small fence. I am still being thrown back, even though the horse's forefeet have touched the ground on the landing side. Although the reins appear tight there is no indication that I am interfering with him. That takes practice!

THE REAL THING

When you are comfortable staying back and letting the horse jump in front of you over a small obstacle, you are ready to practice the position you will use for all simple jumping of whatever height, except when you're going downhill. This position, as we said earlier, is nothing more than the closed position you learned in Chapter 9. You used it to learn posting and for climbing hills.

Begin by working on the flat in closed position until both you and the horse feel comfortable and balanced. Remember, at no time should you feel as if you are getting *ahead* of the horse. You should feel that even if the horse stumbled and went to his knees, you could stay on without difficulty. If your horse carries his head very low, it may take some experimenting to find a position for your hands and an upper body angle that feel secure. As long as pressure on your hands pushes your *hips* and not your *shoulders* back, the position is workable. If you are having a problem with this, try shortening your stirrups a hole or two. The shorter your stirrups, the more you can close without hitting the saddle.

You will also be using your legs, which is to say, your stirrups, to hold you back. This takes a little practice, because you must find a way to brace against your feet without pushing them out in front of you or locking your knees. If you think about kneeling—that is, pushing your knees forward and down at the same time as you press with your feet and hands—that should help. It is also very useful if you can get someone to mimic the thrust that will throw you forward. That means they will have to push against your seat on the side on which they are standing, which you may or may not want to do. But if you can resist a strong push against your seat when you are in closed position, without getting tense or locking your knees, you should find staying back over the fence comparatively easy.

Another good exercise, if your horse is voice-trained or someone will longe or lead you, is to get settled in your closed position at the trot, then have the horse come to a halt as abruptly as possible. Your goal is to be able to stay behind the horse throughout the transition, without locking up anywhere.

If you are a novice, work at the trot only. If you are more advanced, you should work at the canter as well.

When you are ready, begin the same procedure that you used for the "backward" seat work. That is, start with one ground pole and gradually add height and obstacles as you feel competent at each level. Once you can trot and canter over two stacks or small crossbars, build yourself a little gymnastic in the jump lane. A gymnastic is a combination of fences set up in a row so that each one, by its position, has an effect on the next one. Introduce it one element at a time: first the cavaletti, then one jump, then the second one.

The basic or starter gymnastic consists of three or four cavaletti, spaced four and a half feet (1.4 meters) apart, and preferably raised a little to get the horse engaging himself. Nine feet (1.9 meters) away place a crossbar, eighteen inches high in the center, with ground poles on either side about eighteen inches away. Place another crossbar the same size nineteen feet from the first one.

A nice, small, jumpable crossbar.

The horse will trot the cavaletti, and then he should pick up the canter either just before or over the first crossbar and continue to canter over the second one. The horse should work willingly and should feel smooth and balanced for the most part, especially at the trot. (Sometimes at the canter the horse has more difficulty finding the right spot—a problem we will deal with in the next chapter.)

The difference between the closed and the open positions is that rather than *leaning* back against the neck strap to keep from getting ahead of the horse, you will be *pushing* back against the horse's neck. It feels rather like pushing a lawn mower. Keep a couple of fingers through the neck strap just in case you make a mistake. You should still be moderately upright, since, when the horse pushes off into flight and throws you back, your hip angle needs to be able to close, just as it did when you were climbing hills.

As you approach the jump lane, hold yourself steady with your seat close to the saddle but not resting on it and your hands on the horse's neck pressing you back and sending the horse forward. To keep your wrists from bending backward, press your *knuckles* into the horse's neck, not the heels of your hands. Your eyes should be looking down to the far end of the jump lane. Your reins should be held with one in each hand so that you can do some moderate steering if you need to before you get into the lane. Other than that, you don't have to do anything at all as you approach the fence except "keep on keeping on."

I'm in a lightly closed position suitable for the approach.

My hand position for the jump approach. I am pressing
myself back, not leaning on the horse's neck!

Go back and look at the jumping photographs at the beginning of the chapter
and copy them in your imagination, so that you can really see yourself and how
your body will work in the air.

So that you don't affect the horse's balance adversely, it is essential that
from a certain point onward you do nothing that could change his balance. I call
that point the *go point*. It is the point from which the horse makes his decision
and his move to jump the fence. Imagine yourself about to jump a moderate-size
obstacle on foot. You jog toward it, looking at it and adjusting your stride until
you "see" the right distance. At that point you move boldly toward the fence
and jump it. If you watch human high-jump competitions you will often see the
contestants make a number of mock approaches to find their go point. Then,
once they are sure, they make the try. If you can imagine having made your
move and then having someone trip you or grab your hands, you can imagine
how the horse would be disturbed by any excessive movement on your part.

You can generally assume that the go point is one to two strides away—more
if the fence is very high. You should treat that as the beginning of the jump and
*be established in your position with a hold on your neck strap well before you get to that
point.* From then on, you can use your center laterally to keep the horse straight,
although the jump lane will do most of that for now. Your weight (page 151) will
keep the horse going, but your center *must not* move forward. (If you find that the
horse wants to slow down a lot, either your center is moving or he is lacking in
confidence about the height or type of fence you are attempting.) Also, you must
not do *anything* with your reins, which must have enough slack in them to allow
for the horse's head movements in the air.

You can see that the horse is very out of balance in this landing. If I had been forward leaning on his neck, he might have rolled over on me. Not fun!

A moment later he has recovered and we are galloping safely away.
He wasn't even upset.

As you ride the approach from a distance, if you are in an open or balanced position your reins can be whatever length you need to maintain light contact and guide your horse. Then, as you get nearer and close your position, you simply bring your hands forward to the neck strap *without shortening the reins*. This will give the horse adequate head freedom unless he approached on a very short neck. As the horse uses his body over the fence, especially in the landing, he extends his nose for balance and needs plenty of extra rein to do so. You can still use one rein at a time if you need to, until you reach the go point. And you can allow the reins to slide through your hands if you feel the horse needs it.

The most common problems seem to be:

1. Finding a really comfortable, secure closed position

2. Finding the right balance of holding and back pressure between the hands and stirrups

3. A tendency to brace the leg and lock the knee

4. Pressing *down* too much rather than forward on the horse's neck

This last throws your weight onto the horse's forehand, causing him to prop in front of the fence or crowhop afterward.

When you get everything right, what you feel is almost nothing at all, especially on low fences. It is so easy that you can't believe you're jumping!

Now all you need is practice. If you're doing it right, you can have fun practicing these little jumps—eighteen inches or less—almost every day for ten or fifteen minutes, and the horse will enjoy it as well. If he doesn't, it's a sure sign that either you are doing something wrong or he has a soundness problem that you weren't aware of. But generally he will just pack you around, while both of you improve your jumping skills and confidence in preparation for bigger things.

If you jump enough, your body will learn how to do it well enough that you don't need to use the braced hands technique described here to negotiate simple fences. I can do that. But I still use this technique any time I'm not sure what the horse is going to do. Odd-looking fences, unusual terrain, or other difficult approaches can all have a physical or psychological effect on both you and the horse, which can lead you into trouble.

We caught a photo sequence when we were working on this chapter that clearly shows the importance of learning to stay behind the motion throughout. It also shows what your body can learn to do to keep you out of trouble. I remember this particular landing clearly, and I won't tell you what I was thinking because they wouldn't print it, but I sure was glad my body knew what to do!

Nonetheless, jumping is an amazing amount of fun for both you and the horse as long as you use some judgment and don't scare yourselves. Enjoy!

14

More About Jumping

Getting There Is Half the Fun

If you've ever done much competing over fences in a class where style is being judged, you know how hard it is to hit every spot right and put together a perfect round. I found it a lot easier when I was young and unselfconscious. In my adult life, I can only remember one round that I finished saying, "Wow! That was *good!*" Of course, showing was not especially my forte, and the professional riders have a much higher average.

My depth perception is only marginal, and I usually messed up by panicking when I couldn't see a distance and fussing with the horse when I should have left well enough alone. I got my first clue about that during a lesson I was taking. The horse was very awkward and unsure at the canter in a rather small indoor arena. I tried all sorts of maneuvers to pull him together and find a spot as we approached the three-foot (one-meter) fences, but only succeeded in flustering him more.

Finally, I decided the heck with it. I thought, "This horse just needs help with his cantering and let the fences fall where they may." I trotted my circle, picked up the canter, and simply focused on keeping him as balanced, soft, and rhythmic as I could while I rode down each line as though the fences weren't even there, letting him choose his own spots. Some of them were a bit close, some a bit far away, so it seemed rather uneven to me, but he stayed nicely balanced the whole way. Much to my surprise, the instructor complimented me enthusiastically on a really great round. Apparently, the unevenness was not obvious to the observer as long as the horse's carriage was constant.

∽

To learn more about this topic, read Chapters 8 and 19 of the companion volume to this book, *How Your Horse Wants You to Ride: Starting Out—Starting Over.*

Before you start jumping three-foot courses, there are a few more preparatory steps to work through. The three factors to be considered in a jump round are (not necessarily in order):

1. Riding lines

2. Finding distances or spots

3. Jumping more difficult fences

These can all be dealt with more or less simultaneously, so you can vary your lessons and practice periods to include all three at whatever level you and the horse are working. Taking them in order, let's begin.

RIDING LINES

A line is simply a chosen path that gets you to a fence in the optimum way. There are a number of factors to consider: For example, the line you would ride in a hunter or equitation class might be quite different from the one you would ride in a speed class. Other factors include the size and type of fence; your horse's stride, experience, and attitude; the position of the fence relative to other fences; its placement in the ring or field; and perhaps other factors relevant to weather, light conditions, and exterior distractions.

I like to think of a jump course as a dressage ride with obstacles. You have changes from some degree of collection to extension, flying lead changes, turns, riding across the diagonal, sometimes down the center line or quarter line, and other configurations, during all of which your horse must be grounded and balanced.

The mistake most riders make is not looking or planning far enough ahead, and not having the ability to see where they must start the turn for the jump to work out. However, learning to ride lines is not a difficult skill and just requires consistent practice.

A good way to practice lines is to set up jumpless courses. These consist of a series of "fences," which are nothing more than paired jump standards with perhaps a pole on the ground between, to be ridden in a certain order. For additional help you can place cones before each fence to denote the go point for that fence.

Tidbits & Supplements

I was competing once at a show against much higher-quality horses than the one I was riding, who was there mostly for experience. We had not been permitted to school over the fences beforehand. In the first hunter class, the second fence was a perfectly ordinary white gate. I never did figure out what the problem was, but horse after horse refused that fence—several more than once. When my turn came, I tried to choose a somewhat different line than those who had preceded me, on the theory that their horses might have been distracted by something that was most visible from that line. My horse approached the fence perfectly normally, as had all the others. At the last second he hesitated very strongly, but I was expecting it and, staying well behind him, was able to get over the fence on the first try, albeit somewhat awkwardly. The rest of our round was adequate. One other horse, the last to go, jumped the fence without trouble, so either the fearsome quality had evaporated or he wasn't concerned about it. He won the class and we were second, an unexpected bonus.

The object is simply to trot or canter through the pattern, keeping your horse calm and balanced and making sure you reach each go point in such a way that you can become *totally passive* except for your center and intent in telling the horse to keep going. If there were a real jump, the horse could continue serenely over it because at that point *it would be the easiest thing for him to do*.

Another useful thing is to go to shows and watch how the pros handle different lines. In upper-level jumper classes they will walk the course, and you can follow their thinking as they line up two fences or plan a difficult turn.

Get in the habit of *always* planning your lines to make things easy for your horse, even when no fences are involved, rather than riding mindlessly from one place to the next. Your skills will be sharpened, and your horse will probably improve as well.

FINDING DISTANCES OR SPOTS AND JUMPING MORE DIFFICULT FENCES

Finding spots is the hard one for many riders. There are some people who seem to find their distances without effort, and I suspect this is at least partly a function of confidence. As I said, when I was young I had no trouble with distances

---

Tidbits & Supplements

One of the things that I discovered some years ago is that the horse needs to have his body and mind in the same kind of grounded, balanced mode to execute a good jump as he does to execute a good halt. There is an excellent exercise that makes use of this concept.

Remembering that the jump starts at the go point, if you trot or canter on the approach, *then ask the horse for a halt at the go point,* you will discover whether you are preparing him soon enough and whether he is grounded and balanced.

Control during the approach to a fence should be no different than control without a fence. However, it is extremely important that when you are using your hands to control the horse's pace, your reins stay very light. If the horse approaches the fence leaning on your hands and you release suddenly at or near lift-off, the horse can lose his balance badly and dangerously. This is called *dropping* the horse, and it can literally do that.

When the horse will approach the fence on a light rein and halt quietly at the go point, you can then ride the approach *as if* you were going to halt—that is, you have him balanced and waiting, so that you could halt if you wanted to. Then, rather than asking for the halt, you simply put your intention on jumping and keep going.

You can use this exercise to prepare him both for the jump lane and for individual fences.

---

at all. It was only when I started to worry about them that they began to cause a problem. I have concluded that *the best way to handle this is to teach the horse to deal with them.* As I am fond of saying, "You ride. The horse jumps. If you want to jump, get off and run over the fences on your own two feet!"

So how do we teach the horse to judge distances? Well, there is a simple way to do that, and you can combine it with learning more difficult fences and with learning to leave the horse alone. If you remember, we said that the horse's two problems were how to figure out the right speed to approach the jump and how to get to the best spot from which to leave the ground. Gymnastics solves both these problems for you. It may take some experimenting to figure out what will work best for your horse, but I have offered some guidelines (see page 276), and many books on jumping will provide you with even more details.

It's best to continue with the jump lane configuration that you've been using, for a while, for your sake as much as the horse's, so that you aren't tempted to steer or otherwise bother the horse's head. You're going to make mistakes with your body, and the lane will give the horse some direction and keep him from swerving out from under you. On the other hand, since the horse is more or less trapped in the lane, it is up to you not to overface him, possibly causing an accident. The lane can be created as described in Chapter 12. It's a good idea to move it around to different places in the ring every week or two, so that it doesn't get too rutted and so the horse doesn't get conditioned to jumping in only one place.

In the beginning, you want to make things as easy as possible for the horse, so that he develops confidence and finds out how jumping ought to feel, so he knows what he's looking for.

By now you should have a fair idea of what a comfortable distance for your horse is over trotting poles. You want them far enough apart so that he builds up some impulsion going through them, but not so far apart that he starts to sprawl out and get disorganized. If you can't get him to halt fairly promptly afterward, they need to be adjusted.

The basic or starter gymnastic consists of three or four cavaletti, spaced four to five feet (1.2 to 1.5 meters) apart, and preferably raised a little to get the horse to engage by himself. The distance to the first jump should be about double the distance between the cavaletti poles. This introductory fence, which gets the horse started in his jump pattern, will be a crossbar, at least ten feet (3 meters) wide and eighteen to twenty-four inches (.45 to .6 meters) high in the center. It should have ground poles either side, eighteen inches out.

A starter vertical fence.

From this fence it will be about nineteen feet (5.8 meters) to a second, identical fence. Unless you are both moderately experienced, you should start with the cavaletti, and, when that is going fairly smoothly, add the first fence. Later you can add the second fence in the same way.

If in doubt, make the distances a *little* shorter, rather than longer, and approach them more slowly. This will make it easier for the horse who is lacking in confidence, and will set back the horse who tends to race (although both these problems should be dealt with before you try to move on).

When the horse is handling the basic gymnastic exercise easily and calmly, *and you are feeling very steady and secure*, you can start raising and changing the second fence. First it becomes a vertical, about two to two and a half feet (.6 to .75 meters) high. Putting two poles close together at the top makes the obstacle more substantial looking, and thus easier. Don't forget to use the ground poles—again, set the height of the fence in front of and behind it, so if the fence is two feet high the ground poles will each be two feet away. You can probably raise the vertical to two and a half feet without changing the distance from the crossbar, but look out for "propping"—stiff-legged braking with the front feet—indicating that the distance is too short. As before, if the distance is too long, the horse may have trouble stopping afterward because he will get sprawled out and lose his balance.

When you are both ready, you can add a third fence, perhaps lowering the second fence back to its original height until the horse gets accustomed to the new pattern. The third fence will start out as a vertical, just like the one before, and the distance will be another couple of feet greater—say twenty-two feet (6.7 meters).

When your horse has got the knack of that setup, you can change the second vertical to an oxer, adding another, higher element behind the first one.

Tidbits & Supplements

It is very useful to know the length of your own strides. Most riders try to teach themselves a three-foot stride, since it is close to a normal stride and the math is fairly easy to do. Then you can simply walk between the fences and adjust them as you see fit. Some riders like to measure the distance between the fences themselves, from highest point to highest point; others like to measure from predicted landing to predicted take-off. You do need to know your horse quite well to use the latter method.

An easy introduction to spread fences. Using flowers as a
ground line adds another element, so the horse should
be allowed to look at them carefully first.

Note that the final element of a spread fence is always a single pole, for safety reasons if the horse lands on it.

When all this is going well—and again, both you and the horse are finding it consistently easy—you can add height, remembering that you will have to extend the distances between fences as they get higher. You can also add more fences, though anything more than five is getting to be quite an effort. Also remember that the fences shouldn't be high unless the horse is very fit and advanced.

Continue to keep the distances between the fences easy until the horse really understands where he wants to be when he leaves the ground.

After you have practiced quite a lot over the gymnastic with the cavaletti, you are ready to canter individual fences. Begin with a two-foot (.6 meter) crossbar with ground poles on both sides so you can jump it in either direction. Make it wide enough that the poles are not at a steep angle. Be sure to use some sort of jump wings at first. You could also continue in the jump lane if you feel it helps everyone's confidence, at least until the horse is handling the single fence easily.

Otherwise, place the jump near the fence on the long side of the arena to give the horse an additional guide. Without getting on the approach line at all, let him walk or trot by it on the inside in both directions a few times so he can look at it.

You can either trot the fence or canter it the first time. Cantering makes a much smoother jump, but trotting makes it easier for the horse to find his spot.

The horse may make this decision for you, choosing the gait that is easiest for him as he approaches the fence. Ideally, you would trot most of the approach and encourage the horse to pick up the canter several strides before the go point.

I have already explained the secret of riding single fences to you: You simply *ride the horse*, keeping him balanced and grounded. Your focus, both mental and physical, should not be on the jump itself. It should be first of all on your own position—that is, establishing your closed position, then reviewing the Seven Steps, especially the following seat or following feet, throughout the approach. Second, keep both your soft eye and your intent *beyond* the fence, not on it. Third, focus on "keeping on keeping on." If you just keep the horse going at a steady trot or canter, with good impulsion, on the line that includes the fence, he will jump it.

Because it is a small fence, the horse can leave the ground anything from one to four feet away and still jump comfortably. Do not try to adjust the length of the horse's stride during the approach—just think about his balance. If we are cantering, I find it pleasantly distracting to count the strides, not to see how many there are but just to help me think about the rhythm of the gait rather

An inviting starter gymnastic. Blocks under the cavaletti to raise them slightly and fix them in place would make it perfect.

Tidbits & Supplements

Many years ago, when the civilian Olympic Equestrian Team was first getting started after World War II, they held a fundraiser not too far from my stable, which I attended with a group of students. It was conducted by the late, great Bertalan de Nemethy, who coached the Grand Prix team so well for so many years.

I still remember the final demonstration as clearly as if it were yesterday. After the necessary preliminaries and explanations, the half-dozen or so riders each rode down through a gymnastic that consisted of four cavaletti and one stride to a two-foot crossbar. Then one stride to a three-foot single pole vertical, a bounce (no stride) to a second identical vertical, then two strides to an oxer four feet wide by four and a half feet high, and finally two strides to another oxer five feet wide by five and a half feet high.

The amazing thing was not the size of the fences, or that the horses jumped them, but that they made it look so easy! They simply cantered quietly down the line of fences, floated into the air, and landed over each one, then collected effortlessly after the final fence to make the short turn necessitated by the small arena where the demonstration took place. And that, children, is how it is supposed to be done!

---

than about the jump. I count 1, 2, 3, 1, 2, 3. My only concern with the jump is that it may make the horse suck back a little, so I keep my center and weight firmly behind him. And then the jump will just happen. No big deal!

When he has a simple single fence figured out, you can put in combinations of fences at distances that work for him. Then you gradually make the fences higher and more difficult, and begin inserting different types of fences, rather than just poles. You should not do this until your position on the horse is very relaxed and established, because new types of fences often result in over-jumping, which can throw you around and scare the horse in the process.

As the fences begin to approach three and a half feet (1.1 meters), either in height or width, you will have to start thinking about giving the horse extra rein. This is the crest release, and is quite easy to learn. At the moment when the horse's thrust closes your hip and pushes it back, you push your hands, and only your hands, forward. The mistake most riders make is to throw their whole body forward, thus putting their center ahead of the horse's center. With some practice at the standstill, you can learn to feel how *the thrust of your arms, plus pressure on your stirrups, can be used to push you back.* Depending on the amount

---

Tidbits & Supplements

If you find yourself tending to panic about the spot, try closing your eyes! Then you are forced to simply turn that aspect over to the horse, while you can still feel what is happening and continue to ride him as well as you can. Don't worry, he won't run out—or if he does it will because your line is not good or he isn't as confident as you thought. Listen to him.

---

of thrust and how much your horse changes the length of his neck, you can do a shorter or longer release.

When he is very secure about all kinds of fences, the final step in teaching your horse about distances is to go back to your gymnastic and start creating distances that are a little long or a little short. You must then help him by asking for more pace and longer strides for the long distances, and more collection for the shorter ones.

If you have done your homework up to this point, both in working on your own position and creating trust and confidence in the horse, not only in himself but in you, you will find that the process of learning to jump takes the two of you less time than you might think.

Riders who have learned the methods described in this and the previous chapter, when placed on a schooled horse, quickly developed confidence. In some instances, having never jumped anything higher than three feet, when they were mounted on a capable horse they found themselves able to handle much higher fences with complete assurance. Not everyone wants to jump the big ones, but it's nice to feel that you will be able to deal with any fence your horse can handle—and that both of you will have fun doing it.

Tidbits & Supplements

After some time you may be ready to maintain contact on the reins throughout the fence. This requires, of course, that your position be very relaxed and secure. But once you feel you have achieved that, the Mexican exercise described in Chapter 9 is a very good way to find your following hand without risking hurting the horse. Start with a very low fence until you learn the trick of staying back without any support from your hands. What you will find is that with your hands in that very low position, unless you are using a very severe bit the horse can accept a firm hold on his mouth without discomfort, as long as it is reasonably steady. I taught a lot of riders to follow the horse's head over fences in this way and none of them had a problem.

15

Cheerful Confidence
Going Where You Want to Go, Effortlessly

Besides being our friends, our companions, and sources of beauty and admiration, horses are for most of us a means of transportation. And as such, we would like them to take us where we want to go with a minimum of effort.

I have a friend named Simon who rode a great deal as a boy, with his brother, James. His mother, who was an excellent horseman herself, was able to provide very good, honest horses for the boys, and good instruction. Much of their riding was on the trails and fields of southern Vermont, and their horses were part of their lives.

When I talk to Simon about the problems people have with their horses, which I try to help them solve, he just looks at me with disbelief. His and James' horses never resisted to any memorable extent. He and James always got where they wanted to go and had fun doing it. He simply can't understand why any horse would become violent or angry. But he is a very kind person and a lifelong animal lover, which unfortunately is not true of all those who handle horses.

∾

The point of this tale is that there is a lot more to getting your horse to cooperate than just knowing how to use your aids. In fact, it has much more to do with the horse's innate confidence in himself, plus his trust in and desire to please his rider.

It has been my experience that nearly all the time when people get into serious disagreement with a horse, they have asked for it. Quite literally, because they have asked the horse to do something that he really doesn't want to do. Rather than trying to solve the horse's problem, the rider gets hung up on the "can't let him get away with that" response, and continues to ask, then insist, then demand, while the horse gets more and more resistant and more and more violent or stubborn.

To learn more about this topic, read Chapter 19 of the companion volume to this book, *How Your Horse Wants You to Ride: Starting Out—Starting Over.*

"Well," you say, "you *can't* let him get away with it, can you?" Okay, let's suppose you work for me, and you are the one I want to do something. What I want you to do is pick up snakes, and you are phobic about snakes. You can't even look at a picture of one. So when I tell you to pick up a snake, you are going to rebel against my order in a big way and you are really going to let me know that you don't want to pick up that snake!

Then I say, "Okay, I can see you are getting really upset, so let's forget about it, for the moment anyway." Now, by not making you pick up the snake, of which you are obviously petrified, am I "letting you get away with something?" I don't think so.

Actually, there are people who would say, "Well, she ought to get over it!" but I think that whether or not that is true, force or punishment is not the way to go. If I really needed you to pick up snakes, I might get some therapy for you. If that was unsuccessful, I might let you go, because I need a person who can pick up snakes and you will never be able to do so. But punishing you for your fear accomplishes nothing.

Even a horse who is obviously taking advantage is doing so because he perceives his rider as inadequate. Which means he doesn't trust her judgment, so he certainly isn't going to do anything that *he* doesn't feel confident about.

What I'm asking you to do is to give up your "Don't let him get away with that" attitude and replace it with "Why does my horse not want to do this, and what can I do to help him and make it easier for him?"

Now you're going to say, "Well, but *my* horse is just barn sour," or "My horse just doesn't *like* jumping coops." And I'm going to answer, "There is no such thing as 'just' without a reason behind it." The "barn sour" horse is a horse who has no belief in his ability to stay safe if he is away from his herd and has not learned to put his trust in his rider instead. The horse who doesn't like jumping coops has either had a bad experience with one or has never figured out exactly how to handle them, so he always jumps them awkwardly. In neither case is aggressive behavior on the rider's part likely to actually solve the problem.

Using another human metaphor, suppose you are working for me and I ask you to do a task in a particular way. You know from experience that my way of performing the task is not a good way and usually results in failure or a poor result. You try to tell me so, but I override you and insist that you do it my way, and also tell you that I don't want to hear your opinions about it any more. Now, if you want to collect your paycheck you will do it my way, but have I changed your opinion? Heck no!

Bullying someone into accepting a premise is not the same as convincing them that you are right. If I want to convince you, *I have to first listen carefully to what you have to say*. And then, if I still want it done my way, I have to be able to convince you logically that my way actually is better. Either there is some factor that you haven't thought about in your own theory, or some need I have that isn't cov-

> ### *Tidbits & Supplements*
>
> I once wrote an article about the desirable qualifications for a horse, after interviewing trainers in a number of disciplines. Every single trainer agreed on one point, whatever their discipline: *The horse had to want to do it!* No matter how perfect his breeding, conformation, and training, if the horse doesn't like what he's doing, he will never do it well.

ered by your technique. And of course, after listening to you, I may decide that you are right. Anyway, once we are *in agreement* about the best way to handle the task, you will perform it without question, and probably far better than you would have performed it if you didn't believe in what you were doing. *You will have become part of the solution, rather than part of the problem.*

That is where you must start when you are asking the horse to do anything. You must figure out a way to get him to want to do it, willingly, and because he is in agreement with you.

Since this is a book on riding rather than training, you must also seek other sources to solve these problems as they arise. And I will warn you ahead of time that your search will never end, since every horse presents new problems for which you have to find answers. That's what makes it interesting.

On the assumption that you have worked on your basic communication with the horse, as described in Chapters 6, 7, 8, and 10, your aids should be reasonably correct in that, of themselves, they do not create resistance. But you can still run into problems that are caused by circumstances. The two most common places to work the horse, and thus run into problems, are in the ring (indoor or outdoor) and out on the trail.

RING WORK

Most ring problems are caused by lack of space. The young horse, unaccustomed to a rider and not very well balanced, is put into a situation where he is constantly faced with a fence, or even worse a wall, which compels him to slow down and turn whether he feels able to or not. It's a bit like trying to drive in traffic when you haven't been driving for very long. Your driving reflexes and skills haven't kicked in yet, so you have to think about too many things at once and you don't feel confident about any of them.

My late husband, Buck, trained horses as a young man near Middleburg, Virginia. They were training three-year-olds and up for the hunt field, polo, and steeplechasing. The training area was a forty-acre field. If the horse got disorganized or frightened and couldn't stop, Buck had all the time in the world to circle or balance and settle the horse, with no fear of running into something. He said it certainly made training a lot easier. Unfortunately most of us are not so lucky, so it is important to realize that you have to help the horse compensate for the limited space.

Upward Transitions

If the horse is resisting upward transitions, he may have been hurried too much when he was young, or he may feel tense and thus unable to loosen up and move, or he may be afraid of getting going too fast and losing his balance. Whatever the reasons, he needs to be helped first of all to relax and go forward just at the walk.

If he is reluctant to move from the halt into the walk and you get no results using your center, weight, leg, stick, and voice progressively, you may need to have someone lead him a step or two to get him started.

The big thing, which is true of all "resistance" problems, is to be very effusive with praise at the slightest try on the part of the horse. I find that Parelli's four levels of pressure are very helpful with upward transition problems. *You must give the horse plenty of time to react, while being very quick yourself to react to any positive response.* Upward transitions are an area where it is very easy to get into an aggressive, punishing mode, because you are already using your legs and stick. Just remember that causing pain and fear causes tension, which interferes with the horse's ability to move forward.

Another possible approach is to work the horse on the ground, either in hand, on the longe, or freelongeing, and teach him voice commands. Then get him responding to

> ### *Tidbits & Supplements*
>
> I believe it is a big mistake to use spurs on a "lazy" horse. Spurs cause muscle contractions (think of what you do if someone pokes you in the ribs), which can help organize a horse who is relaxed and confident but will just scare a horse who is already tense.

Tidbits & Supplements

I worked with a horse once who would come into the ring and as soon as you asked him to go forward, he would hesitate and then rear. He didn't rear very high and he didn't seem to be being stubborn or aggressive. It was more like he was just getting stuck and didn't know what to do. On a guess, I had his owner put him on a calcium-magnesium supplement to help relax his muscles, especially in the neck and shoulder area—a method I had used successfully before with very tense horses. Within minutes after we gave him the first dose, he started moving forward willingly. Eventually he became a successful show hunter. Thinking outside the box turned this horse from a "stubborn, dangerous animal" into a useful citizen.

---

just the voice commands while mounted, and finally add the aids, continuing with the voice until he makes the association. Whatever you can do to avoid creating *more* tension will give you a better final result.

It isn't something that would occur to most of us, but the transition from walk to trot is very complex and the horse needs time to figure out what to do with his feet. If he is hurried during this learning stage, the horse may lose confidence and get even slower about making the transition.

Your final goal for an upward transition is a horse who will respond promptly, quietly, and smoothly to correctly applied aids, without overreacting or second-guessing you. If you spend the necessary time helping the horse solve his upward transition problems before going on, it will pay off in all areas in the future.

Rushing

We have talked about horses who don't want to *go* when they're in a small space, but the other side of the coin is the horses who don't seem to want to *stop*. They're usually okay walking, but as soon as they go into the trot or canter they race around, under minimum control.

Again, we are dealing with loss of balance and grounding, but now, rather than being unwilling to go, the horse either cannot, or thinks he won't be allowed to, stop and regroup when he is out of balance. Some trainers get very hung up on teaching the horse to maintain his gait without the application of aids, but I would far rather that my horse stopped when he got into trouble than tried to keep going. If he tries to keep going he gets more tense, and he may feel that he has to buck to release his tensions—and in any case it doesn't solve his problem.

Here your thinking needs to be directed primarily toward helping the horse balance and ground. *Until he is balanced and grounded, he will be unable to slow down safely and comfortably.* That means your reins must be very sympathetic, but supportive. That is, they must help the horse balance by being quiet and steady, but must be ready to release if they start to interfere and the horse begins to lean on them. You must be very aware of how both reins feel relative to one another as well as separately. If you feel the horse keeps making one rein loose, you must be especially careful to keep that one steady and snug so that the horse can ground on the associated (opposite) hind leg. Conversely, if one rein seems heavy, you must keep releasing it, then offering support again, so that the horse can use it but not become heavy and stiff against it, again interfering with balance and grounding.

The horse must be wearing something on his head that he feels comfortable about using for balance, usually either a soft snaffle or a mild hackamore. Very often a horse with a rushing problem will be given some sort of severe bit, to give the rider greater "control," but of course the horse can't relax and ground against it. If the severe bit does succeed in slowing him down, it will probably be to a shortened, artificial frame and stride rather than the engaged, balanced steps that indicate true control by the horse of his own body.

If, as is often true of outdoor arenas, the ground is not level, you should try to ride a pattern of trot uphill, walk downhill, until the horse starts to find some balance.

Kicking, Biting, or Spooking at Other Horses

If the horse normally gets along well in the herd but becomes aggressive in the ring, he is telling you that he feels threatened and unhappy. Since he can't take his fears out on the instructor or his rider, he takes it out on the other horses. Rather like a person who has a bad day at work and then comes home and yells indiscriminately at the family.

This becomes a matter of figuring out what is causing his insecurity. It could be bad riding, poor balance, uncomfortable tack, or other aggressive horses. Work on the cause as best you can, and meanwhile try to avoid putting him in situations where he or other horses could get hurt. Be especially careful about other horses riding directly toward him, which is very confrontational to an insecure horse. Turning his head away or circling will avoid this. Letting him stand quietly in the middle of the ring while other horses ride around, and praising him for signs of acceptance, is also a possible solution.

Cutting In

The bugaboo of every novice rider is the problem of keeping the horse on the rail. It is also one of the causes of heavy hands! School horses cut in because their novice riders are not securely centered, so the horses are constantly off balance. The riders are then told to "*pull* on that outside rein" to keep the horses out, and as we have seen, a steady pull simply forces the horses to pull back in order to balance themselves. I have ridden some quite advanced horses who had this sort of experience and had developed a defensive habit of snatching the outside rein right out of one's hand if the pressure got the least bit firm.

Riders—and their instructors—very often are unable to understand why the horse would want to cut in, since that, of course, diminishes the space and makes the turns more difficult. The problem is simply that the unbalanced horse is afraid of falling, so he wants to give himself plenty of maneuvering room. It is also possible that he quite sensibly doesn't want to fall near the wall, where he could be trapped. A horse who was forced to keep to the rail while he was still young and unbalanced might also have some fears about being able to cope.

The solution for both beginner riders and beginner horses is not to make an issue about cutting in, but to focus on lateral centering and rein pressure. Generally speaking, this means the rider should keep her center slightly to the inside most of the time and keep a little more contact on the *inside* rein. The outside rein should be used actively, leading as necessary.

Natural crookedness causes a very common cutting in pattern. As the horse approaches the far end of the ring going right hand around, he ceases going forward and thus becomes tense and then crooked (see the drawing on page 129). If you try to use rein aids to correct him, he tends to compress even more and thus become even more crooked, so it is a difficult pattern to overcome. Besides the confidence-building techniques described in the next section ("Avoiding the Far End of the Arena"), I have found the following method of ground riding to be extremely successful. It requires some ground work first.

Ground Riding

The goal is to teach the horse to steer using a stick. By doing so, you avoid using the reins so it is easier for the horse to keep going forward. We begin with an exercise I call *ground riding*. This has other uses as well, so it is worth learning and worth teaching to the horse.

Normally, as we know, when you walk on the ground with a horse you stay in front of him so that you are leading and he is following. However, in this instance he doesn't *want* to lead, which is why he is curling up and resisting going forward. Therefore, rather than preventing him from leading, you are

Tidbits & Supplements

The box is a good visual for steering problems of any sort. It helps you figure out what your aids should be, based on how the horse is resisting.

Imagine you have drawn a rectangle around your horse. The front of the rectangle is formed by pressure from the reins of opposition. The sides of the rectangle are formed by a combination of reins, center, and leg. The back of the rectangle is formed by your legs and weight. If you want the horse to go forward, you open the front of the box while keeping the back of the box closed. If you want the horse to turn, you open the side of the box. The reins on the sides work like sliding doors; if you slide your hand forward, you slide the door open and the horse can go out; if you bring the hand back, the door closes and keeps the horse in. When you want him to stop you close the front of the box. If he tries to push through the box in any direction, you simply move the box just enough so he can't get past it. By thinking of the box as moving along with the horse, you can keep the horse going and control his direction without restricting him.

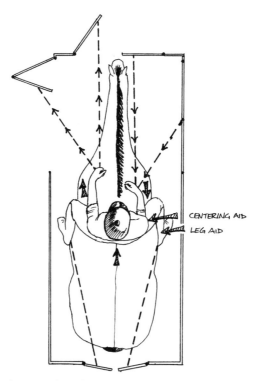

The "box." The doors on the left side have been opened by the releasing left hand, while the right hand keeps the right doors closed, with the support of the right center and leg. The weight and legs are keeping the rear doors closed.

going to insist that he do so. Nicely, of course. He can be worked in his bridle and saddle, so that you can mount and continue the exercise mounted while it is still fresh in his mind. You will need a fairly long stick, not too whippy, since you will be using it near his face.

Begin by checking your horse's responses to the stick (Chapter 7). Once you are sure he is comfortable with the stick moving quietly around his head, escalate to something more vigorous, changing your mental intent at the same time because, of course, you *want* him to move his head away from it. Look for the slightest response, then immediately stop and praise, and stroke his neck with the stick just to remind him it doesn't hurt.

Almost any horse will move his head away immediately, so if you can catch that moment and praise him, you shouldn't have much trouble. However, many horses, once they realize you aren't actually hitting them, will decide they can ignore the stick. If your horse doesn't respond to the praise/reward by continuing to move away from the stick, you may have to tap him once firmly on the muzzle or the neck to get a continued response. Just be very careful to stay away from his eyes.

Work both sides so he learns to move his head in either direction. Then place him on the rail about halfway toward the far end, at first going left hand around.

1. Take a position on the horse's left side, facing forward, opposite the seat of the saddle, so that you are in the same relative position you would be in if you were mounted.

2. Hold the reins loosely in your left hand and the stick in your right hand, parallel with the horse and in the reversed position (see the photo on page 39).

3. Reach back with the stick and tap the horse on the croup to ask him to walk forward.

As long as he walks straight forward willingly, continue to walk passively beside him. If he turns his head away from you, reach forward with your left hand and use the rein to bring him back. If he is the sort of horse who strongly resists the rein when you are behind his head, you can reach under his neck with the stick and wave it on his off side to bring him back to you.

However, it is when he turns his head *toward* you that the stick becomes most important. Do *nothing* with the rein. In particular, be sure the rein on the other side doesn't tighten up as his head turns, which might cause him to lean against it. Instead, as soon as his head starts to come around, wave the stick up and down just as you did when you were teaching him about it. If he tends to slow down at the same time, tap his croup to keep him going, alternating with swinging the stick by his head to keep him from turning in. If he tends to speed up, it may be necessary to reach forward a little around his nose to keep him back.

When he is walking quietly and straight with you on the left, work him to the right the same way.

Now you can try it mounted. Before proceeding, reintroduce him to the stick from the saddle, stroking his shoulders and neck and swinging it carefully over his head, to make sure he is comfortable with it mounted as well as on the ground.

1. Make a couple of large walking circles to the right at the near end of the arena for a warm-up, then start down the long side. Keep your center a little to the inside, and your reins even and passive and both a bit opening. Your soft eyes should be looking down to the end of the line. Don't forget to breathe! Thinking about the box (page 298) will help, too.

2. Hold your stick in your right hand with the tip pointing up. The reins should be already bridged in your left hand so that you can take your right hand off instantly. Using soft eyes, watch for the slightest movement of the horse's head toward the inside that indicates he is starting to shorten up. As soon as he does . . .

3. Drop your center a little back and to the inside, then quietly carry your right hand down and to the side so the stick forms a barrier parallel to and on the right side of his head and neck. (See the photo on page 301.)

4. If he straightens up and continues to walk forward, just hold the stick there passively. If he tries to push through it to the right, start to wave it up and down, being careful not to scare him. Try to keep your soft eyes on the end of the line. You can add some right leg behind the girth and some soft active left seat to help him straighten up and keep going.

You might have to use the stick to tap him on the muzzle once, but if you feel that you have to get really aggressive either your other aids are incorrect or he simply isn't ready to go to the far end of the ring yet. That could be a balance problem or an emotional problem, but it indicates major insecurity that needs to be dealt with at a more basic level—on the ground—as described in the next section.

Avoiding the Far End of the Arena

This is one of the most common problems that we meet with in ring riding. It is a variation of "barn sour" and "herd bound," and simply means that the horse is too insecure to feel comfortable leaving his 'herd," as represented by the end of the arena nearest the gate and the stable. At a show, the "herd" can be the end nearest the trailer. Jump course designers and judges make allowance for

Using a stick to help the horse learn to stay forward and straight.

this when they're setting up or judging jump classes. A line that rides in three strides coming toward the "herd" might well ride in four strides going away from it, when the horse is going forward less willingly.

Let's talk a little about the horse in the wild. He has two basic requirements for survival: food (and water), and keeping away from predators. As he grazes, he must balance these two needs. If he stays in the middle of the herd, he is pretty safe from predators, but he has to share the grass with everyone around him. If he moves away from the herd he has a better choice of grass, but he is more susceptible to attack. So he has to be confident that if a lion suddenly appears out of the bushes, he (the horse) is athletic and well coordinated enough to get away safely.

The second thing to think about is that horses usually graze in pairs. More eyes to see, and more confusing for the lion if the horses take off in different directions.

The third thing to think about is that while one horse might be the first horse's buddy, another horse might be challenging his herd status and trying to push him out of the herd. So he has to choose his companions wisely.

Now, how does all this apply to the herd bound, barn sour, fear of the far end syndrome? Or, to put it another way, how can you use this knowledge to help the horse?

Tidbits & Supplements

In the last few months I have been working with a colt not quite a year old, and it has been a very interesting experience. (When I was a teacher in a stable with limited funds, I tended to stay away from the very young animals.) The most interesting thing is the way the colt reacts to unfamiliar occurrences. First he wants to rush away, but as soon as his initial fear is over, there is a tremendous bump of curiosity that wants to know exactly what's going on. I know that curiosity is one of the horse's important characteristics, but I had never seen it demonstrated so graphically! In other words, given his own time, the horse will eventually approach the fearsome object or place *all by himself*, tuck it into his tremendous memory bank, and know what to do about it if he meets with it again.

Taking the last first, you have to set up your relationship with the horse so that you are his buddy; the one wpho will help him out and support him when there's danger. What you *don't* want to be is the one who is trying to drive him out of the herd. And that is exactly what you'll become if you try to drive him to the far end of the ring when he feels insecure and doesn't want to go there. So your job is not to "make him do it" but to build his confidence so that he feels he *can* do it—pretty much on his own, but with your support.

So, you have a simple, two-pronged program that you can use in any fear situation. One part is working with the horse, in situations where he is comfortable, on developing his balance and confidence about carrying the rider. Ideally, *he should be able to do anything he does naturally just as easily with a rider on his back as he does by himself.* Incidentally, that's the definition of dressage that I was taught, although very few people seem to know it any more.

The second part is introducing the horse to all kinds of situations and acting as his companion, not as one who is trying to drive him into danger. This is best done on the ground, first with you leading and later ground riding. He should be allowed and encouraged to take as long to look at things as he needs, while still keeping some attention on you. That is, he cannot run over you to get away from something he fears. The procedure is more or less as follows.

1. Walk out with the horse until you come to something that causes him to become tense. He might stop, raise his head, or try to turn around. You have him stop. And look.

2. If he seems to be getting worse, not better, have him turn *slowly* around and walk back about fifty yards (forty-five meters) or so and turn around, stop, look again, then move forward again. While you want to allow *him* to make the decision to approach the scary object, you can suggest to him that *you* would like to approach and think it's okay.

3. If he will walk past it quietly, that's a start. But eventually it would be good if he would explore it more closely—though he may simply reach a decision about it and ignore it thereafter.

4. Don't be misled by the horse who seems to be in a hurry to get to everything. It may seem as if he is bold and fearless, but very often these horses are moving quickly so they can rush by or away if they feel too threatened. You want the horse to walk forward calmly and under control of himself, as well as being willing to listen to your suggestions.

5. It is important that he develop the confidence to lead (ground riding) going away from home and follow (stay behind you) going toward home.

Doors and openings at the far end of indoor arenas are very threatening because unexpected things can appear there. Any instructor who uses an indoor arena regularly will tell you that most falls occur near or because of the door. Some horses need to be allowed to walk down and look out at some point early in the ride before they can feel secure about it.

There is also what can be called the "box canyon effect," especially indoors: The horse is separated from his herd and trapped by the walls so that his maneuvering room is limited. Kind of the equivalent of finding yourself on a dark street in a strange neighborhood. When I had to divide an arena to conduct two lessons, I always put the more advanced class at the far end and kept the beginners near the stable for safety's sake.

Horses who are insecure about the far end of the arena should be allowed to work at the near end until they are well warmed up, then, if possible, allowed to move around with a minimum of direction so that they make their own decision to go to the far end. Again, if the horse is allowed to do this, he will develop confidence and the problem will quietly go away.

This work should be done first leading, then ground driving, and finally mounted. In the beginning everything will take a while, but as the horse learns to trust you as a companion and trust in his own developing skills, it will take less and less time. You should also look into the other ground training disciplines described in appendix C.

HEADING OUT

Going out of the ring presents its own problems. Too much space can be as threatening to a timid horse or rider as too little. And you have the additional complications of varied terrain and constantly changing surroundings. The training techniques described above are equally applicable to the trail and the arena, and trail riding is so good for both rider and horse, mentally as well as physically, that it is well worth spending time to get it right.

Spooking, Spinning, and Other Fears of the Great Outdoors

Many horses can't be ridden on the trail because they are so afraid of anything unfamiliar. Either they refuse to go at all, or they spin or bolt to escape.

This is strictly a trust and confidence problem, and should be dealt with using ground training before the horse is ever ridden out in unfamiliar areas. First of all, the horse must trust you. The ground training systems listed in appendix C are all good ways to build trust, and there are others as well. Just remember that you only get respect from the horse if you are willing to give it.

Introduce him to as many odd conditions as you can think of in a secure situation. Flapping tarps and sudden noises are a couple of examples. Just escalate gradually, so the horse develops courage and confidence. Don't try to see how badly you can scare him!

If you are going to have to go out alone, spend plenty of time taking the horse out in hand, first leading, then ground riding, using the techniques described above for dealing with fear in the arena. Be very attentive to the horse's responses. *You want him to be confident, not just obedient.*

Generally, you encourage him to stop and look, and even walk quietly away and back, but at some point you ask him nicely to stop looking and start listening—to you! That is, his ears will be pointed toward the fearsome object but he won't be panicking, at which point you can speak to him, or pat him, or do something else to get his attention. His ears should then turn toward you, at least momentarily, and then gradually for longer and longer. At that point you can suggest that he either approach the object or walk quietly past it, depending on circumstances.

So the conversation goes something like this:

Horse: "I see something I don't like."

You: "Okay, why don't you stop for a minute and get a good look at it?"

Horse: "Thanks. Oooooh, that's pretty scary. I don't like being this close to it."

You: "Okay, let's turn around, but not too fast. You have to think about me, too, you know."

Horse: "Weeellll, okay. I'll try. Ahhh, that's better. [pause] Okay, I'm ready for a closer look now."

You: "Go for it. [pause] I think you've got the picture now, so let's see if you can walk by it."

Horse: "Sure, if you say so."

After a number of conversations along this line, the horse will develop a good level of self-confidence and trust in you, and he will go pretty much where you ask him to go.

If you can find someone else with another horse to go for ground walks with you at first, that's an extra safety step. At first, the green horse should follow out and lead home, but eventually he should reverse the order. He should learn to keep his distance when he is following and wait quietly. *At no time should he ever be allowed to walk home rapidly.* You may have to do a lot of stopping and starting and even circling before he understands this, but he must discover that he will only be allowed to go home if he does so quietly and calmly (see page 64). Eventually you should be able to ground ride him both out and back with him remaining calm and attentive. At that point you can start riding him out, but be prepared to dismount if he seems to lose confidence. With a bit of practice, if you've done your job right, you will find you have a very dependable horse.

Group Trail Riding

I think more people get in trouble going out in a group than riding alone. We expect the horse to maintain his place in line and stay far enough away from the other horses that he doesn't risk getting either one of you kicked. However, this is totally against his natural instinct. If he is with horses he knows in unfamiliar circumstances, he wants to stay packed together within the safety of his herd, especially at speed. Conversely, if you go out on a large trail ride with a group of unknown horses, your horse feels very threatened and doesn't really know how to handle the situation. As always, building his confidence in himself and in you is the key.

When you first start taking a young or green horse out with other horses, the ideal situation is to go with two older, experienced horses, who will either lead or follow, can be rated easily, and don't kick or otherwise behave aggressively. (Whatever you do, don't go out with a nervous, excitable animal, especially if his owner is equally tense. You're better off alone!)

The inexperienced horse should probably be placed in the middle at first. It's okay to allow him to crowd the leader a little bit, as long as he isn't aggressive about it. Some horses are more comfortable leading—most are not comfortable being last, which requires some special training (see page 308).

Work mostly at the walk in the beginning, especially on the way home. A little trotting is okay as long as everybody goes at the same speed and no one gets worried. Cantering is usually too exciting before the horse has quite a few quiet miles under his saddle.

When you meet with anything unfamiliar, let the youngster look as long as he needs to, although at some point you can ask him to give you his attention again if he seems calm. If necessary, use the advance and retreat that you used on the ground. Don't be afraid to dismount if he starts to get really upset. You can nearly always control him better from the ground, and it is certainly safer.

As he becomes calmer and more secure, you can introduce cantering. The best place is on an uphill, and the young horse should be put into the canter a little before the horse in front of him, or at the same time. What you should not do is try to hold him back at this stage when the lead horse moves off. Have the leader tell you when she is going to canter so that you are ready to start as well. The first canters should be quite short and, as the horse accepts them calmly, they can gradually be increased, as can the speed. However, at the first sign of taking over, everybody should immediately walk until things settle down. Try not to always canter in the same places on the trail every time, as the horse will learn to anticipate them.

Eventually you are going to want to ride in a larger group, but this should be approached in stages. The horse in the wild stays with his herd, somewhat separated from other herds. If he wanders close to another herd they will drive him away, so being thrown in among a bunch of strangers is pretty threatening. Even in their own herd, horses interact and move in ways that might not be acceptable for a ridden horse.

There are a number of options for introducing your horse to group riding. A lot depends on what is available but here are some good ways to start.

● Add more quiet horses to your little group, letting your horse take turns riding in different spots in the group.

● If there are no other horses available nearby, arrange to take a small group lesson at a local stable, where you can also trail ride in their company.

● Go to clinics. It's best not to start out at one where they put a lot of horses and riders together in an arena, since one or more of the horses may act up and scare your horse. The more bad experiences you can avoid early on, the faster your horse will develop confidence.

● Go to horse shows or other events, again starting small if possible. Don't plan to show at all, which would make you both nervous. Instead, just lead, and later, if it seems appropriate, ride him around the show grounds.

Bring a calm, mature horse along for a companion if possible. Going to a show that lasts several days is also a good experience. The young horse meets many new challenges, but has several days to adjust to them. A very maturing experience!

● One of the better ways to introduce the horse to large groups is at an event such as a hunter pace. Here you arrive at the starting area, where there will be a number of horses milling around. You can lead the horse around, let him watch and generally find a level of comfort, preferably in the company of a calm companion. He will see other horses galloping off, but when it is his turn, he and his companions can depart at a sedate walk or trot. During the course of the ride, other teams will overtake your team and you may overtake others. The whole experience lasts long enough that he will probably be tired and relaxed when he returns.

Meeting Other Horses While Out

If you ride in an area that is shared by other riders, you are going to meet up with them occasionally. Some of them will be polite, some not. If you hear someone coming rapidly down the trail, the first thing to do is get out of the way. Usually you can ride off into the underbrush, but be sure to turn your horse so he is facing outward. If he has his head in a corner and feels threatened, he may kick. If you are in a really impossible place, you may want to trot away, turning around if necessary, until you find a place where you can either get off the trail or at least be visible far enough in advance for the other rider to stop. What you *really* want to avoid is having the other horse crash into you. Horses don't forget experiences like that, and it can ruin them for trail riding for a long time—or even forever.

Tidbits & Supplements

When Buck was training hunters in Virginia, they expected it to take four years to make a finished hunter. The first year, when the horses were three, they were ridden to the meet, where they stood off to one side and watched until the field moved off. The second year, after the field moved off the young horses followed along, about three fields behind. The third year they rode at the back of the field. The fourth year, when they were six, they rode in the middle of the field. And that's the way you get perfectly mannered field hunters!

Even if the other horses are polite and ride slowly by, when they ride away your horse is going to want to join them. It is very scary for a horse to feel that the herd is leaving him behind, as you can well imagine. If you have not spent time on the waiting exercise (next section), the best thing to do is simply turn your horse around and ride him in the opposite direction for a few minutes, until the other horses are out of sight. You can then reverse again and continue. If he still wants to catch up, simply repeat the procedure until he settles.

Panicking When Left Behind

If he is going to be a good trail horse, one thing every horse needs to learn is to wait while the other horses leave. Once he knows this, he will wait quietly while other horses negotiate an obstacle one at a time, he will go to the back of the line, and he will wait if another horse is having trouble. All in all, very useful skills.

Waiting can be taught as a ground exercise first. You will need one other horse and rider to help with the training.

1. After the horses are well warmed up, with the other horse in the lead ask your horse to halt. The other horse should keep walking, but only for a few steps, so that he stops about fifteen feet (four and a half meters) ahead. Keeping things as calm as possible, ask your horse to stand and wait.

2. As soon as he appears to be waiting quietly, or at least trying, allow him to walk up to the other horse. If this exercise is too difficult for him, make the distances shorter. In any case, experiment until he begins to understand, as he did when learning to walk home, that only if he waits will he earn the right to join the other horse.

3. Once he has the idea, you can gradually increase the distance between the horses until he will stand quietly while the other horse canters away.

Allow a fair amount of time for the whole process, especially for it to become fully confirmed in his mind. This is a tough lesson to learn.

Rushing on the Way Home

All of us have been out in the company of a horse who, the moment he turns toward home, insists on leading and walks out as fast as possible. The least restriction starts him fussing, tossing his head, and jigging while his rider struggles fruitlessly to keep him under control.

The ground work described on page 303 can and should deal with this problem. The trick here is not to ask too much in the beginning. The horse should already understand the principles of dropping his head on command and staying back behind your shoulder. Then:

1. Begin by leading him a very short distance away from the barn and the other horses. Look for any signs of tension—which means anything other than walking quietly and calmly behind your shoulder with his head down, and immediately stop and wait. If he doesn't show any tension, go perhaps fifty yards (forty-five meters) before stopping.

2. Keep the horse standing briefly, then ask him to turn slowly, almost step by step, until he is facing home, and again ask him to stop and stand.

3. If he waits calmly, praise him and walk fifty feet (fifteen meters) or so toward home, making sure he stays behind your shoulder even if he is otherwise tense. If he fusses, keep asking him to wait and look for a moment when he *starts* to relax, then praise and allow him to walk another short distance.

4. Continue this exercise, gradually increasing the distance you go before turning around, the length of time you expect him to stand, and your expectation that he stand calmly and quietly.

This is very valuable training for group work, especially for things like hunting, where you often have to wait your turn at a fence. My husband used to sit on his hunter, who was standing quietly with loose reins, while other horses bucked and plunged, then raced dangerously at the fence. He always had a little smile on his face.

An additional exercise that is very helpful is to drive your horse in a trailer to an unfamiliar area with an extensive trail system, then go out for an extra long ride. Since he doesn't really know where home is, the horse is not likely to anticipate it, and the length of the ride tires him to the point where he just says, "The heck with it!"

Downhills

Riding downhill on a horse who is obviously having difficulty balancing himself is very scary for all concerned. There are several ways to help your horse if he has trouble getting down a hill.

As is often the case, one secret is planning. If you know there is a downhill ahead, plan to stop *well* before you get to it. If you don't know the territory, slow down any time you come to a place where you can't see far ahead of you, just in case there is a steep hill just around the corner. Even a well-balanced horse can get pretty disconcerted if he is galloping flat out and suddenly finds himself starting down a cliff!

The general rule is: Approach uphills fast and downhills slowly.

When a horse starts down a hill, gravity makes his body (which is up in the air and heavy) want to go faster than his feet (which are more or less attached to the ground). To keep from losing his balance the horse needs to get his feet farther out in front of his center. So what's stopping him? Usually, the rider. When the horse starts down the hill he may start to speed up a little, or the rider may expect him to. In either case, the rider starts using the reins to slow him down. This is fine if either rider or horse is pretty skilled, but if both are a little insecure about the bit, the horse may respond in a way that restricts the use of his legs. He may tuck his chin in and bunch his neck muscles so that his front legs can't get out in front of him, or he may raise his head and hollow his back so that his hind legs can't come forward under his center. In the worst case, he both hollows his back and tenses his neck so that neither set of legs can help him.

You might think the solution is to drop the reins, but that doesn't work either since, as we know, the reins are important to the horse's balance, especially in difficult situations. (You might say, "Well, how does the horse cope with hills in nature?" The answer is, he learns from the other members of his herd, and he doesn't have the rider's weight to deal with.)

So there you are, starting down a hill that is steeper than you expected, and you are going faster than you intended. How can you save the situation before it becomes serious? You have two different reins, and by using them in two different ways you can help the horse to balance and also help him to slow down.

Notice the order of events: *first help him balance, then slow down.* If you try to force him to slow down when he is out of balance, it won't work. Start by *getting your own balance first*, preferably a little off his back and as open as you can manage.

1. Take a soft hold of both reins—not too high and slightly opening— enough so you can feel him leaning a little but not fighting.

2. Now see if you can feel that he is leaning a little less on one rein or if his head is turned a little one way, and just keep that rein steady and passive. (If you can't feel any difference, try first one rein, then the other.)

3. Release the opposite rein a little for a moment. He will either turn his head toward the rein you're holding, in which case you take up the slack and keep his head turned a little bit, or . . .

4. He will pull away from the rein you're holding and turn his head the other way, in which case you pick up that rein, hold his head on that side, and loosen the first rein. *Be sure you are not using an **indirect** rein, which could easily cause him to fall.*

Now you have him in a shoulder-in position, which is the whole secret. His hind legs are facing straight down the hill, giving him maximum support. His head and neck are turned just enough to open up one shoulder and front leg to reach out in front of him and slow him down, acting like the front brake on a bicycle. At the same time, the steady rein on the side toward which his head is turned

> ### *Tidbits & Supplements*
>
> If you're riding with other horses, the less well-balanced horse should be toward the front so he doesn't have to worry about getting left behind. If he gets behind he may try to hurry faster than he can handle, and scare himself into trouble.

gives him something to balance and ground against, but doesn't interfere with the reaching out of the leg on the other side. If his head is turned to the right, the right rein is holding and his left side is open to swing forward.

Use an active hand on the open side to slow him down by releasing the rein as he raises his foot (shoulder farthest back) enough to let him bring the foot forward to support him, then pulling the rein smoothly when the foot is on the ground (shoulder farthest forward) to help him slow down. If he starts fighting either rein, ease it for a moment while you hold on the other one. If it is a long hill, you may find yourself switching sides several times as one of his sides gets tired of being the brake and he wants to use the other one.

If he doesn't turn his head by himself, use an active rein on one side to get him turned into the shoulder-in position. Then proceed as above.

This takes much longer to explain than it does to do. Practice on a small hill at the walk until both you and the horse understand exactly what you are doing. Gradually increase the length and steepness of the hill and, eventually, the speed of the gait.

It helps to know that your horse doesn't want to go crashing down the hill out of control any more than you do, and will be grateful for all the assistance you can give him.

DEALING WITH SERIOUS PROBLEMS

As any experienced horseman knows, if the horse really, *really*, REALLY doesn't want to do something, short of knocking him out and dragging him, you are not going to get him to do it. **The most essential thing to know about "controlling" the horse is that you can't!** At least, not in the sense that you can control your car. If your horse really doesn't want to do something, no mechanical device no matter how severe, no punishment no matter how brutal, will make him do it. In fact, such treatment usually just confirms in the horse's now panic-stricken brain that his life depends on his continuing to fight.

In terms of control, what really scares just about everyone is the horse who responds to pressure in a violent manner: bucking, bolting, serious shying, and rearing. The best protection from this kind of thing is ordinary common sense. You wouldn't get into the car with a driver whom you knew was drunk or otherwise not in control of himself. Similarly, you should not go on with a horse who is losing control of himself, especially if you find it frightening. Instead, look for the cause of the problem, take the horse back, both literally and figuratively, to the point where he is calm, and start again.

Bucking

There are two kinds of bucks. The first is simply the horse's effort to work out tension. It's the sort of bucking most horses do when they are first let out in the field. The horse knows his body needs to be free of tension in case a lion shows up unexpectedly, and a long twisting buck is the best way to do it. Free-longeing your horse before riding, when at all possible, enables him to get rid of this kind of tension naturally and safely.

He may also buck while you are riding, frequently at the canter in the early part of the ride or at any time when the horse feels unsure and unbalanced. The most common version is called *crowhopping*, where the horse first drops his head then props his front feet, rounds his back, and hops along. It is his effort to let his hind feet catch up with his front feet so he can catch his balance. If you ride this properly, it is entirely harmless. All you have to do is lean well back and let your reins run, then gently urge the horse forward. His back will quickly loosen and he will pick himself up and go on normally. What you should *not* do is to try to pull his head up. This will only block his front legs and pull you forward. The horse will then have to stop, you will fall off, and the horse will be extremely surprised. You will go home and tell everyone your horse bucked you off. The horse will go home and tell everyone that you pulled yourself right over his head!

There are some other "warm-up" kinds of bucks that are not aggressive but should be discouraged, since they may unseat you. You will no doubt recognize them! Turnout, and plenty of walking and slow trotting—nonthreatening warm-up work—before starting more demanding work should help. If the horse seems determined, using the one-rein hindquarters disengagement (page 225) should stop him. If he still doesn't give up, you should dismount and start looking for other causes.

The bad kind of buck is the aggressive kind, when the horse is really angry about something and is going to let you know in no uncertain terms. It usually occurs very suddenly and violently, and often in a situation where the horse is expecting punishment that he considers undeserved. Attitude training, and perhaps, if you are experienced, clicker training, may cure this, but horses with this problem should only be dealt with by an experienced and confident rider. The horse has to learn that you are not going to treat him unfairly, and to care enough about your welfare that he no longer *wants* to hurt you. Sometimes the violent bucking has become a reflex, in which case it will take quite a while to erase.

Bolting

Bolting—uncontrolled running—is probably the most frightening of the equine vices. Bucking, shying, and rearing are more violent, but they are over quickly and you either survive them safely or you don't. But a horse can bolt for long distances, during which the rider gets more and more tense and frightened, so if she does finally fall, the fall will be painful or even serious.

The first thing to know about bolting is that the horse, left to his own devices, will only bolt for about fifty yards—just about the length of a lion's charge, as it happens. If you watch horses in the field you will see them do just that. Something happens to spook them and they wheel and run, but just for a short distance. Then they stop and turn and look at whatever started them off.

The second thing to know is that there is no reason for you to fall off a running horse, since the running, by itself, is not unseating, and if you use your Seven Steps you should be able to stay on without any trouble. So if you are in an area where there is plenty of room for the horse to run, there is no reason to panic. Perhaps that's why people who come from the wide open spaces of whatever country tend to be such bold riders.

What *keeps* the horse running is nearly always his rider. If the horse runs and the rider panics, the horse senses her panic and figures there must be something after them both. It doesn't occur to him that *he's* the one she's afraid of. So here again, the Seven Steps become important. If you can make yourself focus on them, by the time you have run through them all you'll nearly always find that the horse has settled down and you can use normal aids to stop him. The only circumstances where that would not apply are if you are with other horses whose riders have panicked, or if you are alone someplace where the whole world seems threatening, in which case the horse may try to run home.

Even then, if you can keep your head the horse will soon begin to tire and be willing to listen to suggestions. Depending on the circumstances, you can use either the pulley rein or the one-rein stop if you want results in a hurry. However, generally speaking if you can slow the horse down normally he is more likely to put the whole occurrence into perspective, realize how stupid it was, and be less apt to blow the next time. If he spooked at something specific you might want to dismount, lead him back, and work through it.

The emergency dismount, by the way, is the tool of preference if you can use it in that split second just *before* the horse bolts, especially if he is a horse who uses bolting as an aggressive weapon against you. If you are skilled and quick, you can land a little in front of him and spin him around before he knows what hit him. You then find yourself holding a very embarrassed horse.

The only really serious situation in bolting is if the horse is going to run into danger, such as out onto a slippery, hard road or into traffic. Then, if you've tried everything and you know you can't stop, you're better off doing an emergency dismount and risking a broken leg than staying on and risking a broken neck. A good reason, by the way, for never riding alone.

Naturally, the best defense is prevention and judgment. Don't be talked into something you aren't ready for, and never be in a hurry to introduce your horse to new, potentially dangerous conditions such as large groups of horses or fast work.

Rearing

Rearing is not something novices should deal with, and the one horse I would never buy was one who had become a chronic rearer, since this is almost impossible to cure. Rearing occurs because the horse feels the need to move, either from fear or because of the rider's demands, and is prevented from moving forward by fear, by the rider, or by his own body, so he goes up. Some horses will just bounce their forehand off the ground a little bit, but the dedicated ones will go straight up and the really dedicated ones aren't afraid to go over backward.

If you are asking the horse to go someplace difficult, such as past a scary object or into water, and his front end starts to come up, stop using your driving aids immediately, except for your center, and immediately turn the horse's head and swing his forehand off to one side, from which position he can't rear. It makes a lot more sense to lose the battle of going than to teach the horse to rear. Usually the horse has just been made to feel so pressured and threatened that the more you push him, the more certain he becomes that you want to feed him to the lion. As we have seen on other occasions, if you just give him more time, or let another horse go first, or get off and lead him, you will get the result you want.

If the horse does rear, lean forward, grab the mane or his neck, and use one leading rein to pull his head off to the side. Whatever you do, don't pull back on the reins, which might pull him over backward. The farther and quicker you can get your weight up on his neck, the harder it will be for him to go over backward, which is the only real danger in rearing. As soon as he comes down, get off, and unless you're an expert, wait to remount until you are well away from the conditions that started the problem. You can often lead a horse past something that he won't pass if you're on his back.

Balking

Balking—stopping and refusing to move forward, perhaps sidling back and forth—is usually more frustrating than frightening. It occurs when the horse is faced with something that he finds frightening, but not scary enough to make him turn and run. Lots of horses balk about going into water, for example.

Like so many things, prevention is the best solution. Building the horse's trust in your judgment and exposing him to many different circumstances in a nonthreatening way are essential.

The two riding skills that are most important for balking are the correct use of your center and weight aids (page 151), and your timing. You must keep your center firmly *behind* the horse's center at all times, which can be difficult if he is backing, for example, or on a downslope, as usually happens near water. If he is trying to turn, you must keep your center on the side he tries to turn toward so that it acts to block him and also keeps you in the middle of the saddle.

At the same time, you must be aware of the slightest effort on his part to move toward the fearsome object. You have him facing the object and you are using your leg and perhaps other driving aids, tapping and waiting a beat, then tapping again. When he takes a step forward you immediately stop the driving aid, *even though* he then stops moving forward. Then you ask again. What you must avoid is a situation where the horse is moving forward and being hit *as* he is moving forward. You are then punishing him for doing what you want, and you will end up with a confused and, often, an angry horse.

Getting off and leading, letting the horse follow another horse, or sometimes just giving him plenty of time to look are some methods that are helpful for balking. But there are also times when the horse simply is unable to overcome his fear, and doesn't go. It can make for a long walk home.

I am not going to lie to you. No matter how carefully I explain, it takes a long time—years, in fact—to learn which techniques to apply and when, especially when the horse isn't making it easy. So do try to avoid confrontational situations when you are learning. Getting off the horse and leading him is often the best solution, even for a skilled rider, if the horse is very insecure. It is not a "reward for bad behavior," since you are going to remount.

Mostly, you must pay attention to the horse's responses to your aids. Any time you meet with obvious tension or resistance, the horse is telling you that he is very unhappy either with what you are asking or the way you are asking it. You can sometimes solve such problems with force, but the solution will only be temporary and the effect on your relationship will last a long time. Remember that most horses only want to be relaxed and happy and obedient, and are looking for you to show them the way.

Afterword

It All Comes Down to You

So now what? If you have taken the time and trouble to read all this and work with it until you know and understand it pretty thoroughly, you are certainly a serious rider. And that means you probably have some long-term goals and perhaps even some ambitions. Maybe you're interested in training young horses or in retraining spoiled ones. Or perhaps you have more competitive aspirations—Grand Prix jumpers or dressage, or high-level eventing.

Whatever your goals, you are still going to be riding horses. And while every horse is an individual, at the same time they are all alike. I have attempted to present solutions to as many riding problems as I think you're likely to meet, and to present them in such a way that they will work with any horse. What is required on your part is the realization that the problems are yours, not the horse's, in the sense that it is up to you to solve them and help the horse solve them.

It's true that there are wonderful horses who just want to please so much that they will try very hard to solve their own problems—caused by bad riding, misunderstanding, or fear—in a way that doesn't disturb the rider. But often those solutions involve ways of performing that lead to premature unsoundness, so a good horse is out of a job before his time. Good riding skills are good because everybody benefits, both in the short and the long term.

Not only are all horses similar in certain ways, but so are all disciplines. There are certain basic requirements that must be met for the horse to be truly successful in any discipline. He must have the desire to achieve, and be healthy and sound. Beyond that, he must be relaxed, balanced, and grounded, and know how to carry his rider in the most efficient way under all the conditions he will meet in his particular discipline. He must be able to respond promptly to correct aids. And most of this depends on how well you ride and how clearly you understand the horse's needs. I hope your awareness in these areas has expanded exponentially.

Finally, what I hope you have learned from this book is not only how to help your horse reach his greatest potential. I hope you have begun to discover the pleasures and rewards of putting the horse first. Of taking him along at his own pace and focusing on building a strong foundation, which will benefit not only his ultimate performance but also his physical and emotional health. And I hope you have discovered that by following this philosophy, every riding session can be happy and successful for you both. What more could you want?

Appendix A

Making and Fitting a Neck Strap

Partly because of the unbelievers, neck straps cannot be bought as such in your local tack shop. You have to make your own. There are a number of ways to do this, depending on the materials you have available and your needs, but whichever way you decide to make a neck strap, you must first consider the horse's comfort. If the neck strap interferes with his functioning, it will cause problems for both of you.

SIMPLE LOOPS

You can make a simple neck strap using a fairly thick, soft cotton rope—not so thick that it is awkward to hold, but as thick as possible. Use the directions to make a neck halter (appendix B). Tie off the loose end around the neck rope so it doesn't dangle around the horse's legs. You can also use an ordinary horse leg bandage the same way, but the knots are more likely to jam.

You can use a long English stirrup leather, or two buckled together if the horse's neck is heavy. This is much easier to adjust if different people ride the horse or if you frequently go from riding bareback to riding in the saddle. A fuzzy tube placed around the bottom half will make it more comfortable for the horse.

Using either of the above devices, you have to be careful that the loop doesn't slide down the horse's neck if he drops his head, especially to graze, when he could put his foot through it. A cord that fastens the neck strap to the saddle or surcingle is a good safety precaution.

If you ride with a martingale, the yoke (the loop that goes around the horse's neck) can be used as a neck strap for short periods, but it is too narrow to use all the time because it would cut into the horse's neck.

The problem with using a simple loop device is that all the pressure is on the horse's neck and shoulders. I prefer to use a neck strap that also attaches to the girth, so some of the pull is concentrated there and it doesn't interfere with the horse at all.

MODIFIED BREASTPLATES

If you ride with a hunting breastplate, you can turn it into a neck strap by adding an extra strap across the withers. The strap should be adjustable in some way. You can adapt the breastplate to bareback by making extenders to the straps that fasten to the D-rings of the saddle so that they will reach around the bareback surcingle. You also need to put nice, thick fuzzies around the long straps that run down the horse's shoulder, or they will cut into him.

The chest strap, which runs down to the girth, must be adjusted short enough that it takes the pressure off the horse's gullet. For some reason this strap is nearly always very long, so it may need extra holes or even professional shortening.

The difficulty with using a hunting breastplate is that even with padding it is rather narrow on the horse's shoulders. More important, the part that goes across the top of the horse's neck usually sits quite close to his withers, which means it tends to be under your hands when you are in half seat, rather than out in front of them. This makes it harder for you to balance, because your hands are in the wrong place.

My personal preference, which I used in my school for many years, is a neck strap made with a padded nylon western breastplate. A western breastplate is Y-shaped, with a short branch going to each side of the shoulders and one to the girth. It needs some adapting to make it usable with either an English saddle or a bareback pad. You can either do the adapting yourself or have a tack shop do it for you. Each branch of the Y consists of a thick, padded piece with an adjustable strap at the end for attaching to the saddle. All the adjustable straps are too short for English or bareback tack, and need to be replaced with longer ones. In addition, you need two pieces to go over the top of the horse's neck: one to hold the breastplate in place so it doesn't slip down over the horse's shoulder points, and one that is the actual neck strap to hold on to.

If you like making your own equipment, you can buy long, braided nylon reins and conway buckles and use them to make a very serviceable neck strap out of a western breastplate, as I've just described. It will not win any beauty contests, but it will be comfortable for the horse and a great comfort to you as you learn.

You can also use an English jumping breastplate, adding a chest strap made of nylon and conway buckles, and over-neck straps as previously described.

FITTING THE NECK STRAP

Whatever the type of neck strap you choose, correct fit and adjustment to both horse and rider are essential if it is to do its job. You must be careful that the neck strap doesn't fall so low that it gets in the way of the horse's shoulder points, nor so high that it presses against his windpipe. If you notice a change in his way of going when you're using the neck strap, check the fit first.

From the rider's point of view, the neck strap should be adjusted so that whether you are sitting or standing, when your hands are pulling lightly on the neck strap your elbows hang just slightly in front of your shoulders. For bareback work this means the hand part of the strap will come about to the center of the horse's withers, while if you will be standing in the stirrups it will be forward of the withers. A long-armed person standing up on a short-necked horse is always going to have something of a problem positioning the strap far enough forward, and may end up having to use the mane.

Appendix B

Useful Knots

QUICK-RELEASE KNOTS

Quick-release knots are used to tie a horse to any fixed object.

The **halter hitch** is the most common quick-release knot, and while it is easy to tie, it is not especially safe because if the horse pulls it tight before you can get to it, it jams and is very difficult to release, If you don't expect to have to release it in a hurry and just want a simple knot, tucking the end through the loop makes it less likely that the horse will undo it himself.

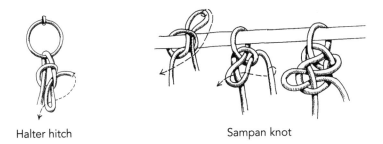

Halter hitch   Sampan knot

The **sampan knot**, which looks very similar to the halter hitch, will not jam no matter how hard the horse pulls, but can be pulled loose easily, even from a distance if you leave a long tail. This is a very useful knot, well worth learning.

The **picket line hitch** was used in the horse-drawn artillery. If it's made with a bight (loop) as the last turn, it is easy to unhitch, though it may jam if the rope is stiff.

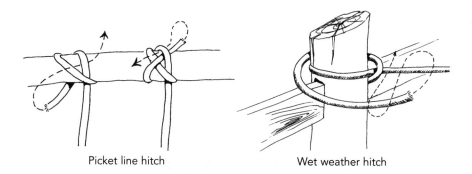

Picket line hitch   Wet weather hitch

The **wet weather hitch** was used by the circus to fasten the tents to the tent pegs. It never jams and is easy to adjust if you want to change the length of the rope without unfastening the horse.

The **chandler hitch** is a quick, safe knot to use if you aren't going to leave the horse alone, but it can work loose after awhile. Tucking the end through the loop will prevent that, although a playful horse could probably untie it.

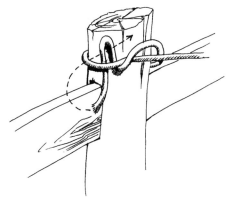

Chandler hitch

OTHER USEFUL KNOTS

The **bowline** can be used to make a loop that will not become a slipknot, or in any situation where you want a knot that absolutely will not come loose accidentally or jam. You can also use two bowlines to safely join together two ropes. The loop can be any size you need.

The **figure-8 knot** is used as a stopper knot, either at the end of a rope or in the middle. Like a bowline, it will neither come undone accidentally nor jam when you want to undo it.

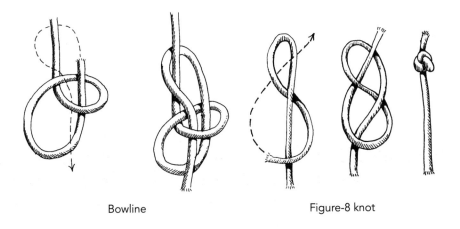

Bowline   Figure-8 knot

The **square knot** and the **granny knot** are multipurpose knots. Although the granny is not held in high regard, it is actually in some ways a more secure knot than the square knot, which can be upset and slipped apart fairly easily if you pull on only one end. The arrows in the figures below point out the difference between the two knots.

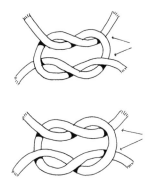

Granny knot (top) and square knot

The **becket hitch** is used to fasten the crownpiece of the type of rope halter that has no metal fittings.

The **neck halter** is a fast, safe way to put a nonslip loop around a horse's neck, either as a neck rope to ride with or to lead him by. It consists of two overhand knots (the same knot that you start to tie your shoe with), but figure-8 knots, which don't jam, could be useful instead if the horse might pull against the rope. The knot at the end of the rope is put through the open knot in the middle of the rope, which is then tightened up against it. The knot in the middle can be moved up and down the rope to get the length you want.

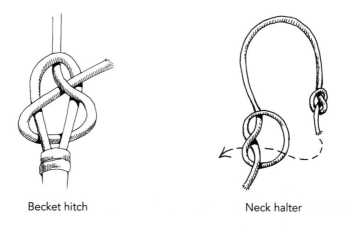

Becket hitch   Neck halter

Drawings of knots by Heather Holloway are based on designs in *Ashley's Book of Knots*, by Clifford W. Ashley, Doubleday, 1944.

Appendix C

Resources

EDUCATIONAL GROUPS

American Riding Instructor's Association
www.riding-instructor.com
aria@riding-instructor.com
28801 Trenton Court
Bonita Springs, FL 34134-3337
(239) 948-3232
Find a certified riding instructor in your discipline and your area.

Centered Riding Inc.
www.centeredriding.org
P.O. Box 157
Perkiomenville, PA 18074
(610) 754-0633
Nonthreatening riding skills for all disciplines, and qualified instructors.
Centered Riding, by Sally Swift, St. Martin's Press, 1985.
Centered Riding 2: Further Exploration, by Sally Swift, Trafalgar Square, 2002.
Videos are also available.

groups.yahoo.com/group/ridingwithconfidence
A support group especially for riders and owners with fear problems, moderated
by Gincy Self Bucklin, with Barbara Seidel.

www.whatyourhorsewants.com
Essays, photos, books, help for readers.

groups.yahoo.com
All kinds of equine discussion groups, including groups focused on all the training methods referred to in this book. Search on the term "Equestrian."

www.reactorpanel.com/html/customize.html
This is one place near where I live to get the adjustable stirrup bars shown on page 83. Typing "adjustable stirrup bars" into your Internet search engine will bring up a number of other sites.

RELATIONSHIP TRAINING

Clicker Training

Web Sites, e-Groups, and Contacts
www.theclickercenter.com
kurlanda@crisny.org
49 River Street, Suite 3
Waltham, MA 02453

www.clickertraining.com
(800) 47-CLICK

Introductory Books and Videos
Don't Shoot the Dog, by Karen Pryor, Bantam Doubleday Dell, revised edition, 1999.
Clicker Training for Your Horse, by Alexandra Kurland, Ringpress Books, 2001.
Clicking With Your Horse, by Alexandra Kurland, Sunshine Books, 2003.
The Click That Teaches (video series), by Alexandra Kurland, Sunshine Books.

Parelli Natural Horse-Man-Ship

Web Sites, e-Groups, and Contacts
www.parelli.com
pnhusa@parelli.com
Parelli Natural Horse-Man-Ship
56 Talisman Drive, Suite 6
Pagosa Springs, CO 81147
(970) 731-9400

Introductory Books and Videos
Natural Horse-Man-Ship, by Pat Parelli, Lyons Press, 2003.
There are numerous videos and other learning tools available. Call or visit the Parelli web site.

Round Pen Training

Web Sites, e-Groups, and Contacts
www.johnlyons.com
generalinfo@johnlyons.com
John Lyons Symposiums
P.O. Box 479
Parachute, CO 81635
(970) 285-9797

Introductory Books and Videos
Lyons on Horses, by John Lyons, Doubleday, 1991.
Many videos are available at tack stores and through the Lyons Web site.

TTeam: Tellington-Jones Equine Awareness Method

Web Sites, e-Groups, and Contacts
www.animalambassadors.com
info@tteam-ttouch.com
TTeam
P.O. Box 3793
Santa Fe, NM 87506
(800) 854-8326

Introductory Books and Videos
The Tellington-Jones Equine Awareness Method, by Linda Tellington-Jones and
   Ursula Bruns, Breakthrough Publications, 1988.
TTouch of Magic (video), Linda Tellington-Jones, Animal Ambassadors.

Index